HERBERT HOOVER
AND
FRANKLIN D. ROOSEVELT

President Herbert Hoover and President-elect Franklin D. Roosevelt sit side by side on Inauguration Day, March 4, 1933. Courtesy of the Herbert Hoover Presidential Library.

HERBERT HOOVER
AND
FRANKLIN D. ROOSEVELT

A Documentary History

Edited by
Timothy Walch and Dwight M. Miller

Introduction by
Wayne S. Cole

Foreword by
John W. Carlin

Contributions in American History, Number 182

Greenwood Press
Westport, Connecticut • London

Library of Congress Cataloging-in-Publication Data

Herbert Hoover and Franklin D. Roosevelt : a documentary history /
  edited by Timothy Walch and Dwight M. Miller ; introduction by
  Wayne S. Cole; foreword by John W. Carlin.
       p.   cm.—(Contributions in American history, ISSN 0084–9219;
  no. 182)
    Includes bibliographical references and index.
    ISBN 0–313–30608–7 (alk. paper)
    1. Hoover, Herbert, 1874–1964.   2. Roosevelt, Franklin D.
  (Franklin Delano), 1882–1945.   3. United States—Politics and
  government—1929–1933—Sources.   4. United States—Politics and
  government—1933–1945—Sources.   5. Presidents—United States—
  Biography.   I. Walch, Timothy, 1947–   .   II. Miller, Dwight M.
  III. Series.
  E802.H375   1998
  973.91'092'2—dc21   97–39599

British Library Cataloguing in Publication Data is available.

Copyright © 1998 by The Herbert Hoover Library Association

Library of Congress Catalog Card Number: 97–39599
ISBN: 0–313–30608–7
ISSN: 0084–9219

First published in 1998

Greenwood Press, 88 Post Road West, Westport, CT 06881
An imprint of Greenwood Publishing Group, Inc.

Printed in the United States of America

The paper used in this book complies with the
Permanent Paper Standard issued by the National
Information Standards Organization (Z39.48–1984).

10 9 8 7 6 5 4 3 2 1

Copyright Acknowledgments

The editors and publisher gratefully acknowledge the use of the following material:

Excerpts from the Henry L. Stimson Papers, Manuscripts and Archives, Yale University Library.

Excerpts from the diaries of Harold Ickes. Courtesy of Harold L. Ickes, Jr. (literary executor).

Excerpts from the diary of Rexford G. Tugwell. Courtesy of Mrs. Grace F. Tugwell.

Excerpts from the papers of E. E. Hunt. Courtesy of his daughter, Virginia Wedgwood.

Excerpts from the papers of James McLafferty. Courtesy of the Hoover Institution.

Excerpts from the papers of Joel T. Boone. Courtesy of the Library of Congress.

Excerpts from the papers of Stephen Early, Eleanor Roosevelt, Franklin D. Roosevelt, William Bullitt and A. A. Berle. Courtesy of the Franklin D. Roosevelt Library.

Excerpts from the papers of Herbert Hoover, Theodore Joslin, Lou Henry Hoover, and Edgar Rickard. Courtesy of the Herbert Hoover Presidential Library.

Illustrations were originally drawn by Jay N. ''Ding'' Darling and Clifford Berryman. The Darling illustrations are courtesy of the University of Iowa Libraries and Christopher Koss.

For
Senator Mark O. Hatfield

Let us remember that great human advances have not been brought about by mediocre men and women. They have been brought about by distinctly uncommon people with vital sparks of leadership
—Herbert Hoover, 1949

Contents

CONTENTS

Foreword

John W. Carlin

The mission of the National Archives and Records Administration is to ensure that government officials and the public have ready access to essential evidence—records that document the rights of citizens, the actions of federal officials, and our national experience. We preserve and provide public access to records on which both the credibility of government and the accuracy of history depend. This is an enormous yet vital task in a democratic republic such as ours.

As a division within NARA, the presidential libraries share in the responsibility to fulfill this mission. For the most part, the libraries ensure ready access to essential evidence by serving researchers in their reading rooms. Each year several thousand individuals from all over the world devote tens of thousands of hours conducting research in the collections held by presidential libraries. To aid these researchers, the presidential libraries prepare and publish a wide range of guides and finding aids. Some of these publications are available on the NARA website (www.nara.gov), and we are working to provide access to many more.

Yet another way that the presidential libraries can provide ready access to essential evidence is through documentary publications. Such volumes educate and inform the public of significant historical topics. They also help the presidential libraries reach broad and diverse audiences. In short, these books enable scholars and students of all ages and backgrounds to study and appreciate the nation's documentary heritage.

Herbert Hoover and Franklin D. Roosevelt: A Documentary History is the latest entry in an expanding shelf of documentary publications from the National Archives and Records Administration. Unlike the thick volumes of the public papers of the presidents, which focus on the ideas and actions of a single president, this new book details the unusual friendship and later rivalry between two presidents at different stages of their lives. *Herbert Hoover and Franklin D. Roosevelt* records a wide range of emotions—admiration, cooperation, suspicion, distrust, anger, and animosity.

As Wayne S. Cole notes in his introduction, Hoover and Roosevelt shared a common admiration for Woodrow Wilson and for each other. In fact, Roosevelt tried to persuade Hoover to run for president on the Democratic ticket in 1920! Hoover would not hear of it. He was first, last, and always a Republican.

Although they were political opposites, these two future presidents worked together on several projects of common interest in the 1920s. Of greatest importance was their joint effort to improve the quality and quantity of home construction throughout the United States.

However, ten years of teamwork seemed to evaporate on election day in 1928. Hoover became president of the United States and Roosevelt became governor of New York. Although polite, their relationship rapidly deteriorated. The presidential campaign of 1932 was hostile and Hoover was bitter about his loss to FDR. The worst was yet to come.

Those long months between the election loss in November and Roosevelt's inauguration in March were hard on Hoover. Unable to persuade Roosevelt and the Democratic Congress to take action, Hoover watched as the nation drifted deeper and deeper into economic depression.

Hoover never forgave his rival and never returned to the White House while Roosevelt was president. It would take an invitation from another Democrat— Harry S. Truman—to persuade Hoover to return to public service.

This book is a collaborative effort. As Timothy Walch and Dwight M. Miller observe in their editorial note, *Herbert Hoover and Franklin D. Roosevelt* would not have been possible without the cooperation of scholars and archivists across the country. Most important, this volume is a reflection of the cooperative spirit that exists among the presidential libraries. I salute the staffs of the Herbert Hoover Presidential Library and the Franklin D. Roosevelt Presidential Library for their hard work and accomplishment. The National Archives and Records Administration as a whole takes pride in this publication and congratulates its editors.

Preface

Timothy Walch and Dwight M. Miller

The documents in this volume constitute only a small number of the vast quantity of historical materials that concern the early collaboration and later rivalry of two presidents of the United States. Herbert Hoover and Franklin D. Roosevelt worked together in the Wilson administration during World War I and on housing and homebuilding issues during the 1920s. It may be too much to say that they were friends, but it is clear that the two men were colleagues who respected one another.

This collaboration and cooperation turned to suspicion and animosity after 1928 when Hoover became president and Roosevelt became governor of New York. To be sure, the two men were civil to one another as they worked on various federal–state projects. But civility turned to rivalry during the election campaign of 1932 and deteriorated further during the interregnum between the two administrations.

Not surprisingly, the changing contours of their relationship generated a fair amount of documentary materials, particularly on their rivalry during and after the campaign of 1932. It is simply not practical to compile and publish such a vast quantity of material.

It is possible, however, to bring together the key documents that fit together to tell the story of the communication and miscommunication between Hoover and Roosevelt between 1917 and 1945. Included are letters, reports and telegrams that the two men and their wives sent directly to one another as well as diary entries and memoranda that document their meetings. Also included are appropriate passages of speeches in which one president mentions the other. Finally, the volume includes candid comments the two men made about each other as captured in the diaries and letters of friends and associates.

Generally not included are passages from oral histories and memoirs recorded or published long after the events took place. In our opinion, this type of document is generally unreliable in recording the twists and turns of the friendship of these two presidents.

With few exceptions, all of the documents in this volume were typewritten with occasional handwritten annotations. These handwritten additions, as well as signatures at the close of the letters and memoranda, are indicated with the mark /s/. Such a mark at the opening of a document is an indication that it was entirely handwritten.

This volume is subtitled a "documentary history," a term we use to place emphasis on both documents and historical commentary. Each document, therefore, is preceded by an introduction that sets the historical context and links that document to the others. We hope that these explanatory passages will encourage readers to follow the story of the relationship between these two presidents as it unfolds in the documents.

The documents in this volume come from several repositories. The vast majority are from three institutions: the Herbert Hoover Presidential Library in West Branch, Iowa; the Franklin D. Roosevelt Presidential Library in Hyde Park, New York; and the Hoover Institution in Stanford, California. Some documents are unique to a single repository; others appear in collections at two or three institutions. Unless otherwise indicated in the introductory notes, the copies for the documents used in this volume were found in the Herbert Hoover Papers at the Hoover Library.

Just as the documents in this book come from several institutions, so do the contributors. This volume is very much a collaboration between the editors and a number of scholars and archivists across the country. Professor Wayne S. Cole of the University of Maryland was kind enough to share his knowledge about these two men, to review the manuscript for errors, and prepare the introductory essay for the volume. In like manner, the staff at the Roosevelt Library led by Verne Newton, Frances Seeber, and Ray Teichman assisted with the location of documents and provided related support. We are also grateful for the support of Elena Danielson and Carol Leadenham of the Hoover Institution in locating copies of several important documents.

Finally, we would like to acknowledge the extraordinary assistance that we received from our colleagues at the Hoover Library. Dale C. Mayer, J. Patrick Wildenberg and Jim Detlefson all contributed to improving the end result. And very special thanks are due to Joan Gibson and Joetta Peden for their excellent work in transcribing and re-keying the text for the documents that follow. Their care has made for a better book.

It is our hope that readers of *Herbert Hoover and Franklin D. Roosevelt* will come to see the documents in this volume as building blocks for a serious and sustained study of the relationships that develop between presidents and their successors. Hoover and Roosevelt were both honorable men, but the promise of their early partnership during World War I never grew. The differences between them in both style and substance were too great to be bridged and that is a tragedy for all Americans.

Introduction
Wayne S. Cole

Poor people seldom become kings or prime ministers or presidents. That eliminates many of us. Until the second half of the twentieth century no Catholic made it to the presidency. To this day no female, African-American, Asian-American, Native-American, Jew, or Muslim has ever been president of the United States. All that narrows the field considerably. But even among wealthy white male Christians there has been substantial variety among those rare individuals elevated to the presidency of the United States. Herbert Hoover and Franklin D. Roosevelt nicely illustrate that diversity in the first half of the twentieth century.

At their time, and in their separate ways, both Hoover and Roosevelt were seen as giants in public life. As a highly successful international mining engineer, as Food Administrator during World War I, and as Secretary of Commerce in Republican presidential administrations during the prosperity decade of the 1920s, Herbert Hoover was a much respected model of administrative skill, statesmanship, professional integrity, and public service. He probably could have been elected president in 1920 if he had clearly made himself available. Handsome, personable, outgoing, and bearing the "Rough Rider's" famous name, Roosevelt was a bright light on the political scene early on. Even his courageous battle against the crippling effects of poliomyelitis in mid-life failed to check his skyrocketing career in public life for long. Hoover and Roosevelt were both tall, robust, and energetic—two very special men destined for distinguished roles in public life.

For all of that, however, Herbert Hoover and Franklin D. Roosevelt, their presidential administrations, and their places in history provide a study in contrasts. Some eight years older than Roosevelt, Hoover lived a much longer life. Born in 1874 into a modest Quaker family in the tiny village of West Branch in eastern Iowa, Hoover was an orphan before he reached his teens. Reared by a maternal uncle in a comfortable environment in the west coast state of Oregon, Hoover studied geology and engineering at the new Stanford University in California, graduating in 1895. Drawn into international mining enterprises, young Hoover quickly became a wealthy ''self-made'' mining entrepreneur with offices scattered all over the world.

Despite his parochial beginnings in the American middle west, Hoover's business and mining operations took him to the several continents and a wide range of cultures and economies. With the precision of an engineer, Hoover paid attention to detail and was an efficient ''clean-desk'' administrator. Getting things right was more his thing than pursuing a course that won political support or popular approval. Though he was not a pacifist, Hoover's Quaker religious background and beliefs did not place military solutions and values high in his scheme of things.

Hoover was a gentleman and treated others with courtesy and respect, but he was never a ''glad hander,'' a ''hail-fellow-well-met,'' or naturally outgoing. A bit shy, diffident, and ''thin skinned,'' Hoover never delighted in the ''rough-and-tumble'' of politics and public life. He tended to become defensive and resentful in the face of public criticism. He was not naturally gregarious; he did not easily project warmth and charisma. His was an image of probity, character, decency, integrity, and responsibility. His reputation was never marred by any serious allegations of personal or financial scandal or corruption. His image served well until it was overwhelmed by the deluge that was the Great Depression of the 1930s.

In almost every respect, the patterns for Franklin Delano Roosevelt were different. Unlike Hoover, Roosevelt never personally experienced poverty or deprivation. Unlike Hoover, Roosevelt was born in Hyde Park, New York, to wealth and social position, with an almost aristocratic background. Though he was proud of China traders in his maternal ancestry, in his formative and young adult years Roosevelt's personal experiences were limited largely to the northeast in the United States and to western Europe in world affairs—a comparatively parochial pattern if viewed from the whole of the United States or from a truly worldwide multicultural perspective.

As an only child in that setting, Franklin was privileged and pampered in ways that Hoover never knew. Roosevelt's Episcopalian religious affiliation and beliefs were as shallow and unquestioning as Hoover's Quaker beliefs were deep and personal—and the comparative class perspectives of the two faiths extended into attitudes each of the two men carried with them in public life. Though not brilliant, Roosevelt performed creditably as a student in the best of America's elite schools: Groton, Harvard, and Columbia. Roosevelt's infidelity and unsatisfying family life contrasted with Hoover's comfortable and contented home life.

Roosevelt's personality and charm carried him so well that efficiency and mastery of detail never seemed as important or essential as they were to Hoover. At the same time, Roosevelt developed a feel for dealing with people and a talent for politics that Hoover never mastered and did not put high in his scale of values. Roosevelt's love of sailing, his early attachment to the big navy views of Captain Alfred Thayer Mahon, and his service as assistant secretary of the navy before and during World War I, gave him a regard for naval power and an awareness of the roles of power in international affairs that Hoover never commanded to the same degree.

Roosevelt's optimistic "can-do" style contrasted with Hoover's more pessimistic mein. Roosevelt's flexible, undoctrinaire approaches contrasted with Hoover's more rigidly doctrinaire and principled style. Roosevelt's casual administrative style contrasted with Hoover's efficient administrative performance. Roosevelt was decidedly a "loose constructionist" and envisaged a large positive role for the federal government in serving human needs at home and abroad; though Hoover conceded the necessity for government action to perform special functions, he had comparatively more confidence in private individual initiative and "voluntarism."

And Franklin D. Roosevelt's image of success, triumph, and inspiring accomplishment in peace and war contrasted with Hoover's image of ultimate defeat and failure. Herbert Hoover is remembered for the 1929 stock market crash early in his one term as president, for the depression that followed, and for his inability to end that depression and restore prosperity. In striking contrast, Franklin D. Roosevelt is remembered for his ebullient leadership as his New Deal extended relief to the needy, brought the economy out of the depression, restored prosperity, and reformed the flawed economy so it would be less likely to suffer economic disaster in the future. And he is remembered for leading the United States and its allies successfully through the most terrible war in human history toward victory over the most fearsome and evil enemy in recorded history.

Even Roosevelt's death at Warm Springs, Georgia, on April 12, 1945, from a massive cerebral hemorrhage (early in his fourth term as president) left an image of glorious triumph over adversity even in death. Those who wondered if the New Deal had really ended the depression, whether involvement in World War II was really necessary, and whether the consequences of Roosevelt's leadership methods were entirely laudatory, won little encouragement from professional historians and generally found it expedient to keep a low profile.

Though it was the Great Depression on the domestic scene in the United States that ruined Hoover's presidential administration, and though it was that same Great Depression in America that enabled Roosevelt and the Democrats to win the presidency in 1932, developments in foreign affairs and international relations played the largest roles in direct relations between Hoover and Roosevelt.

World War I introduced the two men to each other as they played their separate roles in President Woodrow Wilson's conduct of America's participation in that Great War. International attempts to resolve the Great Depression on the world scene brought the two men to their most intense encounters—and highlighted their differences in dealing with those intractable problems. And their sharply differing approaches in 1939–1941 on America's policies toward the wars raging in Asia, Africa, and Europe put the two men on opposite sides in the tremendously important "Great Debate" on American foreign policies before the Japanese attack on Pearl Harbor, Hawaii.

Hoover's impressive performance in providing humanitarian relief to suffering people in Belgium from late 1914 to America's entry into the war in 1917, his role as Food Administrator in the Wilson administration during World War I, his performance in providing food relief to millions of people in Russia and elsewhere after the war, and Roosevelt's important position as assistant secretary of the navy before, during, and after World War I, allowed the two men to meet for the first time, socialize with each other, and learn to respect each other's talents and potential in public life. Each used those wartime "contacts" with each other for incidental purposes in the 1920s when Hoover was Secretary of Commerce in the Republican administrations of Harding and Coolidge, and when Roosevelt was struggling to overcome the effects of polio and trying to build his political future in the Democratic party.

Their rising political fortunes on opposite sides of the political fence strained their relationship. In the elections of 1928 Hoover and the Republicans successfully triumphed over New York's Democratic Governor Al Smith's bid for the presidency. Smith had been Roosevelt's political patron and his choice for the presidency; Roosevelt's campaign for Smith included unfavorable evaluations of Hoover in comparison with Smith that troubled the sensitive Hoover. Though the election of 1928 brought Hoover to the presidency and crushed Smith, it also elevated Roosevelt to the governorship of New York State, a position that served as his springboard to the presidency four years later. And in 1932 the hard-fought campaigns between the badly pummeled Hoover and the confident challenge from Roosevelt left neither man with warm feelings toward the other.

The interregnum between the election on November 8, 1932, and the inauguration of Roosevelt on March 4, 1933, produced the most intense and ultimately unsatisfying personal encounters between the two men—and did so on what were essentially international issues. The Great Depression was not simply an American phenomenon; it was a worldwide disaster affecting governments and countless millions of people on every continent. German reparations owed to the Allies after World War I, Allied war debts owed to the United States, financial collapse in Germany and central Europe, fluctuating exchange rates disrupting both financial and trade relations, frustrated disarmament efforts, and consequent political disturbances and instability in countries throughout the world made the depression a truly international phenomenon. It desperately called for international solutions. Those acute international problems were given specific focus by the Lausanne agreements of 1932 in which the European governments attempted to link any adjustment of the reparations to comparable adjustments of the war debts, by the World Disarmament Conference that began its deliberations in Geneva early in 1932, and by the World Economic Conference scheduled to begin in London in 1933.

Hoover's long personal involvement in international economic activities and his heavy focus on international trade and investment during his years as Secretary of Commerce made him especially alert to the international dimensions of the Great Depression. The leading role of the United States in the world economy made its actions (and inactions) of vital importance for developments elsewhere. And with economies collapsing everywhere, leaders of other major countries almost desperately turned to the United States (and to President Hoover) for help and solutions. The very high tariff rates provided by the Smoot-Hawley Tariff of 1930 and the war debts owed to the United States provided focal points for those concerns abroad.

During the four months between Roosevelt's election in the fall of 1932 and his inauguration in the early spring of 1933, all those economic difficulties came together in alarmingly acute crises. There was no time to waste. But as a lame-duck president with a Congress controlled by his opponents, Hoover had little power to act effectively and, in any event, could not commit the United States beyond the end of his term. In desperation he sought the cooperation of president-elect Roosevelt to help cope with those crises. Given Roosevelt's identification both earlier and later with internationalism, one might have expected him to have responded helpfully. Not so!

For one thing, Roosevelt simply did not have the legal authority to make policy decisions or actions until he was sworn in as president on March 4, 1933. Furthermore, despite Roosevelt's earlier and later internationalism, his approach in 1932–1933 was that the problems of the depression had to be resolved first on the domestic scene before turning in time to international actions. That priority was consistent with directions encouraged by his Brains Trust advisers who had helped guide his presidential campaign and would help mold his early New Deal. Psychologically, it could be unwise to identify too closely with the failed policies of the defeated outgoing Hoover administration.

There was also a significant political dimension to FDR's approach. In 1932 Roosevelt had won his greatest following in the South and the West. To win enactment of his New Deal program, Roosevelt depended partly on support from western agrarian progressives—most of whom were Republicans politically and so-called "isolationists" in foreign affairs. To have cooperated with Hoover's internationalist approaches to the problem could have alienated those western progressives. And though President Hoover insisted that he was not attempting to influence the policies that Roosevelt might pursue after he took office, the cooperation that he sought from Roosevelt entailed international dimensions that may not have meshed comfortably with the approaches Roosevelt would implement in his early New Deal. Some around Roosevelt worried that the outgoing Hoover might trick the incoming president into sharing in his flawed approaches. As Republican Senator Hiram Johnson of California (himself a western agrarian progressive isolationist who supported much of FDR's early New Deal) warned Roosevelt: "beware of Greeks bearing gifts."

In response to President Hoover's pleas, the two men and their close advisers met three times during the interim. They conducted the meetings courteously. Hoover displayed commanding knowledge of the international economic problems at issue. Both men agreed that reparations and war debts were separate matters that should not be linked as the European governments attempted to do through the Lausanne agreements. But Roosevelt insisted that he had no legal authority to share in decision-making until March 4. Whatever Roosevelt's impressions of the meetings may have been, the meetings did nothing to improve Hoover's image of Roosevelt. By the time of inaugural day on March 4, the two men were barely speaking to each other. The relations (if one can call them relations at all) never improved after that.

Hoover had not been a "do-nothing" president. He had taken more positive and vigorous federal government actions to contend with the economic difficulties and depression than any earlier president had ever initiated. Under his leadership Congress had enacted the Agricultural Marketing Act, had authorized formation of the Reconstruction Finance Corporation, and adopted the Home Loan Act. On his initiative, the Congress authorized and his administration negotiated a one-year moratorium on intergovernment debts (the Hoover Moratorium) designed to ease the international financial crises. But he saw the federal government's authority under the Constitution as decidedly limited and, in any event, saw a large responsibility and authority resting with state and local governments. And based on his personal experiences over the years, Hoover had confidence in voluntary cooperative initiatives from private associations and individuals. In the years that followed, Hoover continued to believe that his policies had been sound and, had politics not intruded, could have restored American prosperity in an environment of democracy and freedom.

Hoover left the White House in March 1933 a beaten, battered, and thoroughly discredited man. The mauling that proud and sensitive person took in the political arena, along with the seemingly gratuitous frustration of his earnest efforts to win cooperation from the president-elect, left Hoover embittered. Not surprisingly, he took a dim view of the New Deal policies initiated by the new Roosevelt administration. He questioned the wisdom, effectiveness, and constitutionality of New Deal measures. More fundamentally, Hoover saw Roosevelt as undercutting the limited government patterns called for by the American Constitution, and as building toward abuse of federal authority, erosion of the federal system, and dictatorial powers in the hands of the president. The patterns in America evolving under President Roosevelt seemed, in Hoover's view, alarmingly like those that had brought the ancient Roman Republic and later the Roman Empire to its destruction and ruin.

Hoover hoped that ultimately the American people would become disenchanted with Roosevelt and the New Deal, that the political winds would blow his way once again, and that history would vindicate him. He hoped the Republican party and the American people would turn to him once again in the presidential elections of 1936 or in 1940. But that was wishful thinking on his part and hopelessly out of touch with political realities. Hoover's public image had been so badly damaged that there was not the slightest possibility that he could ever again win nomination or election to the presidency. Roosevelt's political talents and amazing popularity made his reelection in 1936 to a second term a certainty. Neither an Alf M. Landon (the Republican presidential nominee in that year) nor a Hoover had any realistic possibility of defeating Roosevelt. And they didn't.

Hoover's sadly embittered psyche made him incapable of finding any substantial merit in Roosevelt's policies and actions—domestic or foreign. Consequently, as the depression and New Deal ran their course in the 1930s, and as international crises in Africa, Europe, and Asia forced their attention upon the American people, it was not surprising that Hoover found serious fault with the policies that the United States under President Roosevelt's leadership was taking toward the wars erupting abroad. Nonetheless, Hoover's disagreements with the Roosevelt foreign policies were not simply or even primarily products of his bitter hostility toward Roosevelt.

Hoover had substantial experience in international affairs—both in private business and in public service. He had served as one of President Woodrow Wilson's trusted advisors at the Versailles Conference. Like Roosevelt, he had favored approval of the Versailles Treaty. Hoover had wanted American membership in the League of Nations, though with mild reservations. Like Roosevelt, Hoover had consistently endorsed the Permanent Court of International Justice, the "World Court." He urged international actions to ease the intensity of the economic problems undergirding the Great Depression in the 1930s. He encouraged conciliatory settlement of international problems through consultation and peaceful negotiations. As president, Hoover had pursued friendly policies toward Latin America that were bona fide precursors to Roosevelt's Good Neighbor policies. Despite his critical and distrustful attitudes toward Europe based on his experiences there during and after World War I, Hoover was not a parochial "isolationist."

Nonetheless, from the beginning Herbert Hoover was highly critical of President Franklin D. Roosevelt's policies toward World War II in Asia and Europe. Both Roosevelt and Hoover abhorred fascism and objected to Japanese, Italian, and German military aggression. Both Roosevelt and Hoover favored extending aid-short-of-war to victims of Axis aggression. For Roosevelt, however, priority went to ensuring British survival and the defeat of Hitler's Nazi Germany; Hoover's priorities went to keeping the United States out of the foreign wars. In the autumn of 1939, President Roosevelt urged Congress to repeal the arms embargo in the Neutrality Act so the United States could sell munitions and implements of war to belligerent countries—with the expectation and intention that those munitions would help Britain and France against Germany; Hoover would have revised the embargo to permit sale of defensive weapons abroad (such as anti-aircraft guns) while retaining the embargo against sale of offensive weapons (such as long-range bombing airplanes). As always, Roosevelt's wishes (not Hoover's) prevailed.

As he had done in World War I, Hoover pressed organized efforts to extend food and humanitarian relief to starving peoples in occupied Europe. Roosevelt and his Secretary of State, Cordell Hull, however, objected that such food relief would be tantamount to aid to Nazi Germany. They blocked Hoover's efforts. If Roosevelt and Hull had not been sufficiently firm in their rejection of Hoover's relief efforts, Great Britain under the leadership of Winston S. Churchill would have been. Churchill saw all such relief efforts, however humane and controlled, as erosions of the British blockade of Hitler's Europe and undercutting Britain's strongest weapon in its war against the Axis. As always, Roosevelt (and Churchill) prevailed on the issue; Hoover could not.

Hoover believed the United States could not resolve Europe's problems by intervening in them. He had no confidence in military solutions to international differences. He was convinced that if the United States properly prepared its military forces it could successfully defend itself in the western hemisphere without becoming involved in destructive wars abroad.

Hoover feared that massive American military preparations, and involvement in war itself, could build militarism and dictatorship within the United States. Waging war for democracy abroad could, in Hoover's opinion, destroy American democracy at home. His opposition to Roosevelt's New Deal and his opposition to American entry into World War II were parts of the same fabric—efforts to preserve individualism, freedom, and democracy within the United States.

Like other noninterventionists, Hoover increasingly feared that Roosevelt's steps to aid Britain short-of-war really were steps-*to*-war for the United States. In speeches he charged Roosevelt with using subterfuge and falsehoods to justify his foreign policies to the American people—claiming he was working for peace when, in Hoover's opinion, he was moving the United States ever closer to involvement in wars abroad.

When Hitler's Germany struck east on June 22, 1941, beginning the Russo-German war, Roosevelt continued to see Nazi Germany as the main danger. The Roosevelt administration quickly extended aid-short-of-war to help the Soviet Union in its desperate war against Nazi aggression. Hoover abhorred communism as much as he did fascism. The idea of trying to defend freedom and democracy by extending aid to Stalin's communist dictatorship in the Soviet Union seemed, in Hoover's words, to be "a gargantuan jest."

Hoover had no sympathy for Japanese militarism and aggression in Asia, but neither did he want the United States to become involved in the Pacific war. He considered Roosevelt's increasing economic pressures on Japan (such as restrictions on shipments of scrap iron and oil) as likely to provoke Japanese retaliation against the United States rather than as effective deterrents to Japanese expansion. He charged that the Roosevelt administration was doing everything it could "to get us into war through the Japanese back door." After the Japanese attack on Pearl Harbor brought war to the United States, Hoover contended that "continuous putting pins in rattlesnakes finally got this country bitten." Nonetheless, after the Japanese attack on Pearl Harbor, Hoover (like most Americans) supported the war effort against the Axis powers.

In 1942, in the midst of World War II, Hoover (along with Hugh Gibson) published *The Problems of Lasting Peace*, a thoughtful book on planning the peace after the war ended. Drawing on his long experience and observation in the international arena, Hoover in that book encouraged peaceful international settlements after the war. Though it was a best-seller and widely read, and though its prescriptions for postwar peace were somewhat similar to ideas that President Roosevelt was shaping independently on his own, the book had no direct impact on Roosevelt's thinking. During the war President Roosevelt discouraged detailed public consideration of postwar settlements. He feared that such deliberations might divide the American people, and divide and weaken the Allied war efforts before the war against the Axis states had been won. Hoover's speeches and writings on planning postwar peace may have had beneficial effects on American thought and on Republican party positions on foreign affairs, but they had little or no influence on Roosevelt or his policies.

Roosevelt's death in April 1945 brought Missouri's Harry S. Truman to the presidency. And that successor to Roosevelt in the White House drew on the talents and expertise of Roosevelt's predecessor in ways that FDR never had. Hoover from Iowa, Oregon, and California communicated with Truman of Missouri (the first two presidents from states west of the Mississippi River) in ways that he never did with Roosevelt of New York. But though Truman's gracious kindnesses to Hoover and his constructive use of the former president's talents were pleasing to the aging statesman, they could never erase the bitterness against Roosevelt that Hoover carried with him to his death at the age of ninety in 1964.

In recent years historians have thoughtfully revised the tainted image of Hoover that had been provided earlier by political devotees of Roosevelt. That revised image is more balanced, fair, and understanding. Nonetheless, Roosevelt is safely ensconced in the select ranks of America's greatest presidents, and Hoover will never win elevation to that rarified level.

It may be comparatively easy for the victor to be magnanimous toward a defeated adversary—but Roosevelt really never was charitable toward the defeated Hoover. It may be understandable for a vanquished and fallen contestant to feel bitterness and resentment against his triumphant assailant—but such emotions fall short of mature dignity. Ideally, one might have wished for better from two such prominent giants on the American political scene. Nonetheless, human nature being what it is, the patterns cannot have been entirely unexpected in the circumstances.

Insofar as the two men represented fundamental differences in human values, on conceptions of the "good life," on images of what is possible and impossible, on the directions American society can move in the future, and on roles the United States can and should play in world affairs, the differences between the two men symbolize paths taken and not taken in America's continued march through history. Big business, big finance, big government, urbanization, military technology, and finally war itself were eroding bases for the values and society that had produced Hoover and for which he had battled. During the years from 1932 to 1945 fundamental changes in the federal government were personified in the contest between Herbert Hoover and Franklin D. Roosevelt. And in spite of several Republican campaigns to bring about change, it is Roosevelt's view of government that has prevailed to the present day.

HERBERT HOOVER
AND
FRANKLIN D. ROOSEVELT

1

Comrades in Arms

Herbert Hoover and Franklin Roosevelt were not always political enemies. In fact, as junior members of Woodrow Wilson's War Cabinet, they were colleagues who shared a common cause. Both men put great faith in Wilson and Wilsonian ideals and both worked very hard to advance those ideals.

It would be too much to say that these two ambitious young men became friends as a result of their shared experiences, but they did socialize on a number of occasions during the war years. It would be reasonable to assume that the two men admired one another for their respective political and administrative skills.

Their working relationship changed significantly after the election of 1920, however. Although Roosevelt and Franklin Lane had tried to persuade Hoover to declare himself a Democrat, he chose the Republican Party. As Roosevelt carried the vice-presidential banner for the Democrats in the presidential election, Hoover worked to elect Warren Harding and was later rewarded with the post of Secretary of Commerce.

Outside of government for the first time in a number of years, Roosevelt became the president of the American Construction Council, an industry association of home builders and contractors. And as ACC president, Roosevelt came in frequent contact with Hoover and his Commerce Department. Together these two men and their respective organizations helped to shaped the dynamic growth of the housing industry in the United States in the 1920s. Through war and peace these two future rivals worked in common cause. But the approach of the 1928 election season would end their partnership forever.

HOOVER TO ELEANOR ROOSEVELT
February 21, 1917

There is no record of the first meeting between Herbert Hoover and Franklin Roosevelt. They were brothers in arms in the Wilson administration and it is likely that they first met sometime in 1916. From the telegram that follows, it seems clear that the Hoovers and the Roosevelts were seeing each other occasionally by the winter of 1917. This telegram was followed by a brief acknowledgment from Franklin Roosevelt the next day. The Roosevelt and Hoover calendars indicate that the two couples got together for dinner at least eight times between March 1917 and March 1920. [This document is from the Eleanor Roosevelt Papers at the Franklin D. Roosevelt Library.]

> February 21 1917
>
> Miss [*sic*] Eleanor Roosevelt
> 1733 "N" Street NW,
> Washington DC
>
> I am a little uncertain as to whether we will get down to Washington this week end and would be glad to know if I could telephone you on Friday. Do not however make any special preparation as my own situation is so uncertain.
>
> Herbert Hoover

FRANKLIN ROOSEVELT TO HOOVER
June 8, 1917

Roosevelt turned to Hoover for assistance with "constituent" issues such as the poultry situation in upstate New York. As Roosevelt readily admitted, chickens were outside his area of expertise. As Food Administrator, Hoover was pleased to respond to the concerns of Roosevelt's friend. [This document is from the Franklin D. Roosevelt Papers in the Franklin D. Roosevelt Library.]

> Dear Mr. Hoover:
>
> Here is the first of what will probably become a long line of letters from my former up-state New York friends with regard to the food situation.
>
> While I live on a farm in New York, I do not know the difference between the bow or the stern of a chicken, and I feel sure that your

office is getting into such shape that you will have experts on these lines who can tell me what to say to my farmer friends.

Sincerely yours,
FRANKLIN D. ROOSEVELT

Hon. Herbert C. Hoover,
Food Commission,
New Interior Building,
Washington, D. C.

ROOSEVELT TO HOOVER
November 27, 1917

Roosevelt asked for Hoover's assistance a second time in November. This time Roosevelt was looking for a job for a friend of a friend. As Roosevelt noted in his letter, the Civil Service system limited his hiring authority. Because the Food Administration was a temporary federal agency, Hoover was not limited by Civil Service requirements. Roosevelt wrote an identical letter to H. A. Garfield, the U.S. Fuel Administrator. [This document is from the Franklin D. Roosevelt Papers at the Franklin D. Roosevelt Library.]

November 27, 1917.

My dear Mr. Hoover:

This will be presented to you by Mrs. Oliver Roland Ingersoll, who has come to me through an old friend of mine in Albany, New York.

Mrs. Ingersoll through circumstances which developed in her husband's business before he died is compelled to seek a position now, and has come to me to see if I can be of any assistance to her. Mrs. Ingersoll is a college graduate, has had several years of banking experience, operates a typewriter, and I should be only too glad if I could take her in my own Department, but unfortunately everything we have here is under the Civil Service.

I know she would be of real assistance in any office where she could be placed, because she has the ability and the necessary experience, and I shall appreciate any consideration you may show her.

Very sincerely yours,
FRANKLIN D. ROOSEVELT

Hon. Herbert C. Hoover,
Food Administrator,
Food Administration,
Washington, D. C.

HOOVER TO ROOSEVELT
November 28, 1917

Hoover was pleased to find a job for Mrs. Ingersoll and asked a favor in return. As Assistant Secretary of the Navy, Roosevelt had the authority to detail military personnel to specific war-related assignments. Hoover asked for Roosevelt's assistance in securing the appointment of Philip Pollack to work for Henry Morgan, the U.S. Food Administrator for Cuba. Roosevelt was reluctant and Hoover did not pursue the matter. [This document is from the Franklin D. Roosevelt Papers in the Franklin D. Roosevelt Library.]

November 28, 1917

Hon. Franklin D. Roosevelt,
Assistant Secretary of the Navy,
Department of the Navy,
Washington, D. C.

Dear Mr. Roosevelt:

I have your letter of the 27th and am pleased to report that the Appointment Division has found a vacancy for Mrs. Ingersoll, and she has been given work in the License Division of the Food Administration.

Mr. Henry Morgan, who is working for us as Federal Food Administrator for the island of Cuba, and also represents the War Trade Board there, is anxious to secure the services of a certain young man of draft age, who is about to enlist or has already enlisted in the Navy. This young man, Mr. Morgan says, is especially fitted by experience and personality for the post, and I am writing to see if it would be possible for you to arrange to have him detailed to work with Mr. Morgan until his other services became absolutely imperative. You know how hard pressed we have been to find competent assistants and will appreciate the urgency of the matter.

Faithfully yours,
/s/ Herbert Hoover

HOOVER TO ROOSEVELT
June 12, 1918

As Assistant Secretary of the Navy, Roosevelt was master of the great American fleet and thereby in a position to help his friend Hoover. No response from Roosevelt survives, but one might assume that he would have done his best to accommodate Hoover. The two men met again, however briefly, in Paris on August 2. The occasion was a luncheon in Hoover's honor hosted by the French government and held at the Elysees Palace. The two men conferred twice more in Paris, on January 20, 1919, and again on April 10, to determine if any Navy surplus could be used in Hoover's postwar relief efforts. [This document is from the Franklin D. Roosevelt Papers in the Franklin D. Roosevelt Library.]

June 12, 1918

Mr. Franklin D. Roosevelt,
Assistant Secretary Office,
Navy Department,
Washington, D. C.

Dear Mr. Roosevelt:

I anticipate necessities that will take me across the Atlantic sometime between the 5th and 10th of July, and it occurred to me that I ought to ask you now if there will be anything comfortable in the way of accommodations on a transport for myself and party of five or six others between those dates.

Faithfully yours,
/s/ Herbert Hoover

ROOSEVELT TO HUGH GIBSON
January 2, 1920

Herbert Hoover was lionized after the war; he was the man who saved tiny Belgium and fed the allies. As the election season of 1920 approached, both political parties cast their gaze on Hoover as a possible candidate for the presidency. Among the Democrats touting Hoover was none other than Franklin Roosevelt. In the following letter to their mutual friend, Hugh Gibson, Roosevelt expresses his support for Hoover. Roosevelt would later recall that he and Franklin Lane had met with Hoover to urge him to declare himself a Democrat and run for president. But in 1931, as he prepared for the upcoming presidential campaign, Roosevelt deleted all references to his earlier support of Hoover from his campaign biography. (See Roosevelt to Ernest K. Lindley, May 31, 1931, FDRL.) [The story was recounted in Milton McKaye's essay, "The Governor," which appeared in the August 22, 1931, issue of *The New Yorker*.]

January 2, 1920.

Dear Hugh:

Many thanks for your Christmas card. It is good to hear from you and we get occasional scraps of news about you and your work in Poland. I envy you the experience in many ways, and congratulate you also on the splendid way you are handling things.

It must be wonderfully interesting—certainly far more so than in Washington at this particular time. I had some nice talks with Herbert Hoover before he went West for Christmas. He is certainly a wonder, and I wish we could make him President of the United States. There could not be a better one.

Bill Phillips has left, and there are lots of others among your colleagues who are awaiting orders; in fact, about half of this town seems to be awaiting orders or "having an important change come into their lives."

By the way if you see M. Paderewski I wish you would shake him by the hand for me and give him my warm regards. The last time I saw him was in this very room, shortly after he left the United States. Tell him that his old friends here and a host of new ones will never forget him.

Always sincerely yours,
/s/ Franklin D. Roosevelt

Honorable Hugh Gibson,
American Minister to Poland,
Warsaw, Poland.

ROOSEVELT TO HOOVER
March 12, 1920

Roosevelt intervened on behalf of a friend to invite Hoover to speak in Bing-hamton, New York. Knowing that Hoover might think such a long trip not worth the effort, Roosevelt suggested a stop at the Endicott-Johnson Shoe company to discuss their innovative employee management program with the president of the company. Hoover had a keen interest in getting the most out of employees. No reply from Hoover survives and there is no evidence in his daily calendar that he journeyed to Binghamton. [The "inclosed note" is not included here. This document is from the Franklin D. Roosevelt Papers at the Franklin D. Roosevelt Library.]

March 12, 1920.

My dear Hoover:

A very old friend of mine, Fancher Hopkins, now Postmaster of Binghamton, N. Y., has sent me the inclosed [sic] note for you. He also wrote that he wishes me to impress it upon you that if you can possibly go up to Binghamton you are to be his guest, and I can assure you that he is one of the best sort of young men that we have in the whole State of New York.

Further, this Binghamton Forum is a live institution and one which has done an immense amount of good all through, what we call the southern tier of counties.

Incidentally, if you could go up to Binghamton for one of the

Sundays between now and Easter you would have a chance to look at the Endicott-Johnson Shoe Company's plant. It is well worth seeing, and you would be interested in having a talk with Mr. Johnson about his relations with the employees. Johnson rose from the shoe-bench himself.

I know how hard it is for you to get away, but I hope you can treat this as a holiday and not a chore.

Always sincerely yours,
/s/ Franklin D. Roosevelt

Inclosure [*sic*].
Hon. Herbert Hoover,
Hotel Shoreham,
Washington, D. C.

LOU HENRY HOOVER TO ELEANOR ROOSEVELT
ca. March 22, 1920

The Roosevelts invited the Hoovers to dine on March 25, but it was not to be. A conference on the European Children's Fund, held March 26, prevented the Hoovers from accepting the Roosevelt invitation. In her letter of regret, Mrs. Hoover lashes out at the Congress for not providing enough funds to sustain the Polish people. Fewer dollars meant more fund-raising work for her husband. [This document is from the Eleanor Roosevelt Papers at the Franklin D. Roosevelt Library.]

[ca. Mar. 1920]

/s/ My dear Mrs. Roosevelt:

My husband's "Children's' Conference" in New York, scheduled for Thursday and Friday, is seeing so much work piling in front of it, that there is no hope of it getting it all done on Friday.

So he will have to go up Wednesday night, which means we can't possibly have the pleasure of dining with you Thursday night.

It was sweet of you to let me leave it open so long! I should have been strong enough minded to have said a definite "no" at once—instead of hoping against hope!

Of course the House's refusal to give credit for enough food to keep the Poles alive till the next harvest is largely to blame, too—it means infinitely more work for him. He can't just shrug his shoulders and say, "Oh, it's a pity—but they'll *have* to die now!" simply because the people on this hill have gotten tired of hearing about their troubles!

So regretfully yours
/s/ Lou Henry Hoover.

HOOVER TO ROOSEVELT
July 13, 1920

Hoover showed his typical initiative in congratulating "my dear Roosevelt" on his nomination as vice president on the Democratic ticket. Although the letter has a casual, somewhat irreverent tone, Hoover composed and revised the letter with care. No response from Roosevelt has been located. [This document is from the Franklin D. Roosevelt Papers at the Franklin D. Roosevelt Library.]

July 13, 1920

Mr. Franklin D. Roosevelt,
2131 R Street N.W.,
Washington, D. C.

My dear Roosevelt:

The fact that I do not belong to your political tribe does not deter me from offering my personal congratulations to an old friend. I am glad to see you in the game in such a prominent place, and, although I will not be charged with traitorship by wishing you success, I nevertheless consider it a contribution to the good of the country that you have been nominated and it will bring the merit of a great public servant to the front. If you are elected you will do the job properly.

Yours faithfully,
/s/ Herbert Hoover

PRESS RELEASE
May 14, 1922

Hoover and Roosevelt joined forces in June 1922 when they convened the formal organizing meeting of the American Construction Council, a trade association established to bring order and standards to the building industry. As a leading proponent of industry standards and self-regulation, Hoover agreed to preside at the first meeting. As an ambitious young man desirous of keeping his name before the public, Roosevelt agreed to serve as the first president of the Council. The release below trumpets the possibilities of the new organization.

For Release Sunday morning, May 14, 1922

American Construction Council,
1052 Munsey Building,
Washington, D.C.

Uniting the Construction Industry for the Common Good. Secretary Hoover to Preside at Formal Organizing Meeting—Franklin D. Roosevelt will accept Presidency of New National Council

* * *

For the first time in the history of American industrial development a great industry has united all its elements—manufacturers, labor, and the professional branches—in a great effort to raise the standards and efficiency of the industry and improve the service which it renders the public.

It is stipulated that all the work of the [American Construction] Council must square with the public welfare and so dominant has this idea been in the preliminary conferences that Secretary of Commerce Hoover, seeing the benefits that will result, has taken the responsibility of presiding at the formal organizing meeting in Washington, D. C., June 19th and 20th, and Franklin D. Roosevelt, of New York, former Assistant Secretary of the Navy, has agreed to accept the presidency of the organization. . . .

The way has thus been well prepared for the great national movement now launched. Nearly every one of the 250 national associations in the industry has tested out its own work and learned from experience the large amount of duplicate effort and its inability to grapple effectively with the problems that extend beyond its special field. They are ready and eager to have these common problems taken over by an all-embracing organization so that there may be the elimination of duplication and more resultful work. . . .

It is these tremendous possibilities, in dedication to the public service and elimination of waste, that have fired imaginations of Mr. Hoover and Mr. Roosevelt and induced them to accept positions of leadership in the movement. . . .

With this strong backing the organizers feel confident that the American Construction Council will quickly be able to play an important part in the industrial life of the nation. . . .

The time is most propitious for action.

ROOSEVELT TO HOOVER
May 29, 1922

Roosevelt wrote to Hoover following the ACC planning meeting to report on what had transpired and to share his own views on the parameters of the Council's work. Roosevelt also alluded to his ongoing battle with infantile paralysis by mentioning that he would not be at the Council's first meeting in Washington on June 19. "I wish I could go there myself," he wrote Hoover, "but the doctors insist on my staying comparatively quiet until autumn.'' Hoover delivered an upbeat address at the meeting by noting ''if there is anything the Administration can do, any support we can give, it is at your disposal.''

May 29, 1922

My dear Mr. Hoover:

I have sent you several messages of late to tell you how pleasant it has been to know that you have consented to preside at the organization meeting of the American Construction Council on June 19th and to get things started. I wish I could go there myself, but the doctors insist on my staying comparatively quiet until the Autumn.

In the meantime I have had several conferences here, and, in particular, a meeting at my house last Friday attended by about twenty prominent men connected with construction. My purpose in holding this meeting was to find out their opinions as to whether the American Construction Council should confine its activities to being a sort of clearing house of information, or whether it should aim at real leadership in the construction industry. I am glad to say that the latter view seemed to be unanimously supported.

One or two of the people present, viewing things from the narrow point of view, spoke of their fears that the American Construction Council would find the labor situation a serious stumbling-block from the outset. These were people who have had trouble with organizations such as the carpenters and structural iron workers.

Of course my idea is that the American Construction Council cannot certainly in the beginning undertake to interfere in local labor disputes or become involved in the pros and cons of open shop vs. closed shop, etc. It seems to me that the larger field should be ours; i.e., a setting up of a code of ethics, the study of seasonal work in building operations, examination of over-building at certain periods and of under-building at others, etc., etc.

These building people have been scrapping among themselves for so long that it would take some time to make them see the larger view of things, but I believe that we can do much by keeping our tempers and moving slowly.

At the meeting on June 19th and 20th I hope you will do everything possible to keep out of any acrimonious discussions of union labor, and I know that with your leadership the meeting will be a success.

I wish I could see you in person to talk to you some more about this and other matters.

With my sincere regards.

Faithfully yours,
/s/ Franklin D. Roosevelt

Honorable Herbert Hoover,
Secretary of Commerce,
Washington, D. C.

ROOSEVELT TO HOOVER
May 4, 1923

A year would pass before Roosevelt took Hoover up on his pledge of assistance and cooperation. In an effort to bring order to a chaotic building industry, Roosevelt proposed to have the American Construction Council establish a "Committee of Investigation." The committee would collect data and make recommendations for change. To gain the cooperation of all the elements of the construction industry, Roosevelt asked Hoover to write a letter of support for the committee's work. Hoover's support "would put the whole plan on such a strong foundation as to make it impossible for the busiest and most important of men to refuse to act." Roosevelt also acknowledged that Hoover's endorsement would give the ACC some much-needed national publicity. The importance and urgency of this request was underscored by a last-minute meeting between the two men on the night of May 4. "Roosevelt—Friday night" is scrawled in Hoover's handwriting across an otherwise neatly typed appointment calendar.

May 4, 1923

My dear Mr. Secretary:

It is my own feeling, and that of those associated with me in the direction of the American Construction Council with whose aims and purposes you are of course very familiar, that we can be of considerable real assistance in helping you in your efforts to straighten out the present tangle and prevent a very bad condition in the building industry throughout the United States in general. In fact this is one of the very things for which the American Construction Council was designed.

We have decided that the best program will be to appoint immediately a special Committee, on which the Heads of the large divisions of the building trades craftsmen's associations will be represented, to prepare, within the next ten days an urgent report on building conditions and the dangers of the situation, which will be submitted to the full Executive Committee of the American Construction Council at a meeting to be held in New York immediately after the completion of the report. This Committee, we hope, will have the assistance of the ablest building statisticians so that we may found the report on actual data rather than on assumption.

The Executive Committee of the American Construction Council which includes all divisions of the construction industry, will then take some formal action which ought to be of very material assistance.

The work proposed for the Committee of Investigation will take much of the time of a number of important and busy men. To get them to do this merely on the initiative of the Council itself will be somewhat difficult. However, if you are in sympathy with the idea and would be willing to address a letter to me as President of the Council, asking me to call the Executive Committee of the Council together to consider the situation, and would give this letter to the press in Washington, it would put the whole plan on such a strong foundation as to make it almost impossible for the busiest and most important of men to refuse to act, as it then becomes an effort on our part to assist you in your official capacity.

Of course, in addition, such a letter from you will give the whole deliberations of the Council nation wide publicity and in that way alone will do much to achieve the desired end.

I will not make any announcement or designation of the Committee for the investigation until I have heard from you if you are willing to make this formal request on [sic] the Council or not.

Very truly yours,
/s/ Franklin D. Roosevelt

The Honorable Herbert Hoover,
Secretary of Commerce,
Washington, D.C.

ROOSEVELT REMARKS
May 16, 1923

Roosevelt met with the Board of Governors of the American Construction Council at his home on May 16. The Council proposed to have the Commerce Department conduct regular surveys of the building trades. In his comments on the resolution, Roosevelt cautioned the board that Hoover might be unwilling to take on this new responsibility and leave it to the Council itself. Roosevelt would, nonetheless, make the case to Hoover in a letter the following day. [This document is from Record Group 14, "FDR," American Construction Council, copy in the holdings of the Franklin D. Roosevelt Library.]

Meeting Of The Board Of Governors
Of The
American Construction Council

* * *

Held at the home of Hon. Franklin D. Roosevelt, President of the
Council, 49 East 65th Street, New York City, Wednesday, May 16,
1923, beginning at 2:30 o'clock P.M. . . . .

Now, there is no reason why the Construction Council should not
speak eventually with such authority that the daily papers of the
United States would carry our reports of conditions in the construction industry in exactly the same way that today they carry the prices
of stocks and bonds, of cattle and of wheat.

I do not believe, quite frankly, that the Department of Commerce
will accept the beau jest—the beautiful jester which we make in this
resolution in asking them to go ahead and do this work. I do not
think they have the money, and I do not think that our very good
friend, Mr. Hoover, wants to go in too much for that kind of official
reporting. He believes, as most of us do, that it is primarily a function of private organizations. We have put in that suggestion, however, because, after all, it is our government, we want their
cooperation, and we make the gesture, if you would like to call it
that, of saying, "Mr. Secretary of Commerce, here is what we believe should be done; will you and your Department undertake it for
the good of the United States?" And when he says, "Thank you
very much, I would like to undertake it, but circumstances prevent,"
then we have the field open to do it ourselves, and we are assured
of the very hearty co-operation of the Government itself in the gath-
ering of the statistics and in the actual work of distributing them to
the general public.

ROOSEVELT TO HOOVER
May 17, 1923

Because he was unsure of Hoover's views on the matter, Roosevelt carefully
laid out the Council's rationale in asking the Commerce Department to establish
a "statistical division" to gather the "details, facts, and trends" in the construction industry. If the Commerce Department could not take on the task, Roosevelt
noted, the Construction Council would take it on. "We feel confident," Roosevelt closed, "that we shall have the assistance and advice of both yourself
and the extremely efficient staff of your Department."

May 17, 1923.

My dear Mr. Secretary:

At a meeting of the American Construction Council held in New York yesterday, representatives of all the different groups forming the American Construction Council were present together with 20 other representatives of labor, contractors, manufacturers and others concerned in construction. I might add that these gentlemen came from practically all parts of the United States.

At this meeting a report on existing conditions, relating to construction, made by a special Committee appointed by me, was read and adopted. I enclose a copy of this report. As you will see it was the consensus of opinion that the existing situation is fraught with danger to our continued prosperity, and recommendations were unanimously adopted for the purpose of meeting in so far as possible the present emergency. It was felt, in brief, that the only practicable method of handling the existing situation is to sound as widely as possible to the public at large a note of warning against the undertaking of additional construction during the coming few months. This is in line with the efforts which you, as the Secretary of Commerce, have already made.

All who were present at yesterday's meeting, however, felt strongly that a solution of the existing crisis is in itself insufficient. We have had in 1920, and again this year, illustrations of what the country ought not to do. To the question "Can similar situations be avoided in the future?" we are agreed that the answer is "Yes."

Again, we believe that the method of preventing a recurrence of the peaks of over-building and their corresponding valleys of extreme depression, is the education of the public at large as to the economic forces which are constantly at work. The American Construction Council was organized last year with the principal purpose of keeping all those concerned in the actual work of building structures of all kinds in touch with the existing situation throughout the country at all times, in order to eliminate these peaks and valleys. We have found however, that the man who chiefly controls the inflation and depression is not the man who does the construction, but the man who orders the work to be done for himself or his Corporation. It has therefore become apparent that it is the individual citizen who needs the information even more than the material producers, contractors and workers concerned.

The Executive Committee of the American Construction Council, together with many others interested, have therefore requested me to urge you, as Secretary of Commerce, to undertake the creation of certain definite machinery for the purpose of accomplishing this. The Resolution unanimously adopted is as follows:

"WHEREAS: There is today no authoritative index available from day to day to the public, showing the trends of costs of construction, and of materials and labor,

"AND WHEREAS, large numbers of corporations, trade associations and labor bodies collect these statistics and much valuable information is gathered by the Department of Commerce,

"AND WHEREAS, nevertheless, there does not exist any adequate method of keeping the public as a whole informed from day to day in regard to the general facts affecting the whole country,

"THEREFORE, BE IT RESOLVED: That this meeting request the President of the American Construction Council, Mr. Franklin D. Roosevelt, to address a letter to the Secretary of Commerce, urging that the Department of Commerce proceed to organize a special statistical division having for its purpose the informing of the public as to the details, facts and trends affecting the whole country at all times; and in the event that the Department of Commerce is unable to carry out this suggestion that our President immediately proceed to determine the practicability of the American Construction Council doing so itself."

It is, of course, our hope that the Department of Commerce will be able to make this undertaking. We realize of course the difficulties of changing existing machinery without the approval of the Congress. If, however, you are able to carry this out we shall, of course be more than glad. If you feel unable to do so we hope that you will approve our undertaking the work.

It is, of course, our desire that this service should not be along the lines of the usually accepted definition of statistics. Masses of figures and graphs will not be understood by the public at large who are the principal people whom we seek to inform. What we seek is the simple statement in plain English which can be as easily comprehended as the daily weather report.

The American Construction Council is, as you know, conceived for the purpose of service to the public, and if it becomes necessary for us to gather and disseminate this information we feel confident that we shall have the assistance and advice of both yourself and the extremely efficient staff of your Department.

Very truly yours,
/s/ Franklin D. Roosevelt

Honorable Herbert Hoover,
Secretary of Commerce,
Washington, D. C.

HOOVER TO ROOSEVELT
May 24, 1923

Roosevelt must have been at least mildly surprised to receive Hoover's unequivocal response to the Construction Council's recommendation. "In my opinion," Hoover wrote, "the Department of Commerce should undertake more work of the character you mention in supplement to the existing information." Hoover suggested that Roosevelt appoint a committee "to confer with this Department as to what should be undertaken." Yet this phrase meant different things to the two men. Hoover intended that the Department take a passive role and provide information to the construction industry, but no more. Roosevelt wanted the Department to take an active role and become a partner with the construction industry in the regulation of building starts. These two views would lead to confusion in the weeks ahead.

May 24 1923.

Mr. Franklin D. Roosevelt,
President, The American Construction Council,
Fidelity and Deposit Company of Maryland,
120 Broadway,
New York City.

My dear Mr. Roosevelt:

I am in receipt of your letter of May 17th and the memorandum attached to it. In my opinion the Department of Commerce should undertake more work of the character you mention in supplement to the existing information.

I would suggest that you appoint a committee representing the American Construction Council and its constituent groups to confer with this Department as to what should be undertaken. I think a great deal can be done by better use of existing statistics, and that it would be distinctly worth while to determine our program at the earliest possible moment. I expect to leave Washington to accompany The President on a trip to Alaska on June 20th, and if your committee could meet with me before that time, a much earlier start could be made. On the committee I should like to see one or two men such as Professor Warren M. Persons of Harvard, Wesley C. Mitchell, or Edwin F. Gay.

Yours faithfully,
/s/ Herbert Hoover

HOOVER TO ROOSEVELT
June 12, 1923

Roosevelt appointed a committee as soon as he had received Hoover's suggestion. In fact, Roosevelt had one of his associates set up an appointment with

Hoover for May 31. A week later, Roosevelt telegraphed Hoover asking him to contact several building industry executives and seek their cooperation in the new statistical venture. Hoover would not do this. In the letter that follows, Hoover explains his reluctance. [This document is from the Franklin D. Roosevelt Papers at the Franklin D. Roosevelt Library.]

June 12, 1923

Franklin D. Roosevelt, Vice Pres.
Fidelity and Deposit Company of Maryland
120 Broadway
New York City

My dear Roosevelt:

I am in somewhat of a quandary about your telegram of June 7th. I had hoped that the Construction Council would be solely originated from the industries without pressure from the Administration. Otherwise it will soon take on the same opposition that all Governmental touches to this problem immediately accrue.

The vast sentiment of the business community against Government interference tends to destroy even a voluntary effort if it is thought to be carried on at Government inspiration.

Yours faithfully,
/s/ Herbert Hoover

HOOVER TO ELEANOR ROOSEVELT
July 30, 1923

Hoover responded belatedly to Eleanor Roosevelt's letter regarding the American Peace Award with an expression of "hearty sympathy with the undertaking and my hope that [the award] will bring a real success." Roosevelt might have hoped for more, but she did not complain to Hoover. In fact, as far as can be determined, she did not acknowledge this letter.

July 30, 1923.

Mrs. F. D. Roosevelt,
49 E. 65th St.,
New York City.

My dear Mrs. Roosevelt:

I am in receipt of your letter of July 19th. The plan of Mr. Bok and the American Peace Award for stimulating discussion concerning the best practicable plan by which the United States may cooperate with other nations in achieving and preserving the peace of the world seems to me to be productive of widespread and thoughtful discussion of this vital problem, and in this alone will well warrant Mr. Bok's splendid prize.

Permit me to express my hearty sympathy with the undertaking and my hope that it will bring a real success.

Yours faithfully,
/s/ Herbert Hoover

HOOVER TO ROOSEVELT
December 4, 1923

Although no formal request has survived, it is likely that Roosevelt or one of his ACC associates asked Hoover for an endorsement of the Council's Committee on Apprenticeship. Hoover was happy to comply because of his strong belief in the value of practical occupational training. In closing, Hoover once again expressed the hope that the Commerce Department could be a source of support for the building industry. The letter was read aloud at the meeting of the AAC Committee on Apprenticeship held in Buffalo on December 5.

December 4, 1923.

Mr. Franklin D. Roosevelt,
President, American Construction Council,
28 West 44th Street,
New York, N.Y.

My dear Mr. Roosevelt:

At the time of the meeting of the American Construction Council's Committee on Apprenticeship, I am very glad to extend my best wishes for its success in coping with one of the most difficult problems that faces the country today. There is no solution except by cooperation of the employer and labor and that is the purpose of your conference.

There has been too little attention paid to the training of building trades' workers, and that this is partly responsible for the shortages which have been complained of recently no one can delay [sic]. Limitations in some trade unions have their corresponding action in some contractor's unwillingness to give facilities for apprentices. The printing trades have solved the problem by joint action of the employers and employees and that your committee should have taken it up gives hope of real consideration.

It is my hope that the Department of Commerce will be able to give active support to such constructive measures as may be agreed upon by all the groups represented in the council.

Yours faithfully,
/s/ Herbert Hoover

ELEANOR ROOSEVELT TO LOU HENRY HOOVER
January 25, 1924

During the winter and spring of 1924, Eleanor Roosevelt was active in promoting programs to regulate child labor. She took her case to both the New York State and the National Democratic conventions, seeking planks in their platforms. Early in the struggle, she turned to Herbert Hoover for his support. When she did not receive a reply, she wrote to Lou Henry Hoover.

/s/ Dear Mrs. Hoover,

I am so sorry to be leaving without having seen you but this conference has taken every minute. I will hope to see you another time.

Will you remind Mr. Hoover that I am anxiously awaiting a favorable reply from him? We do need his help for the child labor Amendment in New York State. My address at home is 49 East 65th Street.

Very Sincerely Yours,
/s/ Eleanor Roosevelt

HOOVER TO ROOSEVELT
September 14, 1925

The founding of "Better Homes for America," an organization established to promote better quality housing, led to the next Hoover–Roosevelt partnership. As president of the new organization, Hoover was seeking an active Advisory Council. Who better to serve than Franklin Roosevelt, the president of the American Construction Council. Roosevelt promptly accepted Hoover's invitation. [This document is from the Franklin D. Roosevelt Papers in the Franklin D. Roosevelt Library.]

Sept. 14, 1925

Mr. Franklin D. Roosevelt,
President, American Construction Council,
49 East 65th St.,
New York City.

My dear Mr. Roosevelt:

You are probably familiar with the activities of Better Homes in America and with its general purposes. It is incorporated under the laws of Delaware as an institution for public service and I am enclosing a copy of the certificate of incorporation.

As president of the organization, I am very glad to be able to ask you to serve as a member of the Advisory Council.

The headquarters activities of this organization are made possible by funds contributed by the Laura Spelman Rockefeller Memorial, and others, while the local demonstrations of Better Homes Week are undertaken by local committees. It is thus entirely free from commercial influence.

The co-operation of the various agencies represented on our advisory council has enabled Better Homes in America to do constructive work on a large scale and to become a most effective agency in raising the standards of our home life.

Yours faithfully,
/s/Herbert Hoover

Encl.

ROOSEVELT TO LOU HENRY HOOVER
August 26, 1927

Lou Henry Hoover was an active national leader of the Girl Scouts of America for much of her adult life. Seeking a dynamic public speaker for the GSA convention in New York City in 1927, she logically turned to Franklin D. Roosevelt. Mrs. Hoover's invitation has not survived, but Roosevelt's response follows below. Sorry to decline the invitation, FDR hoped that he and his wife could renew their friendship with the Hoovers at some point in the future. [This document is from the Lou Henry Hoover Papers at the Herbert Hoover Library.]

August 26, 1927.

Mrs. Herbert Hoover,
Stanford University,
California.

My dear Mrs. Hoover:

I wish much that I might accept your delightful invitation to speak at the Convention of Girl Scout Leaders in New York the end of September. I am not making any public speeches as I still sport a crutch and a cane, but I would certainly have made an exception in this case had it been possible.

However, I am going to Warm Springs, Ga. the middle of September to help get the Georgia Warm Springs Foundation under way and I simply have to be there at the time of your Convention as various doctors will be there to see the progress of our work among the crippled children.

I hear much of the splendid work of the Girl Scouts through my cousin, Mrs. Lyman Delano.

I wish much that my wife and I could see something of you and the Secretary. Do let us know if you come to New York at any time. It would be delightful if you could both come and lunch or dine with us in order that we might renew those delightful old times in Washington.

Very sincerely yours,
Franklin D. Roosevelt

CC: 2300 S. Street N. W.,
     Washington, D. C.

ROOSEVELT TO HOOVER
September 26, 1927

Roosevelt wrote the next month to ask Hoover to meet with an old friend, Julian Goldman. In closing his letter, Roosevelt expressed his regret a second time that he was not able to speak to the Girl Scout convention. He did "hope to have the pleasure of seeing [Hoover] some time this winter in New York." Hoover met with Goldman on October 5.

September 26, 1927

Hon. Herbert Hoover,
Washington, D.C.

My dear Mr. Hoover:

Mr. Julian Goldman, the head of the chain of Goldman Stores, is an old friend of mine and I shall be very glad if you can talk with him. He has for a very long time been interested in economic problems which credit and installment buying have brought to the front, and you will find that he knows much of the subject and can, I think, contribute a good deal to the study of these matters.

I shall hope to have the pleasure of seeing you some time this winter in New York. I was very sorry that I could not accept Mrs. Hoover's very delightful invitation to speak before the Girl Scout meeting, but I am just off for Georgia Warm Springs for several weeks. For this reason, I cannot sign this letter but am asking my secretary to send it to Mr. Goldman to present to you.

Very sincerely yours,
Franklin D. Roosevelt

ROOSEVELT TO HOOVER
January 13, 1928

Roosevelt wrote next in January seeking an appointment with Hoover for himself and some of the leaders of the American Construction Council "to confer with you about the future program of the council." Hoover's secretary, Bradley Nash, wrote that Mr. Hoover would be pleased to meet with the group. After several more notes between Nash and Roosevelt's assistant, Dwight Hoopingarner, an appointment was scheduled for 11:30 a.m. on February 16. No agenda of the meeting exists; one might presume that they talked about the establishment of a national construction institute as noted below.

January 13, 1928

Hon. Herbert Hoover
Secretary of Commerce
Washington, D. C.

My dear Mr. Secretary:

On February 16th I shall be passing through Washington on my way from the South and would like very much, in company with members of the Board of Governors of the American Construction Council, to confer with you about the future program of the Council.

At the Council's recent convention in St. Louis, as you no doubt know, a resolution was passed by the Board of Governors and at the suggestion of various representative people throughout construction circles to establish a national Construction Institute perhaps along the lines of those already in the steel and several other major industries. It is this general idea as well as other phases of the Council's work that we wish to talk over with you before taking further steps.

I shall arrive early that morning and can arrange to call upon you that afternoon.

Cordially yours,
/s/ Franklin D. Roosevelt
President

2

Partisan Politics

The friendly, working partnership between Hoover and Roosevelt ended as the two men moved up the ranks in their respective political parties. By 1928, Hoover had become the favored candidate to receive the Republican nomination for president. Roosevelt was to become the Democratic candidate for Governor of New York and a stalwart behind the candidacy of Al Smith, the Democratic candidate for president.

It is reasonable to date the abrupt end of the Hoover–Roosevelt partnership with the first letter in this chapter. Although not an exchange between the two men, it is clearly an attack on Hoover by Roosevelt that was sent to Hoover's close friend and associate Julius Barnes. Barnes was shocked to receive such a letter and said so to Roosevelt in his reply. There is little doubt that Hoover was informed about the contents of the letter.

It is likely that Hoover was embittered by the letter. Above all other qualities, Hoover valued loyalty and dignity. He and Roosevelt had worked together for over a decade; indeed, he had helped Roosevelt in his work on the American Construction Council! To be repaid with such an attack was despicable in Hoover's thinking.

Roosevelt had a completely different perspective. His letter to Barnes was a form letter, nothing more. Although he had nothing to say on the matter, Roosevelt likely saw his attacks on Hoover as politics, pure and simple. After Hoover won the election, Roosevelt congratulated the new president. That did not mean, however, that the new governor of New York was going to let the new

president get a free ride. Throughout the Hoover presidency, Roosevelt repeatedly poked at the president whenever he could. In fact, Roosevelt's attack on
Hoover at a Gridiron dinner so offended Hoover that he boycotted the occasion
throughout the Roosevelt presidency.

Thus, in a matter of a few months, a working relationship that had built up
over ten years was damaged beyond repair. It was a testament to the destructive
power of partisan politics.

ROOSEVELT TO JULIUS BARNES
September 25, 1928

The cordiality between Hoover and Roosevelt came to an end as both men
prepared for the political campaigns in 1928. Hoover was, of course, the Republican candidate for president. Roosevelt was not only the Democratic candidate for governor of New York, he also was a point man for Democratic
presidential candidate, Alfred E. Smith. In this latter capacity, Roosevelt authorized his associates to write, sign and send appeals in his name to hundreds
of individuals. One went to Julius H. Barnes, a Hoover man of long standing.
It is not likely that Roosevelt was even aware that Barnes was to receive one
of these letters.

September 25, 1928

Mr. Julius H. Barnes,
42 Broadway,
New York City.

My dear Mr. Barnes:

I have not heard what decision you have made as between the
two Presidential candidates, but remembering your firm belief in the
policies and ideals of Woodrow Wilson, I am encouraged to hope
that you have decided as I have decided,—that under Governor
Smith our country stands far more chance of returning to the path
blazed out for us by our greatest President, than under the materi-
alistic and self-seeking advisers who surround the other candidate;
men whose influence has already made it manifest that high ideals
and a forward-looking policy—not only for this country, but for the
world—would stand as little chance under Mr. Hoover as they have
stood under President Harding, Mr. Coolidge and Mr. Mellon.

To me, the contemptuous casting aside of all of President Wilson's wonderful dreams of a better world, and the substitution of
crass materialism and a dollar-and-cents viewpoint of everything has
been a world tragedy. I know Governor Smith and I know that in
his own way his interest in humanity, his intolerance of the oppres-
sion of the weak and his desire to help those handicapped by cir-

cumstances has led him to the same belief as to what our country's attitude should be, and as to how its course should be guided, as animated President Wilson.

I would deeply appreciate it if you would write me confidentially what you have decided, addressing the letter to my house, 49 East 65th Street, New York City.

Yours very truly,
/s/ Franklin D. Roosevelt

JULIUS H. BARNES TO ROOSEVELT
September 26, 1928

Julius Barnes received a shock when he opened his mail on September 26. He responded to Roosevelt that same day, noting his surprise and disappointment. "Of course I am for Herbert Hoover," Barnes wrote with indignation. "I am for him, as I believe millions of others will prove to be, because in every personal quality and in every experience of his long and varied career, he stands a man peculiarly equipped for the discharge of the responsibilities of this high elective office." There is no evidence that Roosevelt ever replied to Barnes.

September 26, 1928

Mr. Franklin D. Roosevelt
49 East 65th Street,
New York, N.Y.

My dear Mr. Roosevelt:

Under date of September twenty-fifth I have a letter over your signature with a request that I reply to you at your residence, and this letter, I am frank to say, greatly surprises and disappoints me. It falls below my previous estimate of your character and your ideals, to find that you would address such a letter to those men who were a part of volunteer war service under President Wilson, regardless of their own Party affiliations, and that you would attempt to make political capital by such disparagement of Mr. Hoover and his associates, when Mr. Hoover was, himself, the acknowledged leader in those days of American idealism, engaged in the relief of human distress.

Moreover, that you should do this in the name of International Cooperation, and in behalf of a candidate whose record of public service—no matter how else one may weigh it—certainly has shown no direct contact with, or interest in, international relations, is the more surprising.

Of course, I am for Herbert Hoover. I am for him because his long years of effective service in relief movements have made in international good will the most secure foundation for international peace; because his many years of leadership in the movement for child health, and thus for happy childhood, shows a keen realization of the most precious possession of any people; because his years of service in the cause of education show the value he has instinctively put upon intelligent, educated, and fair-minded youth; because in the fields both of domestic and foreign trade he has effectively furthered the cause of healthful industry on which, through rising wages and secure earnings, individual happiness and security must rest. I am for him, as I believe millions of Americans will prove to be, because in every personal quality and in every experience of his long and varied career, he stands a man peculiarly equipped for the discharge of the responsibilities of this high elective office.

Yours truly,
Julius H. Barnes

ROOSEVELT COMMENTARY
October 11, 1928

Shortly after he had accepted the Democratic nomination for Governor of New York, Roosevelt wrote to an associate to provide a ''non-partisan'' assessment of the two candidates for president. Although he acknowledged Hoover's ability as an administrator, Roosevelt argued that Hoover lacked the multidimensional skills required of the presidency. ''His is not the type of mind to meet the legislative mind,'' Roosevelt added. ''He has not the patience to work with them to settle differences to achieve results.'' [This document was first published in *Franklin D. Roosevelt's Own Story*, edited by Donald Day (Boston, 1951), pp. 105–106.]

October 11, 1928

... I have long been a friend of Governor Smith. I have long been a friend of Sec. Hoover. I have tried to picture to myself without partisanship what kind of President each of them would make. I am proud as an American citizen of the fine and able way in which Sec. Hoover has carried out his relief work in Belgium and later in Poland, his Flood control, his help to the victims of the Mississippi Flood, his aid to industry through the Dept. Of Commerce.

But Mr. Hoover as President would have a very different task to perform. His previous tasks have been directed, first one then the other, towards one definite aim. He has been sole dictator of each of these tasks. He has had no colleagues with equal authority in performing them. In a sense each of these tasks has been an amplification of a specific engineering job, the building of a great bridge, the tunneling of a mountain or the building of the Panama Canal.

The task of the Presidency is far different. The President of the United States must have a mind not single-tracked, but like a great railroad yard. During the course of each and every day in the White House he is confronting tasks with ten wholly uncoordinated problems, presented by ten uncoordinated government departments. He concerns himself with the broad field of foreign affairs, then with the Army and Navy, then with agriculture, then with Foreign commerce, then with Home industries, then with difficult legal problems, then with conservation, then with the Mails and Express service, then with the business of separate commissions, like the Interstate Commerce Commission and the Federal Trade Commission and then with grave problems of finance. Somehow, though I admire him greatly as an administrator for a single task, I cannot picture a President Hoover successful in jumping at half hour intervals from problem to problem from point to point in the administration of the vast array of business affairs of the Federal Government and keeping his equilibrium.

Then there is the other point. Weaving in and out of every part of these multifarious problems is the inevitable, constant and pertinacious "involvement," as President Harding would have said, with the Legislative branch of the Government. History says that some of the finest executive Presidents have made complete failures of their relationship with the Congress of the United States. Frankly, I do not for one minute believe that my friend, Mr. Hoover, if elected President, will succeed in having anything but a four years' struggle with our friends, the Senators and Representatives on Capitol Hill. His is not the type of mind to meet the legislative mind. He has not the patience to work with them to settle differences to achieve results. . . .

ROOSEVELT ADDRESS
November 1, 1928

In a campaign stop in Yonkers, New York, Roosevelt addressed the crowd on the topic, "Is Hoover Human?" Roosevelt noted that this issue had been raised in a recent article in "one of our leading magazines," a reference to Ray T. Tucker's essay under that title in the November issue of *The North American Review*. Roosevelt went on to posit that Hoover was too much of an elitist who distrusted the "crowd" of ordinary Americans and too much of an engineer. "There is such a thing as too much engineering," Roosevelt added. [This document is printed in Samuel I. Rosenman, ed., *The Public Papers and Addresses of Franklin D. Roosevelt* (New York, 1938), pp. 67–72.]

... Yes, I want to say something about the theory of Government. You know, campaign speeches are very different nowadays from what they were when I was young. I go back far enough to remember the Fourth of July orator. There are few of them left, thank God.

But I believe that people are interested in the philosophy of politics, in the theory of our Government. More and more the old-fashioned "pull the eagle's tail to make him scream," or "twist the lion's tail to get a howl out of the mob," has gone by. That day is gone, and we have come down with our better education all over this country to a willingness to talk about the philosophy of politics, and about the theory of Government, provided it can be made at all interesting ...

What leads me to think about this is the fact that this morning I happened to pick up the November number of one of the leading magazines and there on page one was an article with the following caption: "Is Hoover Human?" That title implies something. It implies the suggestion in the minds of a great many citizens that Mr. Hoover is not human. And I went on and I read it, and through seven long pages the author of that article labored, and labored heavily, to prove that the Republican candidate has the human qualities which the title of his own article puts in question. . . .

I want to go on. In this article there was a quotation, a quotation from a book written by the late Secretary of Commerce, Honorable Herbert Hoover, and, mind you, it is very short. It is worth taking home with you and thinking about. Here is what Mr. Hoover writes, with his own pen, out of his own head, in his own book, a book called American Individualism, and he says:

"Acts and deeds leading to progress are born of the individual mind, not out of the mind of the crowd. The crowd only feels, it has no mind of its own which can plan. The crowd is credulous, it destroys, it hates and it dreams, but it never builds. It is one of the most profound of exact psychological truths that man in the mass does not think, but only feels."

I know the gentleman well, and have for many years; and that, in my judgment, is the best insight that you can possibly find into the personality of Herbert Hoover, into his approach to every public and private question. It is characteristic of the man. That question gives the reason why the author of the article asked, "Is Hoover Human?" And it affirms the judgment of tens of thousands of Americans who during the past four months have been viewing him as a possible occupant of the Presidency.

Now, Mr. Hoover's theory that the crowd, that is to say, 95 percent of all the voters who call themselves average citizens, that the crowd is credulous, that it destroys, that it hates, that it dreams, but that it never builds, that it does not think, but only feels—that is in line with the training, the record and the methods of accomplishment of the Republican candidate for the Presidency.

It is another way of saying, and I say this as an analyst and not as a candidate, that there exists at the top of our social system in this country a very limited group of highly able, highly educated people, through whom all progress in this land must originate. Furthermore, that this small group, after doing all the thinking and all the originating, is fully responsible for all progress in civilization and Government.

What is on the other side? It seems to me that the whole life of the man whom we still refer to as "Our Al Smith" is a refutation of this innate theory of his opponent. Governor Smith has given undoubted proof of the definite fact that the mass of humanity does think, that it can make up its own mind on the pros and cons of all public questions; that it often originates, and that there is a very definite relationship between what Mr. Hoover calls the crowd and the continuation of modern progress. . . .

And yet, Mr. Hoover's attitude on that subject, and I suppose the attitude of those ideal individuals of his who would do all our thinking for us, is that the present conditions in the United States—all over the United States—constitute merely a "noble experiment." Governor Smith, on the other hand, recognizes the diametrically opposite point of view; he recognizes that the great majority of the average voters do think, and by that process of thought are convinced of the outrageous conditions that have resulted from the Volstead Law and its present method of administration; furthermore, that a change in these conditions is demanded from the bottom upward. Governor Smith and I are at one in recognizing this demand from what Mr. Hoover calls the crowd. We recognize it as the thought on the part of that crowd, the thought that demands constructive action. Constructive action means change from the present condition, and we favor change. . . .

In the final analysis the great issue in both the national and State campaigns revolves around that fundamental belief of my friend Mr. Hoover in the incapacity of the mass of average citizens either to think or to build. In the national election the great Governor of the State of New York is the most splendid living example of the opposite fact.

And in this State election, too, the same point is raised, for the Republican leadership of this State is based on that same belief that Mr. Hoover holds. I deny, and the Democratic Party denies, that the average man and woman in this State, who make up its electorate, are incapable of thought or of constructive ability. I know that the electorate does think, that it does originate, and that it does build, and it is on that fundamental belief that I base my campaign for the Governorship. It is the same belief which has brought to us the great program of the past few years; the same belief that must carry us forward during the coming years to an even greater progress. . . .

ROOSEVELT TO CHARLES H. BETTS
December 21, 1928

Roosevelt's comments about Hoover were controversial with some voters, including Charles Betts, the publisher of two independent newspapers in upstate New York, and an early Hoover supporter. Roosevelt was careful to qualify his campaign remarks knowing, perhaps, that he would be working with Hoover over the next four years. [This letter was first published in *FDR: His Personal Letters, 1928–1945*, edited by Elliott Roosevelt, 2 vols. (New York, 1950), pp. 20–21.]

Albany,
Dec. 21, 1928

Dear Mr. Betts:

I am glad to have your nice letter of December 8th. I am perfectly sure that you are wrong about my saying—"this man Herbert Hoover." I have never used that expression in my life. I may have said "what has Mr. Hoover ever done" or "what has my friend Hoover ever done," but I certainly never said "This man Herbert Hoover." It is perfectly possible that I asked the rhetorical question—"what has he ever done"—but I am very certain that I followed it up with a statement of what he has done. In other words, I tried to point out in the campaign, on many occasions, that Mr. Hoover has accomplished many great tasks where he was the sole boss, and relating to some specific object, but that frankly I doubted whether his type of ability could coordinate all of the one hundred and one simultaneous tasks that fall to the lot of a President.

Anyway you and I will soon know whether my doubt is justified or not. Mr. Hoover is an old friend of mine and for the sake of the country, I hope he will make good.

We shall hope to see you in Albany and you must be sure to come in to see me when you come there.

Very sincerely yours,
FRANKLIN D. ROOSEVELT

ROOSEVELT TO HOOVER
March 4, 1929

Roosevelt was among the many Americans who congratulated Hoover on the day of his inauguration as the 31st president of the United States. The new governor of New York telegraphed the following message. [This document is from the Franklin D. Roosevelt Papers in the Franklin D. Roosevelt Library.]

MARCH 4, 1929.

THE PRESIDENT,
THE WHITE HOUSE,
WASHINGTON, D.C.

PLEASE LET ME EXTEND TO YOU THE FELICITATIONS AND GOOD WISHES OF THE PEOPLE OF THE STATE OF NEW YORK ON YOUR INAUGURATION STOP MRS ROOSEVELT AND I ALSO SEND YOU AND MRS HOOVER OUR PERSONAL CONGRATULATIONS AND GOOD WISHES

FRANKLIN D. ROOSEVELT
GOVERNOR

HOOVER TO ROOSEVELT
March 7, 1929

Hoover took a moment out of the hectic first days of his presidency to acknowledge Roosevelt's telegram. The cordiality expressed in this exchange would quickly come to an end. [This document is from the Franklin D. Roosevelt Papers in the Franklin D. Roosevelt Library.]

March 7, 1929

My dear Governor Roosevelt:

I have been greatly pleased to receive your cordial message extending to me the felicitation and good wishes of the people of the State of New York. Thank you very much for sending it.

Thank you, too, for the personal congratulations and good wishes from you and Mrs. Roosevelt to Mrs. Hoover and myself. I want you to know of our deep appreciation.

Faithfully yours,
/s/ Herbert Hoover

Hon. Franklin D. Roosevelt,
Governor of New York,
Albany, New York.

DIARY OF EDGAR RICKARD
April 13, 1929

The famed Gridiron Club sponsored a dinner each spring at which the president was the guest of honor. The entertainment for the evening were humorous remarks lampooning American politics in general and the president in particular. As one of the president's closest friends, Edgar Rickard attended his first Gridiron dinner with Hoover on April 13. All of the remarks were taken in good humor by Hoover except for those delivered by Franklin Roosevelt.

Saturday, April 13, 1929

With H. H. to Gridiron Club Dinner (my first), clipping attached and program preserved gives main joshes. Tense moment when Gov. Franklin Roosevelt, speaking from head table, makes ingracious remarks, entirely out of place, re H. H., and H. H. comes back with dignified and telling rebuke. Am guest of Roy Howard and [Richard V.] Oulahan. Remarkable event, with every high official of the government and entire Diplomatic Corps present. H. H. feels Roosevelt attack keenly and questions if his rebuke in order; takes club gibes in fine humor.

ROOSEVELT TO HOOVER
November 24, 1929

The most devastating economic depression in the nation's history began with the "crash" of the New York stock market in October. In an effort to counter the impact of this downturn, Hoover turned to public officials as well as to industrial leaders asking them to speed up production and public works projects. Among the telegrams sent out in late November was one to the governor of New York. [This document is from the Franklin D. Roosevelt Papers at the Franklin D. Roosevelt Library.]

En route November 24, 1929

The President
The White House
Washington D C

I have read on the train of your telegram to all governors stop I expect to recommend to the legislature which meets January first a much needed construction program for hospitals and prisons stop this program will be larger than ever before and will be limited only by estimated receipts from revenues without increasing taxes stop the definite figures of my recommendations will be sent you and I am asking the acting governor to ascertain from all mayors and county authorities the amounts of their construction budgets.

Franklin D. Roosevelt
Governor of the State of New York

HOOVER TO ROOSEVELT
November 27, 1929

The president expressed his appreciation to the governor in a brief letter three days later. No doubt Hoover was eager to maintain good ties with the leader of the Empire State. [This document is from the Franklin D. Roosevelt Papers in the Franklin D. Roosevelt Library.]

November 27, 1929

My dear Governor Roosevelt:

I have received your response to my telegram of November 23rd. I deeply appreciate the fine spirit of cooperation which you have extended in this national effort.

I am arranging for Secretary Lamont to keep you informed as to the progress in other States in order that you may be assured of the unity of action necessary for national results.

Yours faithfully,
/s/ Herbert Hoover

Hon. Franklin D. Roosevelt,
Governor of New York,
Albany, New York.

ROOSEVELT TO LOUIS M. HOWE
August 19, 1930

As the depression deepened, the criticism of Hoover increased. Indeed, cartoonists and columnists began to blame the president for the nation's economic woes. Always the politician, Roosevelt saw the president's declining image as an opportunity for the Democratic Party. In the memorandum below, he shares his idea for a political cartoon with Louis Howe, his closest political confidante. [This document was published in *FDR: His Personal Letters, 1928–1945*, edited by Elliott Roosevelt (New York, 1950), p. 141.]

Albany,

Aug. 19, 1930

Memorandum for L. McH. Howe:

Here is a subject for a campaign cartoon:

Caption: Are you carrying the Hoover banner?

Below this: Picture of a man holding his trousers pockets turned inside out.

Underneath: The words "nuff sed."

[F.D.R.]

HOOVER TO ROOSEVELT
October 21, 1930

Mid-term elections were only one of many things on Hoover's mind in the autumn of 1930. He wrote Roosevelt on October 21 asking him to appoint delegates to the White House Conference on Child Health and Protection. Roosevelt responded a little more than a week later.

My dear Governor:

In July, 1929, I called together a preliminary committee to lay out the work for a nation-wide inquiry into Child Health and Protection. This committee has secured the assistance of more than 1200 national and state officials together with experts in every field, and has gathered facts and compiled data for a nation-wide consideration of the whole subject.

I have called a national conference for this consideration to be held at the White House in Washington, November 19th to 22nd. I am most desirous that every state should participate in the determination of conclusions and recommendations upon this subject.

I would deeply appreciate it, therefore, if you would appoint delegates from your various official Departments who will represent fields in this connection at the conference. The subject is one that I feel will appeal to you. The conference is not called for the purpose of advancing legislation. Its maximum value can be obtained from the advancement of thought and interest in the subject, the exchange of experience and the establishment of standards and methods for the future.

Yours faithfully,

/s/Herbert Hoover

Honorable Franklin D. Roosevelt
Governor of New York
Albany, New York

DIARY OF HENRY L. STIMSON
September 29, 1931

Henry L. Stimson, Hoover's Secretary of State and later Roosevelt's Secretary of War, was a shrewd observer of personalities and an avid diarist. In September of 1931, he recorded his frustration with Hoover over the St. Lawrence Seaway negotiations. In the process, he also documented Hoover's growing distrust of Roosevelt. [This document is from the Henry L. Stimson Papers in the Department of Archives and Manuscripts at Yale University. It is used with permission.]

September 29, 1931

. . . He [Hoover] is not always judicial in his judgments of men who differ with him or whose views do not coincide with his, and sometimes I have found him to be quite prejudiced in such respects. Now in a matter like this, I think it is most important that he should hear every possible side and not give way at all to his prejudices.

At Cabinet I tried to get him to agree to MacNider's advice of not coming out with any publicity with regard to the coming negotiations with Canada over the St. Lawrence Waterways. MacNider had drafted a letter to Governor Roosevelt for the President to send which was intended to stop this publicity by a conciliatory move to Roosevelt. But the President would have none of it. He said that Roosevelt was only playing politics with it and that he knew it because he knew of secret interchanges of plans which were going on between Bennett and Roosevelt. With all due respect I have some doubt about that advice being correct, but I could not get him to follow MacNider's advice and the best I could do was to urge him not to come out with his publicity until MacNider's plan and negotiations with Bennett had a little more time to fructify . . .

HOOVER TO ROOSEVELT
November 9, 1931

As he had done a year previously, the president invited the nation's governors to send delegates to a White House conference. In November of 1931, the subject was home building and home ownership. As governor of New York, Roosevelt was asked to name several delegates. He asked Herbert E. Gaston of the New York State Conservation Department for suggestions. Gaston proposed the names of several individuals who would later serve in prominent positions in Washington—Herbert Lehman, Henry Mogenthau, and Frances Perkins, among others. [This document is from the Franklin D. Roosevelt Papers at the Franklin D. Roosevelt Library.]

November 9, 1931

My dear Governor Roosevelt:

From December 2 to 5 will be held in Washington a national Conference on Home Building and Home Ownership which I have called to consider the whole question of homes—urban and rural.

This Conference follows months of study by committees of men and women of authority and experience who have gathered and analyzed available information as well as made additional studies and inquiries. Among the subjects considered are construction, financing, design, equipment, city planning, environment, furnishing, home management, and the reports and recommendations are based on the best experience of those who have special knowledge of the subjects.

All of these questions are so interlaced with our economic situation, and adequate housing involves such important aspects of health, morals, education, and efficiency that I am hopeful that every state will participate in the forthcoming conference.

I shall greatly appreciate it, therefore, if you will appoint representatives from your various official departments whose interests are in the respective fields of work covered by the Conference in the thought that the exchange of experience and the establishment of standards and methods will encourage home building and home ownership, help to increase employment through stimulation of construction and the industries upon which building depends, and promote social stability.

Yours faithfully,
/s/ Herbert Hoover

The Honorable Franklin D. Roosevelt
Governor of New York
Albany, New York

ROOSEVELT TO HOOVER
December 19, 1931

Hoover was never much of a politician and was not comfortable at ceremonies celebrating the completion of public works projects. To Hoover's thinking, there were more important things to do. It is not surprising, therefore, that when Roosevelt invited Hoover to open the soon-to-be completed Port of Albany, the president balked. In response to Roosevelt's invitation of December 19, he had his secretary, Lawrence Richey, write that "It is impossible for him to say whether it will be possible for him to attend.'' Richey suggested that Roosevelt write the president again in May to receive a definite answer. [This document is from the Franklin D. Roosevelt Papers at the Franklin D. Roosevelt Library.]

December 19, 1931.

The President,
The White House,
Washington, D.C.

My dear Mr. President:

It is a pleasure and an honor for me to extend you a most cordial invitation personally and on behalf of the State of New York to attend the formal opening of the Port of Albany and to dedicate the Federal development of the Hudson River in connection therewith.

I sincerely trust that you may be able to arrange your plans to honor the State of New York and the Port of Albany with your presence as guest of honor and I heartily join with the Albany Port District Commission and the people of this section in the hope that you will be with us. It is planned to have the ceremony in June, but the exact date will be left to you.

The Federal development of the Hudson River, for which Congress has authorized an expenditure of $11,200,000 to deepen the channel to twenty-seven feet, and with which you are thoroughly familiar, is a very important waterway project, not only to the people of New York State but to the Country at large.

The presence of the Chief Executive of the United States will greatly honor us at this most important dedicatory ceremony. I understand it is the intention of the Albany Port District Commission, in charge of this ceremony, to make it a world-wide celebration, as the opening of this Port places it in direct connection with ports in all parts of the world.

The Albany Port District Commission intends to have official representatives of various nations present at the ceremony, as well as notable citizens from all sections of this Country.

I hope also that you and Mrs. Hoover will stay with us at the Executive Mansion in Albany at the time of this dedicatory ceremony.

Very sincerely yours,
/s/ Franklin D. Roosevelt

3

Calm Before the Storm

The spring of 1932 turned the president's attention once again to the ugly sport of politics. As much work as there was to be done fighting the Great Depression, Hoover could not resist discussions of who the Democrats would put up against him in the fall.

Hoover put up a brave front. There was no discussion of his own vulnerability. The talk focused on the horse race that was the Democratic campaign for the nomination. Would it be Al Smith once again? What about Newton Baker? And always in the back of Hoover's mind was the specter of Franklin D. Roosevelt.

Hoover claimed that the Democrats would not nominate Roosevelt—that the New York governor was the weakest candidate in the field! Whether he was being honest with himself and his staff, Hoover said on several occasions that he hoped that Roosevelt would be the Democratic nominee! Hoover's "hope" recalls the ancient curse: "Beware of the answered prayer, you just might get it!"

Once Roosevelt had the nomination, Hoover speculated on his opponent's health. Could a man as frail as Roosevelt withstand the brutal schedule of the campaign? More important, should Hoover make a campaign issue out of Roosevelt's paraplegia? Hoover would hear none of it. He had seen enough mudslinging in 1928 and he vowed not to have another such campaign.

As the campaign was about to begin in earnest, the president and the governor got into dispute over who should negotiate the terms of the St. Lawrence Seaway

Treaty. It seemed that Roosevelt believed that he should have a place at the negotiating table. Hoover brushed this effort aside.

DIARY OF JAMES H. MACLAFFERTY
March 10, 1932

James MacLafferty served as Hoover's point man on Capitol Hill and as such, they frequently discussed political issues. As the presidential elections of 1932 approached, MacLafferty discussed with Hoover the very real possibility that Roosevelt would win the Democratic nomination. As MacLafferty notes in his diary for March 10, Hoover knew that he was in for a tough reelection fight, no matter who the Democrats nominated. [This document is from the James MacLafferty Papers at the Hoover Institution in Stanford, California. It is used by permission.]

March 10, 1932.

... I said that I was going to spend the afternoon on the Hill because I wanted to hear the debates on the tax bill and that I was going to, at the same time, try to find out these names.

I now called the President's attention to the fact that the Senate investigation of short-selling on the New York Stock Exchange has been postponed for a week or so and I asked him if there was any significance to be attached to it. He said there was not.

Next I brought up the subject of the results of the Democratic presidential primary held in New Hampshire day before yesterday and in which, although with a very small vote being cast, Governor Roosevelt snowed Al Smith clear under.

The President said that he thought the result was a boost for Roosevelt's aspirations although I could see he was not satisfied in his own mind as to any clear conviction.

I said that as the days pass I am more and more willing to see Roosevelt capture the Democratic nomination. I cited that the Progressives and the Radicals are for him and that they were even now trying to kiss him to death. I called attention to the fact that Senator Wheeler, of Montana, whom I call a Radical, had just left for North Dakota to take the stump for Roosevelt in anticipation of the presidential primaries that are soon to be held in that State. I said that the conservative East would greatly fear Roosevelt as a nominee and that if our party is fortunate enough to take a stand on the wet and dry question that would satisfy reasonable Republican wets we would have a good chance to carry the East against Roosevelt.

The President listened carefully to what I had said and his comment showed that he was inclined to agree. He particularly agreed with the last sentence I have recorded above.

He went on to say that he thought the result of the New Hampshire primary might prove favorable to Garner. He commented on the very small vote that took the trouble to go to the polls in New Hampshire and seemed to feel that it might be because of a lack of interest among the Democrats there as to who their nominee is to be.

The President then opened the top drawer of his desk and took out the list showing the electoral votes that I had given to him the other day. He drew toward him the always present pad of paper and commenced figuring with his pencil as between wet States and doubtful ones while I sat silent. The first result he obtained left him short of the electoral votes necessary for him to get to be elected. He then tried again and came to a conclusion a little more satisfactory to him although not entirely so. I could see that, like myself, he fears his greatest hurdle will be the fanaticism [that] goes rampant on both sides of the wet and dry question. I am sure he will try to outwit it.

ROOSEVELT TO DAVE H. MORRIS
June 6, 1932

An early supporter of Roosevelt's candidacy, Dave Morris eventually became ambassador to Belgium. In the letter below, Roosevelt urged Morris and other members of the "Roosevelt Business and Professional League" to attack Hoover's lack of leadership during the past four years and to argue that Roosevelt stood the best chance of beating the president. [This document was published in *FDR: His Personal Papers 1928–1945*, edited by Elliott Roosevelt (New York, 1950), p. 241]

Albany,

June 6, 1932

Dear Dave:

I hope that during the next two or three weeks you and the other members of the committee can get a few prominent people to come out publicly and state two simple facts. First, that business men realize that another four years of Hoover's inept leadership, or rather complete lack of leadership, will spell disaster for the country and that Hoover will be re-elected unless I am nominated; secondly, that Hoover and the Republican organization are perfectly frank among themselves in saying that Hoover can beat any other Democrat but cannot beat me!

That point of view should be widely disseminated between now and our Convention.

I hope you liked my statement about the Seabury investigation.

Hope to see you soon.

As ever yours,
/s/ Franklin D. Roosevelt

DIARY OF THEODORE JOSLIN
June 9, 1932

Ted Joslin was Hoover's press secretary from 1931 to 1933 and met with the president several times a day. Not surprisingly, Joslin and Hoover regularly discussed politics. In the spring of 1932, the hot topic was the horse race for the Democratic presidential nomination. Although Joslin thought that Roosevelt was likely to get the nomination, Hoover was not so sure. "Well, I hope you are right," Hoover told Joslin, "but I believe they will nominate Newton Baker."

Thursday, June 9, 1932

/s/   I have been saying for some weeks that the Democrats are practically certain to nominate Governor Roosevelt. The President asked me today if I had changed my mind. "Not at all," I replied. "Nothing has happened to change the situation." "Well, I hope you are right," he said. "But I think you are wrong. I hate to think it, but I believe they will nominate Newton Baker." He then told of a conversation with Dave Lawrence who looks for another convention like the New York and Baltimore gatherings, with the prize going to a dark horse. I am still stringing along for Roosevelt probably on the third ballot. He'll be in trouble though, if the balloting goes more than five ballots.

Later in the day I learned that the Scripps-Howard papers had declared editorially for Al Smith—due notice that Roy Howard's flirtation with the President was over. When I told the President, he said, "They have no hope of getting Smith. That is a move to build up Baker. It's a significant development and bears out what I said earlier."

I asked him if he wanted to read the editorial.

"No, I can't waste my time on that cheap trash," he said.

MACLAFFERTY DIARY
June 28, 1932

MacLafferty and the president revisited the case of Franklin Roosevelt and the Democratic nomination on June 28. According to MacLafferty, Hoover "feared" that Roosevelt would not receive the nomination. Whether his comment was sincere or a false bravado, Hoover seemed to believe that he stood the best chance of reelection if he faced Roosevelt in the fall. [This document is from the James MacLafferty Papers in the Hoover Institution at Stanford, California. It is used by permission.]

Washington, D.C., June 28, 1932

. . . This morning I found the President gloomy. He is worrying for fear Roosevelt will not be nominated. I countered with the statement that Roosevelt will be nominated. I said that it was foolish to prophesy but that I was going to do it and that I wanted him to remember that I said Roosevelt will be nominated. I said that there was a time when I felt there were no last ditch Roosevelt people but that I felt differently now and that I believed there were and that if Roosevelt does not receive the nomination there would be deep scars left, that would hurt the chances of whoever was nominated.

I stated that there was little use in speculating on the future until the Democrats were through with their convention and had told the world what they intended to try to do.

The President went on to say what he thought Roosevelt should have done so far and these were things that Roosevelt has not done. The Roosevelt people are now wanting a rule to the effect that if a nomination is not reached under the two-thirds rule by the time there has been six ballots then the balloting shall be done under the majority rule. Mr. Hoover said it would have been much better [to] have advocated that the limit for balloting under the two-thirds rule should have been about twelve ballots. He said that what has now taken place has weakened Roosevelt and that he much feared it would cost him the nomination. I agreed that Roosevelt has been weakened but that he would be nominated in spite of it. I am now, therefore, on record with the President through a prophecy and I hope it is not a false one.

JOSLIN DIARY
June 28, 1932

The Democratic nomination was very much on Hoover's mind in late June. He confided to Joslin, as he had already done to MacLafferty, that he hoped Roosevelt would get the nomination. "Do you still think Roosevelt will get nominated?," Hoover is reported to have asked Joslin. "I hope so. Our salvation lies largely in his nomination." No statement made during the 1932 election season could have been further from the truth.

Tuesday, June 28, 1932

/s/   With the Democratic convention in session, the President had a worried look on his face today. "Do you still think Roosevelt will be nominated?" he asked me. "Absolutely," I replied. "He'll get it on the second or third ballot." "I hope so," the President continued. "Our salvation lies largely in his nomination. Do you still think his running mate will be Ritchie or Garner?" I replied, "It looks more like Garner than Ritchie to me. Roosevelt will be 100 votes short on the first ballot. He'll have to get that number from the weakest of the "stop Roosevelt" group. There are 3 or 4 States to which he can turn. His best bet is the Garner group, which has 90 votes. McAdoo holds that group. He has it in for Smith. If McAdoo switches to Roosevelt it will be all over, for California is at the head of the list of States. Any deal will give Garner the second place and perhaps would include McAdoo for Secretary of the Treasury. It would be sweet revenge for McAdoo for what Smith did to him in 1924."

"I am afraid of Baker," the President said. "He's a strong second choice of the convention and would be a much harder man for me to beat. Do you think he has a chance?"

"He would be nominated if Roosevelt doesn't win on the fourth or fifth ballot at the outside," I said. "But there is one way to nail him. Hearst hates him. Mayer is a good contact for you. Have Larry telephone Mayer that Baker is likely to get the nomination and have him tell Hearst to get busy if he wants to stop him. Hearst's Chicago paper could lay an editorial before all the delegates tomorrow morning."

The idea appealed to the President. He called in Larry who got Mayer on the phone right away. Later in the day Mayer reported back that Hearst would cut loose in the morning. Thus the President is actually picking his own opponent. I haven't any doubt at all that Roosevelt will be nominated surely before the fifth ballot. If the Democrats had any sense they would give Ritchie second place. He would help Roosevelt immensely. But if my guessing is good, they will have to pay off Garner by giving him the V.P. nomination, which is all to the good for us.

MACLAFFERTY DIARY
July 2, 1932

MacLafferty and Hoover discussed the Roosevelt nomination once again on July 2. MacLafferty raised the issue of Roosevelt's paralysis, but Hoover correctly surmised that Roosevelt's movement would be carefully scripted and that the public would not be aware of his "helplessness," as MacLafferty called it. MacLafferty thought that the matter should be an issue in the campaign, but Hoover demurred. [This document is from the James MacLafferty Papers in the Hoover Institution at Stanford, California. It is used by permission.]

Gunston Cove, Virginia, July 2, 1932

This morning I saw the President at his office. He came early. I was shown in at 8:15 o'clock and he had turned his chair away from his desk awaiting me.

"A short time ago," I began, "I congratulated you because of your nomination to succeed yourself as President. Now I congratulate you because Frank Roosevelt has been nominated by the Democrats as your opponent."

"Well," said the President, thoughtfully, "I suppose of all those mentioned he will be the easiest one to beat."

We spoke of the fact that Roosevelt was to fly to the convention today and that he would address that body. I said that the audience would see Roosevelt's physical helplessness and that I marveled at their willingness to put a man as physically incapacitated as he at the head of the government.

Mr. Hoover said that the audience would not be allowed to see Roosevelt's helplessness but that it would be cleverly concealed by the skillful handling of him. He said he had noticed this when Roosevelt was recently at the White House to attend the dinner he, Hoover, had given to the governors of many States. He said that newspaper cameramen had attempted to get pictures of Roosevelt as he was being helped out of his automobile but they were prevented by Roosevelt's military aids who kept so close as to prevent it. I said that I knew the locale of everything in the convention hall at Chicago and that the audience would have to see his helplessness when he took the platform to address them. Mr. Hoover still insisted that in spite of that it would be concealed. But it turns out Mr. Hoover was wrong as to that for it has just been announced over the radio that Mr. Roosevelt is being helped to arise to his feet so that he may address the convention and the whole country is now hearing as to his physical affliction.

I spoke deprecatingly of Roosevelt's hastening to the convention by airplane as soon as he was nominated and said that I was inclined to feel it showed an eager haste that was a little on the cheap order. I really should have said "undignified" for that is really what I meant. Mr. Hoover did not agree with my idea as to this.

I told the President that I was inclined to feel that he was to be the issue in the coming campaign. He said that should not be so. I said that what I really meant was that the people were to be called upon to decide whether or not at this critical stage they were willing to trade him for Roosevelt.

ROOSEVELT TO HOOVER
July 9, 1932

Negotiations between the United States and Canada were at a critical stage during the summer of 1932. The state of New York had been in protracted negotiations with the U.S. State Department over the state's right to the power generated by the St. Lawrence Waterway. To move matters along, Roosevelt proposed a meeting with Hoover. "It is my belief," he telegraphed the president, "that through a personal conference between us this could be promptly solved."

July 9, 1932

The power authority of the state of New York has officially reported to me the status of its negotiations with the state department in the matter of effecting an agreement between the federal administration and the state of New York in connection with the development of the St. Lawrence River for navigation and power.

According to this report after many protracted conferences between the state department and the New York state power authority over a period of many months the Secretary of State has referred the issues to you for final determination.

The question, failure to agree upon which has prevented complete accord, is the proportion of the cost to be borne by the state of New York. I am sure that you agree with me that prompt and speedy settlement of this only question remaining unsettled is a matter of vital necessity. It is a vital necessity for the simple fact that this great project involves two objectives of equal importance and cannot in public justice accomplish one without the other. I am deeply interested in the immediate construction of the deep water way as well as in the development of abundant and cheap power. The state of New York not only owns this potential power but seeks through a state agency to make it available to millions of people at reasonable cost. That is why the determination of the share of the total cost of construction to be paid for by this state is a present factor which should not be relegated to later negotiations between us.

Four sovereignties are involved: The Dominion of Canada and the Province of Ontario, The United States and the state of New York. In Canada the Premier of Canada and the Premier of Ontario have directly conducted negotiations on this very subject. In international matters affecting the joint rights and interests of the United States government and one or more of its sovereign states, an understanding should be reached between the federal and state governments as a condition precedent to the conclusion of negotiation with a foreign nation. In view of this therefore it is my belief that through a personal conference between us this could be promptly solved.

With such an agreement between the federal administration and the state of New York it would be my hope that it would be possible to submit a treaty to the Senate for immediate and I hope favorable action as soon as signed. May I respectfully point out that such action would hasten greatly the initiation of this vast project—one which means cheap transportation by deep waterway for the agricultural and other products of the west; cheap electricity from the state owned and controlled resource to be developed for the primary interest of homes, farms, and industries; and, of immediate importance, employment for thousands of workers. If by thus cutting red tape and eliminating formalities we could work together to secure early and final action on this great public work it would be greatly to the public interest. It has already been too long delayed.

I hold myself subject to your call and am ready to go to Washington on forty-eight hours [sic] notice at your convenience. I shall be on a cruise between New York and Cape Cod this week but will be in port each night. Word to Albany will be forwarded promptly.

Franklin D. Roosevelt
Governor of New York

The President
The White House

HOOVER TO ROOSEVELT
July 10, 1932

Hoover turned aside Roosevelt's suggestion of a personal conference. Matters such as the use of power generated by the waterway would not be a part of the international treaty. Such matters were "purely domestic action" to be settled by each country after the treaty had been signed. In the following telegram, Hoover offered to meet with Roosevelt and other governors after the treaty was signed.

July 10, 1932
Franklin D. Roosevelt
Governor of New York
Albany New York

I am in receipt of your telegram of July 9th. I am glad to assure you that the negotiations between the United States and the Dominion of Canada in respect to the Great Lakes Waterway are making progress and that it will not be necessary to interrupt your cruise by a visit to Washington.

These negotiations, as you know, involving a score of intricate problems, have been under way for nearly three years and have now reached a hopeful aspect. While under our Constitution international treaties fall within the sole jurisdiction of the Federal Government, nevertheless the representatives appointed by you and leaders in other states primarily concerned have been consulted during the course of the negotiations. I am in hopes an agreement can be reached between the two governments, but it has not yet been concluded, and I shall be glad to have you advised when this occurs.

The question of the disposal of the byproduct of power which will result from the works which border the State of New York, like all domestic questions of this character affecting the two countries, is reserved by the proposed treaty for purely domestic action by each country. This disposal is not the subject of international agreement. If a treaty is concluded and is ratified by the Senate, then the domestic questions which may arise must be settled through the action of both the Senate and House of Representatives in accordance with federal and state law and in accord with the interest of all the states of the Union.

You will realize that neither you nor I have authority to enter upon agreements in respect to these domestic questions, but if the treaty is consummated and ratified I shall be glad to consult with you and other governors. I have no doubt that we can make such recommendations to the Congress as will be helpful to them in solving the particular domestic problems relating to each state.

Having ardently advocated for over ten years the great work of completing this shipway from Duluth and Chicago to the sea, I am glad to know that it will meet with your support.

Herbert Hoover

STIMSON DIARY
July 10, 1932

As Secretary of State, Henry L. Stimson was very much involved in the negotiations on the St. Lawrence Waterway. In the diary entry below, Stimson records his reaction to Roosevelt's telegram and Hoover's response, as well as his own thoughts on how the unfortunate matter should be handled. [This document is from the Henry L. Stimson Papers in the Department of Archives and Manuscripts at Yale University. It is used by permission.]

July 10, 1932 (Sunday)

Again this morning the newspapers were full of trouble, for Franklin Roosevelt had bounded into print with a letter to the President about the St. Lawrence Seaway. It was based upon a report of the Power Authority, signed by Walsh, the Chairman of the Power Authority, reporting that we were on the point of making a treaty with Canada and that we had not yet settled with New York what New York was to pay for the electricity. On the basis of this Roosevelt wrote directly to the President asking for a personal conference. I called up the President as soon as I saw the paper and found that he was very much excited. At first he seemed inclined to lay the blame for it on us. We had insisted upon giving the New York people a chance to lay before us during the past year their views on this matter, and as a result of this everything had gone along very smoothly. But now Roosevelt is evidently trying to play politics about it. The President now saw only his effort to play politics and did not, would not, see how much politics we had saved during the year by our conduct. His attitude made me a little angry and I stood up to him pretty strongly. Again I advised him not to take too truculent an attitude towards Roosevelt, although I quite concurred with him as to Roosevelt's attitude, but I took the position that to be truculent would be undignified. It would simply make it worse. As a result of it, the President wrote a letter which he read to me in the afternoon. It was a very good letter indeed, and I told him so. But of course the whole incident worried me. I was very much troubled that it had to drop on him while I was away and I was unable to help. The fact that he took it so hard made it even worse. However, fortunately, Jim Rogers was in Washington, and he helped the President out in this matter. Rogers has had charge of the entire negotiations and, of course, knew more about it than I did, and he concurred entirely with my view in regard to the attitude to be taken towards Roosevelt, and that helped a good deal, because other than that, apparently the President only had Walter Newton to help him and advise him; and Newton's advice as usual is not good, he being rather inflammatory. But the whole thing made me feel my weekend was at an inauspicious time.

4

A Bitter Campaign

The campaign began in earnest during the first days of August. Trying to relax at the cabin he had built on the Rapidan River in Virginia, Hoover could not get his mind off of Roosevelt. As Ted Joslin relates in the first document in this chapter, Hoover was angered by Roosevelt's casual use of the truth. Hoover was determined to respond to every misstatement and he marshaled his troops for the attack!

The campaign itself was a brutal slugfest of attack and counterattack. For the most part, the two candidates crisscrossed the country delivering speeches, many of which were broadcast on radio. With his rich baritone voice, Roosevelt sounded confident that he could solve the country's problems. Hoover, on the other hand, spoke in a flat, nervous, monotone, which gave his listeners the impression that he was under siege. Radio played a big part in the election of 1932.

Perhaps the most ironical attack on Herbert Hoover came in Roosevelt's speech in Sioux City, Iowa, on September 29. It was in that speech that Roosevelt attacked Hoover for driving up the federal deficit! Roosevelt would later discover that controlling the federal budget was not as easy as it seemed from his vantage point in Albany, New York.

In later speeches Roosevelt effectively attacked Hoover as the man responsible for the depression and the man who refused to respond to this economic collapse. Neither charge was true, but the public wanted someone to blame for their misery and Hoover was that man. Try as he might to defend himself, the public would not hear him.

The loss of the presidency was a bitter blow to Hoover, a man who had done so much to help America and her allies. Hoover soon learned how the American people could be manipulated by a masterful politician such as Franklin Roosevelt. Hoover never forgave him.

JOSLIN DIARY
July 31, 1932

The president was in a fighting mood at the end of July, set off by a Roosevelt campaign speech. In a call from Camp Rapidan, Hoover gave specific instructions to Joslin on how to attack the Democratic candidate. "The thing to do, Ted," the president said, "is to carry the fight to Roosevelt. We've got to crack him every time he opens his mouth. Now's our chance." Although he issued the call to arms, Hoover would not lead the charge against Roosevelt. It would not be presidential, he thought. In his place were an army of Republican senators and administration officials to press the cause.

Sunday, July 31, 1932

/s/   What a day! The President had me up at 7:30, even though it was Sunday, and by noon I had given or received 36 telephone calls. The total was 61 at 6 o'clock. The activity was incident to Roosevelt's radio speech last night. It was full of holes and the President, always quick to answer, got me busy lining up senators and dictating the sort of statements they were to use. During the day I turned loose [Reed] Smoot, [James E.] Watson, [L. J.] Dickinson, [Felix] Hebert, [George H.] Moses among others.

"The thing to do, Ted, is to carry the fight to Roosevelt," the President said from the camp. "We've got to crack him every time he opens his mouth. Now's our chance." Then he dictated to me what each of the senators should say, and boy, it's plenty. I'm worn out tonight, but the job is done. If Roosevelt could only know who did the job on him when he reads the papers in the morning!

ROOSEVELT ADDRESS
August 20, 1932

In a speech before a partisan crowd in Columbus, Ohio, candidate Roosevelt lambasted the Republican leadership in general and Herbert Hoover in particular for the state of the nation's economy. He compared the Hoover administration to Alice's Wonderland in *Through the Looking Glass*; Hoover himself was depicted as "Humpty Dumpty." Roosevelt also lampooned Hoover's periodic predictions in 1930 and 1931 that the economic depression would end soon. It would not be a civil campaign. [This document is printed in *The Public Papers and Addresses of Franklin D. Roosevelt*, edited by Samuel Rosenman (New York, 1938), 1: 670–682.]

Much of our trouble came from what the President described as "a new basis in Government relation with business; in fact, a new relationship of Government with its citizens. . . ."

Even before the election of Mr. Hoover a terrible race began between the rising tide of bubble fortunes in the stock market and the rising tide of unemployment. Mr. Hoover's own records in the Department of Commerce showed that there were 2,000,000 fewer men at work in the four principal fields of employment in 1925 than there had been six years previously, although the population and production had vastly increased and many new industries had appeared. . . .

This mobilization of business as the President practices it by promotion and advertising methods will always be defective. His power to influence public opinion is great, but this driving will, as it has been well put, always be back-seat driving—ineffective and dangerous. . . .

It was the heyday of promoters, sloganeers, mushroom millionaires, opportunists, adventurers of all kinds. In this mad whirl was launched Mr. Hoover's campaign. Perhaps foreseeing it, a shrewd man from New England, while in the cool detachment of the Dakota hills, on a narrow slip of paper wrote the historic words, "I do not choose to run. . . ."

It has been suggested that the American public was apparently elected to the role of our old friend, Alice in Wonderland. I agree that Alice was peering into a wonderful looking-glass of the wonderful economics. White Knights had great schemes of unlimited sales in foreign markets and discounted the future ten years ahead.

The poorhouse was to vanish like the Cheshire cat. A mad hatter invited everyone to "have some more profits." There were no profits, except on paper. . . .

Between that day when the abolition of poverty was proclaimed, in August, 1928, and the end of that year, the market balloon rose. It did not stop. It went on, up and up, and up for many fantastic months. These were as the figures of a dream. The balloon had reached the economic stratosphere, above the air, where mere man may not survive.

Then came the crash. The paper profits vanished overnight; the savings pushed into the markets at the peak dwindled to nothing. Only the cold reality remained for the debts were real; only the magnificently engraved certificates not worth the cost of the artistic scroll work upon them!

So I sum up the history of the present Administration in four sentences:

First, it encouraged speculation and overproduction, through its false economic policies.

Second, it attempted to minimize the crash and misled the people as to its gravity.

Third, it erroneously charged the cause to other Nations of the world.

And finally, it refused to recognize and correct the evils at home which had brought it forth; it delayed relief; it forgot reform. . . .

The real point at issue is this. Has the Republican Party, under a captaincy distinguished during the past four years for errors of leadership and unwillingness to face facts, whose whole theory of curing the country's ills has been to call his leading sufferers together in conference to tell him how they may be helped, has this party, I ask, under this leader, suddenly become the Heaven-scent healer of the country who will now make well all that has been ill?

In other words, has the Republican elephant, spotted with the mire through which it has wandered blindly during these past four years, suddenly by miracle overnight become a sacred white elephant of spotless purity, to be worshiped and followed by the people, or has it merely been scrubbed and whitewashed by cunning showmen in the hope that they can deceive a credulous electorate for four years more?

. . . . In contrast to a complete silence on their part, and in contrast to the theories of the year 1928, which I have shown that the Republican leaders still hold, I propose an orderly, explicit and practical group of fundamental remedies. These will protect not the few but the great mass of average American men and women who, I am not ashamed to repeat, have been forgotten by those in power.

ROOSEVELT ADDRESS
September 29, 1932

Roosevelt's remarks in a campaign speech at Sioux City, Iowa, are replete with irony. As a candidate, Roosevelt accused ''the present administration of being the greatest spending Administration in peace times in all our history.'' He accused Hoover of establishing ''bureau on bureau and commission on commission'' and promised to reduce ''the annual operating expenses of your national Government.'' Once in office, Roosevelt found it difficult to keep this promise. Indeed, he would later be attacked by the Republicans for the size of his budgets and the expansion of government. [This document was published in

The Public Papers and Addresses of Franklin D. Roosevelt, edited by Samuel Rosenman (New York, 1938) 1:761.]

I accuse the present Administration of being the greatest spending Administration in peace times in all our history. It is an Administration that has piled bureau on bureau, commission on commission, and has failed to anticipate the dire needs and the reduced earning power of the people. Bureaus and bureaucrats, commissions and commissioners have been retained at the expense of the taxpayer.

Now, I read in the past few days in the newspapers that the President is at work on a plan to consolidate and simplify the Federal bureaucracy. My friends, four long years ago, in the campaign of 1928, he, as a candidate, proposed to do this same thing. And today, once more a candidate, he is still proposing, and I leave you to draw your own inferences.

And on my part I ask you very simply to assign to me the task of reducing the annual operating expenses of your national Government.

ROOSEVELT ADDRESS
October 19, 1932

In Pittsburgh, Roosevelt attacked Hoover for blaming the American economic depression on a troubled world economy. "We need not look abroad for scapegoats," proclaimed Roosevelt. "We had ventured into the economic stratosphere—which is a long way up—on the wings of President Hoover's novel, radical, and unorthodox theories of 1928, the complete collapse of which brought the real crash in 1931." The Democratic message was clear—Hoover gets the blame for America's misery. [This document was published in *The Public Papers and Addresses of Franklin D. Roosevelt*, edited by Samuel Rosenman (New York, 1938), 1:802–803.]

Nineteen hundred and thirty-one proved to be the worst year experienced in the depression up to that time. For my distinguished opponent, 1931 was the year in which all his distinctive 1928 economic heresies seemed to come home to roost, all at the same time.

I emphasize this history because our opponents have now become almost frantic in their insistence that this entire sequence of events originated abroad. I do not know where; they have never located "abroad," but I think it is somewhere near Abyssinia. They insist that no American policy was in the least to blame, and that to say otherwise is what they call "hideous misrepresentation." The "foreign cause" alibi is just like ascribing measles on our little boy to the spots on his chest, instead of to the contagious germ that he has picked up somewhere.

No, we need not look abroad for scapegoats. We had ventured into the economic stratosphere—which is a long way up—on the wings of President Hoover's novel, radical and unorthodox economic theories of 1928, the complete collapse of which brought the real crash in 1931.

HOOVER ADDRESS
October 28, 1932

Battling back against Roosevelt's attacks, the president conducted a brief "whistle stop" campaign through West Virginia, Ohio, and Indiana October 28–29. At each stop along the way, he thanked voters for their support and defended his programs. He reserved his criticism of Roosevelt for his major rally in Indianapolis, where he accused Roosevelt of spreading falsehoods and calumnies about the country's economic crisis. The governor of New York knew better and the president was taking him to task. [This document was published in *Public Papers of the Presidents: Herbert Hoover, 1932–33* (Washington, D.C., 1974), pp. 610–614, 627–629, 632.]

But before I begin the major discussion of the evening, I wish to take a moment of your time to revert to those methods and policies for protection and recovery from this depression in the light of certain recent misstatements of the Democratic candidate in respect to them.

I presume the Governor of New York will announce that I am acting upon the defensive if I shall expose the self-interested inexactitude which he has broadcasted to the American people. I am equally prepared to defend, attack, or expound. I shall not be deterred from my purpose to lay before the people of the United States the truth as to the issues which they confront, and I shall do it with a sense of responsibility of one who has carried out and must carry into effect these issues.

I wish to call your attention to the fact that the Governor of New York in a speech on October 25 stated:

"This crash came in October 1929. The President had at his disposal all of the instrumentalities of the Government. From that day until December 31, 1931, he did absolutely nothing to remedy the situation. Not only did he do nothing, but he took the position that Congress could do nothing."

That is the end of the quotation, and it is a charge which extends over the first 2 years and 2 months of this depression. It seems almost incredible that a man, a candidate for the Presidency of the

United States, would broadcast such a violation of the truth. The front pages of every newspaper in the United States for the whole of those 2 years proclaimed the untruth of that statement. And I need remind you but of a few acts of the administration to demonstrate what I say.

The Governor dismisses the agreements brought about between the leaders of industry and labor under my assistance less than 1 month after the crash by which wages of literally millions of men and women were, for the first time in 15 depressions of a century, held without reduction until after profits had ceased and the cost of living had decreased.

He ignores the fact that today real wages in the United States are higher than at any other depression period, higher in purchasing power than in any other country in the world. And above all, he dismisses the healing effect of that great agreement by which this country has been kept free from industrial strife and class conflicts.

He would suppress from the American people the knowledge of the undertaking brought about within 2 months after the crash amongst the industries of the United States to divide the existing work in such fashion as to give millions of families some measure of income instead of discharging a large portion of them into destitution, as had always been the case in previous depressions and was the case abroad. He ignores the fact that these agreements have held until this day for the staggering of employment.

If the Governor will look up his own files of his official correspondence, he will find that within a month after the crash I appealed to him, amongst the other Governors, for cooperation in creating employment and stabilization of wages, in which I set out to him the gravity of the national situation and urged that he should present in turn the great need to the counties and cities of his State. If he says nothing was done, it was a violation of the promise which he wrote to me on that occasion. . . .

The Governor says nothing had been done. The Governor would also suppress the fact of the mobilization of the American people under my direction during the winters of 1930 and '31 of private charity and of public support to relief of distress in every town, village, and hamlet in the United States through which we carried them over these winters without serious suffering or loss, as is proved by the public health statistics of today.

The Governor cannot be ignorant of the recommendations which I made to the Congress within a month after the crash, and again in the session a year later, for the great increase of Federal public works in aid of employment, and he cannot be ignorant of the appropriations made at my recommendation for the care of farmers stricken by drought or the public funds raised under my leadership for these purposes.

The Governor ignores the most patent fact in the history of this depression: that, under the wise policies pursued by this administration, recovery of the United States from the first phase of the depression—that is, the collapse from our own speculation and boom—began about a year after the crash and continued definitely and positively until April 1931, when the general world crash took place which was not of our doing.

The Governor is probably ignorant of the international measures taken to limit the extension of this prairie fire under American leadership. He ignores the German moratorium and the standstill agreements in June 1931, which not only saved Germany from complete collapse but prevented much of the extended distress from reaching the United States. He neglects the creation, after the collapse of England, of the National Credit Corporation with a capital of $500 million in cooperation amongst American banks, which saved over 700 institutions involving the deposits of upwards of 10 millions of our people, and that was doing something.

The Governor entirely misrepresents the fact that the plan to meet this crisis which swept upon us from Europe was proposed by me to the political leaders of the United States at a White House conference on October 6, 1931. He ignores the fact that plan was laid before the Congress by a message on December 8, and that it was not the creation of the Democratic leaders at the end of December, as he would imply. Although the leaders of the Democratic Party had promised 14 months before they would produce a plan, they produced no plan until they began their destructive program some months later. And not one of those acts has been disavowed by the Governor. He ignores the fact that the unprecedented measures proposed and carried through by the administration with the help of some of the Democratic colleagues in the Congress would have put us on the road to recovery 8 months ago instead of having had to await the adjournment of the Democratic House of Representatives only 4 months ago.

And again the Governor, despite every proof, keeps reiterating the implication that the measures taken by this administration have had no fruitful result to the common man. He has been told, at least by some of the men who advise him in this campaign, that the gigantic crisis with which the United States was faced was escaped by the narrowest margins and that it was due to unprecedented measures adopted by this administration. If some of these men will tell him the whole truth, they will tell him that they personally sought to buy and withdraw large sums of gold because of their belief that we could not maintain the gold reserves of the United States.

Would it not be well that every American citizen should take pride in the fact that America carried this Nation through this crisis safely and soundly and did it as a matter of national and united action?

Why cannot the Governor of New York be frank enough to recognize the successful care of the distressed in the United States; that a vast amount of employment has been provided by cooperative action amongst our citizens; that the savings of more than 95 percent of the depositors in our banks have been held secure; that the 20 million borrowers who otherwise would have been bankrupt by destructive pressures from forced selling of their assets in order to pay their debts have been protected; that the 70 million life insurance policies which represent the greatest act of self-denial of a people in provision for the future safety of their loved ones have been sustained in their vitality; and foreclosure of hundreds of thousands of mortgages upon homes and farms has been prevented? Those are national accomplishments for which the whole American people are proud.

The Governor knows that the integrity of our currency has been sustained, that the credit of the Federal Government has been maintained, that credit and employment are being expanded day by day.

The living proof of these measures, which were conceived from the human heart as well as the human mind, can be found in the men and women in every city, every town, every township, and every block in this broad land, for they have been saved their jobs and their homes and secured from suffering and that by the action of the American people as a whole. . . .

During the past few weeks the Democratic candidate has had a great deal to say in endeavoring to establish the idea in the minds of the American people that I am personally responsible for the bad loans by American bankers and investors to numerous foreign countries. He says: "This is an unsavory chapter in American finance." I agree with part of that. "These bonds are in large part the fruit of the distressing policies pursued by the present administration in Washington. None other, if you please, than the ability of lending to backward and crippled countries." That is the end of the quotation from him.

The Governor does not inform the American people that there is no Federal law regulating the sale of securities and that there is doubtful constitutional authority for such a law. And he fails to state that most of these bonds are issued from the State of New York, which sovereignty has such an authority, and where the government has done nothing of a reform to that evil, if it be one. I recollect a

Republican Governor of New York who, believing that wrong was being done to the citizens of his own and other States on life insurance, found a man named Charles Evans Hughes who cleaned that mess up once and for all.

The Governor has not stated to the American people my oft-repeated warnings that American loans made in foreign countries should be upon sound security and confined to reproductive purposes. I have defined these loans as being the loans made for creative enterprise on which their own earnings would repay interest and capital. In one of his addresses the Governor pretends at least not to understand what a reproductive loan is, and yet, as I will show you in a moment, he does know something about it. I will say at once that when we have surplus capital, properly secured loans for reproductive purposes abroad are an advantage to the American people. They furnish work to American labor in the manufacture of plants and equipments; they furnish continuing demand for American labor in supplies and replacements. The effect of such creative enterprise is to increase the standards of living amongst the people in those localities and enable them to buy more American products and furnish additional work for American labor.

I have no apologies to make for that statement. It is sound; it makes for the up building of the world; it makes for employment of American workmen and profits for American investors. If it be followed there would be no losses. In these statements made by the Governor he entirely omits the conditions and warnings with which I have repeatedly surrounded the statements upon this subject and the warnings which indeed I have given broadcast over the last 7 years in respect to this type of investment. Although no Federal official has any authority to control the security offered on these loans, none of them have defaulted where the safeguards proposed by me have been followed.

It is obvious from the Governor's many speeches that he now considers that all foreign loans are wrong. He seems to consider the selling of foreign bonds in our country to be wicked and the cause of our calamities. And an interesting part of all this tirade is that I have never yet been engaged in the selling of foreign bonds and foreign loans. I have not been accused of that. The Governor, however, has an advantage over me in experience in that particular. As late as 1928 the Governor was engaged in that business for profit and actively occupied in promotion of such loans. At that time he was the chairman of the organization committee of the Federal International Banking Company, a corporation organized for the selling of foreign securities and bonds to the American people. . . .

Two weeks ago at Cleveland I felt it was necessary to denounce certain calumnies being circulated in this campaign by the Democratic National Committee in official instructions to their campaign speakers. That committee privately acknowledged that these have not a shred of foundation, and yet they refuse to take the manly course and withdraw those statements. They have sought to maintain their continuing poison by silence.

I now have before me other calumnies of the Democratic National Committee, circulated in the same fashion by instructions to their campaign speakers. These instructions bristle with titles such as these—and these questions will interest American women—they are entitled:

"How President Hoover has failed children."

"His real interest in the Nation's children may be gained by his recorded effort to emasculate and disrupt the Children's Bureau."

"The bunk of the Home Loan Bank."

Governor Roosevelt implies his endorsement of these calumnies by repeating these implications in his speeches when he speaks of what he calls ". . . attempts that have been made to cut appropriations for child welfare." . . .

Aside from the fact that the charge that the Supreme Court has been controlled by any political party is an atrocious one, there is a deeper implication in that statement. Does it disclose the Democratic candidate's conception of the functions of the Supreme Court? Does he expect the Supreme Court to be subservient to him and his party? Does that statement express his intention by his appointments or otherwise attempt to reduce that tribunal to an instrument of party policy and political action for sustaining such doctrines as he may bring with him?

My countrymen, I repeat to you, the fundamental issue of this campaign, the decision that will fix the national direction for a hundred years to come, is whether we shall go on in fidelity to American traditions or whether we shall turn to innovations, the spirit of which is disclosed to us by many sinister revelations and veiled promises.

My friends, I wish to make my position clear. I propose to go on in the faith and loyalty to the traditions of our race. I propose to build upon the foundations which our fathers have laid over this last 150 years.

ROOSEVELT ADDRESS
October 31, 1932

As the campaign was winding down, Roosevelt delivered an address on unemployment to a sympathetic crowd in Boston. In this speech, Roosevelt criticized the Hoover campaign for abandoning argument for personalities. "The

Administration attempts to undermine reason through fear," noted Roosevelt, "by telling us the world will come to an end on November 8th if it is not returned to power for four years more. Once more it is leadership that is bankrupt, not only in ideals, but in ideas. It sadly misconceives the good sense and self reliance of our people." Roosevelt responded by charging Hoover with having done nothing to fight the Depression. [This document was published in *The Public Papers and Addresses of Franklin D. Roosevelt*, edited by Samuel Rosenman (New York, 1938), 1:843–855.]

The President began this campaign with the same attitude with which he has approached so many of the serious problems of the past three years. He sought to create the impression that there was no campaign going on at all, just as he had sought to create the impression that all was well with the United States, and that there was no depression. . . .

At Indianapolis he spoke of my arguments, misquoting them. But at Indianapolis he went further. He abandoned argument for personalities.

In the presence of a situation like this, I am tempted to reply in kind. But I shall not yield to the temptation to which the President yielded. On the contrary, I reiterate my respect for his person and for his office. But I shall not be deterred even by the President of the United States from the discussion of grave national issues and from submitting to the voters the truth about their national affairs, however unpleasant that truth may be. . . .

The Administration attempts to undermine reason through fear by telling us that the world will come to an end on November 8th if it is not returned to power for four years more. Once more it is a leadership that is bankrupt, not only in ideals but in ideas. It sadly misconceives the good sense and the self-reliance of our people. . . .

The present leadership in Washington stands convicted, not because it did not have the means to plan, but fundamentally because it did not have the will to do. That is why the American people on November eighth will register their firm conviction that this Administration has utterly and entirely failed to meet the great emergency.

The President complains, President Herbert Hoover, because I have charged that he did nothing for a long time after the depression began. I repeat that charge. It is true. I can further add to that charge by saying that from the time this report by Secretary of Commerce Hoover was published in 1923, for the six years that preceded the crash in 1929, he did nothing to put into effect the provisions advocated in 1923 against the possibility of a future depression.

Instead of doing something during these six years, and especially the last year or two, he participated in encouraging speculation, when the sound business brains of the country were saying that speculation should be discouraged, and in spite of the fact that his own report in 1923 said that depressions are in large part due to over-speculation. He failed to prepare by positive action against the recurrence of a depression. On the contrary—the exact contrary— he intensified the forces that made for depressions by encouraging that speculation. . . .

Immediate relief of the unemployed is the immediate need of the hour. No mere emergency measures of relief are adequate. We must do all we can. We have emergency measures but we know that our goal, our unremitting objective, must be to secure not temporary employment but the permanence of employment to the workers of America. . . .

But when the President speaks to you, he does not tell you that by permitting agriculture to fall into ruin millions of workers from the farms have crowded into our cities. These men have added to unemployment. They are here because agriculture is prostrate. A restored agriculture will check this migration from the farm. It will keep these farmers happily, successfully, at home; and it will leave more jobs for you. It will provide a market for your products, and that is the key to national economic restoration.

One word more. I have spoken of getting things done. The way we get things done under our form of Government is through joint action by the President and the Congress. The two branches of Government must cooperate if we are to move forward. That is necessary under our Constitution, and I believe in our constitutional form of Government.

But the President of the United States cannot get action from the Congress. He seems unable to cooperate. He quarreled with a Republican Congress and he quarreled with a half Republican Congress. He will quarrel with any kind of Congress, and he cannot get things done.

That is something that the voters have considered and are considering and are going to remember one week from tomorrow. You and I know, and it is certainly a fact, that the next Congress will be Democratic. I look forward to cooperating with it. I am confident that I can get things done through cooperation because for four years I have had to work with a Republican Legislature in New York.

I have been able to get things done in Albany by treating the Republican members of the Legislature like human beings and as my associates in Government. I have said that I look forward to the most pleasant relations with the next Democratic Congress, but in addition to that let me make it clear that on that great majority of national problems which ought not to be handled in any partisan manner, I confidently expect to have pleasant relations with Republicans in the Senate and the House of Representatives as well as with Democrats.

After the fourth of March, we—meaning thereby the President and the members of both parties in the Halls of Congress—will, I am confident, work together effectively for the restoration of American economic life.

I decline to accept present conditions as inevitable or beyond control. I decline to stop at saying, "It might have been worse." I shall do all that I can to prevent it from being worse but—and here is the clear difference between the President and myself—I go on to pledge action to make things better.

HOOVER ADDRESS
November 4, 1932

At a campaign rally in St. Louis, the president again defended his record and attacked his Democratic rival. His tone was combative as he criticized Roosevelt for having sullied the campaign with misinformation and innuendo. It had been a nasty campaign and Hoover put the blame squarely on Roosevelt. [This document was published in *Public Papers of the President: Herbert Hoover, 1932–33* (Washington, D.C., 1974), pp. 719–720.]

... Now, if by maintaining the prosperity of this country over a long period of years the people did become so overconfident of the future and thus over optimistic, the Republican Party might be praised at least for that long period of prosperity. It was a bad outbreak of overoptimism and overconfidence. The collapse of the boom brought about great losses and great suffering, but I submit that some of the greatest leaders amongst the boom promoters of that period belonged to the Democratic Party, and the Democratic candidate himself assisted actually in promotions during that period which he now so warmly denounces. I do not criticize his acts. They were honest formations of concern. He was merely participating in the prevailing mood, like the former Democratic candidate who undertook the construction of the tallest building in the world in the same boomtown.

Of more importance, the Governor in his speeches conveys the impression that as President I should have stopped the boom. He does not describe the method by which I should have stopped it. Of course there is no constitutional nor statutory authority to Presidents to stop booms. If the President had attempted to stop that boom, one of the persons that he would have needed to warn is the present Democratic candidate.

Now, the only way I can see that a President could even tilt with a boom would be to turn himself personally into a blue sky law and go on the stump analyzing balance sheets and stock market prices and proving to the people that their investments were wrong. Now, I have little taste for this proposal that the White House should be turned into a stock tipster's office. I earnestly object to the idea that such a form of dictatorship should ever be set up over the American people, even if they do get over optimistic. It may lead in directions for which this Republic would be mighty sorry. Even the Democratic platform does not seem to accord with the Governor, for it says: "We condemn the actions of high public officials designed to influence stock market prices."

Now, this same sort of reasoning led the Governor to propose in this city that the Presidential influence should be used in municipal finance. He said: "If necessary they must be compelled to walk in the way of municipal honesty and efficiency," and he added: "This is what I propose to do toward the credit represented by the 17 billions of municipal bonds." It occurs to me that we should need to revise our whole form of government and the Constitution of the United States in a dozen places if the President of the United States is to supervise municipalities and mayors.

The Governor seems to have some idea of creating a Federal blue sky law to prevent booms and control the issue of all sorts of securities. I am not disputing that many securities are issued which are dishonest and over which there should be a control. But, the full constitutional authority for that sort of action rests, of course, in the States, and I am advised that this is not within the constitutional authority of the Federal Government. In any event, even if it were, I doubt whether the people in any State in the Union would like to have another board in Washington, distant from their own close inspection and understanding, dealing out certificates as to issue of securities and thus controlling the industries of their States. In any event, his plan would be centralization of government beyond anything we have hitherto witnessed and does not seem to accord with the forgotten Democratic theory of State rights. All this has been within the power of the State of New York not only to protect its own citizens but the citizens of other States, and the Governor seems to have forgotten it until this campaign . . .

HOOVER ADDRESS
November 5, 1932

As Election Day drew closer, Hoover became more personal in his remarks. On November 5, he spoke in St. Paul and castigated Roosevelt and the Democratic

Party for running a mean-spirited campaign. Once again, Hoover responded to the scurrilous charge that he was not a U.S. citizen. Hoover also went on the offensive by warning farmers that Roosevelt intended to abolish the Federal Farm Board. [This document was published in *Public Papers of the President: Herbert Hoover, 1932–33* (Washington, D.C., 1974), pp. 762–763.]

Governor Roosevelt in his address last night also stated: "I have been scrupulously careful to engage in no personalities, no unfair innuendoes, no baseless charges against the President of the United States."

I would like to have someone else answer this, but it appears that I am the one to carry the answer across to the American people. I would recommend that anyone interested in this statement should read Governor Roosevelt's speeches from the beginning of this campaign.

I have been compelled to take the unprecedented action of calling attention to a few of them. I have been also compelled to frequently call attention to statements being put out through the Democratic National Committee and their agencies which amount to positive calumnies. In no case has the Democratic candidate disavowed this action of his official committee or agencies. He has naturally profited by his silence.

I have been informed in this State that someone is endeavoring to picture me as having voted in a foreign country as an indication that I am not a citizen of the United States. I know it is directed from the activities of the Democratic local committees. But why answer those things? That picture is taken from the tax rolls of a foreign country where I at one time rented a house, and where there is a tax on every item of rent and where the rolls are made up from the tax rolls; where I never voted or had a right to vote. This has been privately and publicly denounced by the Secretary of State over the last 8 years.

I have just heard of another of these actions which took place yesterday in the State of Ohio—the circulation of thousands of handbills stating that the Farm Board spends $5 million annually in salaries and has a fund of $250,000 for traveling expenses. This statement is untrue. There follows a long list of salaries purported to be paid by the Farm Board.

It states, incidentally, that Mr. Roosevelt will abolish the Farm Board. If that be true—but I don't believe it is true—that will be of interest to the 2 million members of farm cooperatives in the United States and especially in a great part of the Northwest.

As to the first point, the administrative expenditures of the Board are less than $900,000 per annum, and I would call attention to the fact that the members of the Farm Board receive about $10,000 a year. The salaries referred to in this circular do not refer largely to the employees of the Farm Board. Many are exaggerated, but the great bulk of them are officials employed by farmer-owned, farmer-controlled and farmer-managed cooperatives because they have sought for the highest skill in the marketing of their products. The Farm Board has no control of these salaries. They are paid at the will of the American farmer and his organizations. The organization you have built up in this State and the salaries are enumerated here as a matter of personal defamation of myself.

But the only point of importance for me to make now is that this is typical of stories being spread through the Nation with a view to misleading the people. I regret that I have to refer to them. They ought to be omitted from a political discussion.

BERLE DIARY
November 7, 1932

The prospects for a big Roosevelt victory were very good the day before the election. Berle recorded in his diary a conversation with Roosevelt about the impact of a landslide. Most interesting is Roosevelt's scenario of how he could become president shortly after the election. [This document was published in *Navigating the Rapids, 1918–1971: From the Papers of A. A. Berle*, edited by Beatrice A. Berle (New York, 1973), p. 75.]

Memorandum, November 7, 1932

I spent Saturday with Governor Roosevelt. Raymond Moley became ill on Friday afternoon and was in bed; General Johnson is still out of action, for the same reason which keeps Key Pittman at the Roosevelt.

On Saturday afternoon, the decks having been cleared, the governor fell to talking about the prospective Cabinet. I observed that [William Randolph] Hearst had already given him one. . . .

I said I hoped his majority would not be too large; if it was something amazing—say twenty-five million (It would be ten million, said the Governor)—the country would want economic action far more quickly than any political engineering could arrange it and, not getting it, there might be a very serious situation. His response was that the kind of program he had in mind necessarily would take a certain amount of time; that if the majority were very large there would be instant pressure on Hoover to fire [Henry L.] Stimson, appoint him [Roosevelt] Secretary of State; have [Vice-President Charles] Curtis resign to the President and then have the President submit his own resignation, whereupon Roosevelt would become President. He indicated that he thought there might even be some possibility of this happening, though he did not consider it probable.

HOOVER TO ROOSEVELT
November 8, 1932

Long before the last of the votes were counted, it was clear that Roosevelt would be the winner by a wide margin. The final totals were 27.8 million votes for Roosevelt to only 15.8 million votes for Hoover. As is the custom in American politics, the loser concedes defeat and congratulates the victor. [This document was published in *Public Papers of the President: Herbert Hoover, 1932–33* (Washington, D.C., 1974), pp. 801.]

November 8, 1932

President-Elect Franklin D. Roosevelt:

I congratulate you on the opportunity that has come to you to be of service to the country and I wish for you a most successful administration. In the common purpose of all of us I shall dedicate myself to every possible helpful effort.

Herbert Hoover

ROOSEVELT TO HOOVER
November 9, 1932

The president-elect acknowledged the president's telegram with one of his own the next day. The cordiality of the two telegrams masked a growing tension and distrust between these two former allies.

November 9, 1932

President Herbert Hoover
The White House

I appreciate your generous telegram. For the immediate as well as for the more distant future I join in your gracious expression of a common purpose in helpful efforts for our country.

Franklin D. Roosevelt

5

Cooperation or Conflict

There is no question that Hoover was bitter about his election loss. He had worked tirelessly, day and night, to combat a financial depression that he called "a war on a thousand fronts." His efforts seemed to matter little to the American people. He could not shake the image of a grim-faced man who sat behind a desk and did little or nothing to respond to a suffering nation. This image could not, however, have been farther from the truth.

The American people knew little of the president's 16-hour days fighting the ravages of economic crisis. Hoover noted that being president at such a time was similar to being a repairman behind a leaky dike. "No sooner is one leak plugged up," he noted wryly, "then it is necessary to dash over and stop another that has broken out. There is no end to it." But for all his effort and all of his previous accomplishments, Hoover could not engender hope. He had to face that grim fact on election day.

Hoover was not one to feel sorry for himself. A looming crisis over foreign debt required his attention. It was more important, Hoover believed, to join with Roosevelt "in a common cause for the good of the country." Roosevelt would not become president for nearly four months and the nation's economy could not be allowed to drift. The president arranged to meet with the president-elect on November 22 to brief him on the state of the nation and agree on a common plan.

Although the meeting took place as planned, there was little agreement between the two rivals. Roosevelt was reluctant to take any action—or approve any of Hoover's plans. When pressed for a reason, the president-elect responded that he would be prepared to act after he was president, but not before. Hoover saw this as little more than a political ploy and it embittered him.

HOOVER TO ROOSEVELT
November 12, 1932

Roosevelt's stunning election-day victory undermined Hoover's ability to govern. The British and French were eager to renegotiate their debt payments to the United States, but were unwilling to do so without the concurrence of the president-elect. In an effort to win Roosevelt's support, Hoover sent him the following telegram. "I am prepared to deal with the subject as far as it lies in the power of the Executive," he wrote Roosevelt, "but it must be our common wish to deal with this question in a constructive fashion for the common good of the country." [This document was published in *Public Papers of the President: Herbert Hoover, 1932–33* (Washington, D.C., 1974), pp. 813–816.]

November 12, 1932

Governor Franklin D. Roosevelt
Albany, New York

The Secretary of State has informed me that the British Ambassador, on behalf of his government, has handed him a note stating that "They believe that the regime of intergovernmental financial obligations as now existing must be reviewed; that they are profoundly impressed with the importance of acting quickly and that they earnestly hope that the United States Government will see its way clear to enter into an exchange of views at the earliest possible moment."

The British Ambassador further asks for a suspension of the payments due by the British Government to our Government for the period of the discussion suggested or for any other period that may be agreed upon. This last suggestion clearly relates to the payment of $95,000,000 which will fall due on December 15, 1932. I have requested the Secretary of State to transmit to you a full copy of that note.

The Secretary of State has also just been informed that similar requests are to be made by other debtor governments which likewise are obligated to make payments to the United States on December 15th next. One debtor nation has defaulted on a payment due November 10th and another debtor nation has served notice on our government of its incapacity to make a payment due in December.

Thus our government is now confronted with a world problem of major importance to this nation.

The moratorium which I proposed a year ago in June—that is the year's postponement of intergovernmental debts and the spread of the deferred payment over 10 years was approved by the Congress. It served a great purpose in staying destruction in every direction and giving to Europe a year in which to realize and so modify their attitude on solely European questions as to support their credit structure from a great deal of further destruction. They have made very substantial progress during that year in financial adjustments among themselves and toward armament reduction.

Practically all of our World War debt settlements were made not by the Executive, but by the Commission created by Act of Congress, and all were approved in the form of legislation enacted by both Houses. A year ago in recommending to the Congress the ratification of the moratorium I presented a statement of my views as to the whole of the relationship of ourselves to our debtor countries and pointed out that debts to us bore no relationship to debts between other nations which grew out of the war.

At the same time I recommended to the Congress that a new Debt Commission be created to deal with situations that might arise owing to the temporary incapacity of any individual debtor to meet its obligations to our country during the period of world depression. Congress declined to accede to this latter recommendation; it passed a Joint Resolution reading in part as follows:

"It is hereby expressly declared to be against the policy of the Congress that any of the indebtedness of foreign countries to the United States should be in any manner canceled or reduced; and nothing in this Joint Resolution shall be construed as indicating a contrary policy or as implying that favorable consideration will be given at any time to a change in the policy hereby declared."

The limitation to purely temporary and individual action as to those incapable of payment during the depression expressed in the "Communique" referred to in the British note, and in my recommendation to the Congress was evident in these documents. The refusal of the Congress to authorize even the examination of this limited question, together with the above resolution, gave notice to all debtor governments of the attitude of this Government toward either cancellation or reduction of existing obligations. Therefore any commitments which European Governments may have made between themselves could not be based upon any assurances of the United States. Moreover the tenor of negotiations asked for by the debtor governments goes beyond the terms of the congressional resolution referred to.

I have publicly stated my position as to these questions including that I do not favor cancellation in any form but that we should be receptive to proposals from our debtors of tangible compensation in other forms than direct payment in expansion of markets for the products of our labor and our farms. And I have stated further that substantial reduction of world armament which will relieve our own and world burdens and dangers has a bearing upon this question. If negotiations are to be undertaken as requested by these governments, protracted and detailed discussions would be necessary which could not be concluded during my administration. Any negotiation of this question on the basis of the requests of these governments is limited by the resolution of the Congress. And if there is to be any change in the attitude of the Congress it will be greatly affected by the views of those members who recognize you as their leader and who will properly desire your counsel and advice.

This outlines where the question stands at the present moment.

I am prepared to deal with the subject as far as it lies in the power of the Executive, but it must be our common wish to deal with this question in a constructive fashion for the common good of the country. I am loath to proceed with recommendations to the Congress until I can have an opportunity to confer with you personally at some convenient date in the near future.

There are also other important questions as to which I think an interchange of views would be in the public interest. The building up of world economic stability is of course of the greatest importance in the building up of our recovery. As you know, a world economic conference will be held during the course of the coming winter. Already two American experts have met with the technical experts of other governments to prepare tentative agenda. While this conference may be begun during my administration, it is certain that it will not complete its labors until after you have assumed office.

Parallel with this, of course, is the disarmament conference in which the United States has taken a leading part, this also has a great economic purpose as well as the advancement of world peace.

Time is of great importance in all these questions and I understand that you are planning to come through Washington sometime during the latter part of next week, and I hope you will find it convenient to stop off long enough for me to advise with you. I should, of course, be only too glad to have you bring into this conference any of the Democratic Congressional leaders or other advisers you may wish.

Herbert Hoover

HOOVER MEMORANDUM
November 22, 1932

Roosevelt's visit to the White House was historic, perhaps the first time a president-elect had visited the White House prior to inauguration day. But perilous times demanded unprecedented action. Roosevelt and Hoover, joined by Professor Raymond Moley and Secretary of the Treasury Ogden Mills, met for more than two hours in the Red Room. The transcript that follows is the president's version of what took place. [A brief account from Roosevelt's perspective was published in *The Public Papers and Addresses of Franklin D. Roosevelt*, edited by Samuel Rosenman (New York, 1938), 1:867.]

Memorandum—November 22, [1932]

Governor Roosevelt, Secretary Mills, and Professor Moley arrived in the Red Room at about 3:30 and we entered at once into a discussion of the debt and allied questions.

I traversed the principles upon which our government had acted consistently, including the Wilson Administration, in connection with the debts. I outlined these principles as to the moral and actual validity of the debt; that it was a contract between ourselves and individual Allied nations and not a collective debt; that they must be dealt with separately; that the debts had already been revised at great sacrifice; that our insistence had been from the beginning that they bore no relationship to German reparations; our refusal to participate in reparations or any negotiations in relation to our debt; and the relationship of the Congress to the debt settlement. We compassed the attempts to mix us in German reparations by the European governments, first through the Dawes conference, then the Young conference, and subsequently at Lausanne, and I explained the safeguards that we had taken on all occasions against becoming so involved.

I pointed out the extreme importance of our maintaining a solid national front on this issue. I expressed the conviction that we should insist on the December 15 payments of $125,000,000. I pointed out that we should do this, first because without such payment and continued postponements of those made by the eighteen months [sic] moratorium would be construed as the abandonment of the integrity of the debt on our part; second, because there was obvious concerted action and there was a renewed attempt to stage the discussions on the basis of its relation to German reparations which would thus destroy the individual character of the obligation and would effectually transfer German reparations to the American taxpayer.

I stated that it was my view that we should indicate to these governments that if the December payments were made that we would enter into negotiations; that we were bound to do this irrespective of the character of these negotiations, as these were friendly nations with the right to discuss matters of mutual interest. I pointed out that if it were indicated that discussions would be entered upon we were likely to secure the December payments and thus strengthen the integrity of the debts; that the most dangerous thing that could happen therefore would be that of default of these payments; that nothing was more dangerous to the whole of the debt obligations and its vast importance to the American people than a default; that defaults in foreign democracies would have to be justified by these statesmen; that the very justification would be the answer to any attempt to revise payments; that no statesman and no party would likely advocate a re-undertaking of the debt when it was once defaulted and the default justified; that therefore every consideration involved looked toward accepting the request to discuss the questions frankly after they had made the December 15 payments. I pointed out that a refusal to discuss a question of this kind would have serious effects on our whole foreign relations. It would mean a break-down of the economic conference and the arms conference and might break down the alignment of the European countries in support of the unified world policies in the Far East and might leave us isolated in this field. I explained in full my fervent wish to see the country move steadily towards recovery, and the dangers that were involved in certain particulars to public confidence by the disruption of relations which might occur, and in the feeling which might grow out of it unless we handled the whole problem in a most constructive manner.

I pointed out that such a negotiation would offer an opportunity for great gains in the whole problem of world recovery. I presented the necessity for the stabilization of the world currencies, for taking down of barriers to trade, and stated that direct compensation would be secured for the American taxpayer if any concessions were given on the debt. I stated that continued payments on the debt was well within the tax paying capacity of the debtors, that they were not such a damaging factor in world exchange in normal times as had been represented, but that if we could secure a greater contribution to the recovery of the world, and other adequate compensations than the cash payments of these debts, it would be the worst of statesmanship not to undertake it.

Governor Roosevelt seemed to express his approval of these observations as I proceeded with them.

We then entered upon the discussion as to the methods of negotiation. I suggested that there must [be] a complete solidarity of front on our part which would involve cooperative action both of himself, the Congress and my Administration; that he alone could direct the policies of the Democratic majority in the Congress. I suggested that the practical way of quick action was to at once appoint the delegates to the Economic Conference and authorize the same men to deal with the debt questions pending the meeting of the Economic Conference, the delegation possibly to include a member from the Arms Conference. This would enable the Economic Conference to meet early in March as had been originally intended. I pointed out that speed was necessary for stabilizing world currencies if the situation was not further degenerated. I pointed out that this delegation while carrying on negotiations on the debt could take up with the British the program which they would agree to support in the World Economic Conference, that joint proposals of ourselves [and the British with possibly the French] at that conference would dominate it, and that we should make no commitment to the debt until these problems and the compensations had been settled. That it was necessary to recognize the Congress in such settlements, and that if the members of the Congress were included it would serve that purpose. That the delegation could at once undertake a study of the problems and preliminary negotiations. I suggested that we should ask Congress to authorize such a delegation, and that we should include Congressional representation in it. The Governor thought it might be possible to set up a fact finding commission to report to the Congress. I told him that this would certainly not constructively advance the situation, and they would certainly default in the December payments, as that would not give any faith to the foreign governments as to our intention to carry on serious negotiations. He then developed the idea that such negotiations might be carried on by the executive and the usual diplomatic machinery without the setting up of a delegation or requesting any authorities from the Congress. I pointed out the history of the Executive and Congressional relations to the debt questions, the uniform insistence of the Congress of its authority; that these facts were well known to our debtors, and that unless we either had some authority from the Congress for the delegation, or included Congressional members on the delegation, it would carry little conviction, and moreover would not build the foundation for subsequent acceptance of conclusions by the Congress. I suggested that I could appoint the delegation and include members from the Congress if he would agree to support that program, and that I could certainly expect the delegation to be of such men that would first meet his approval, and that I would expect to be guided by his views in that particular. That in any event no conclusions to negotiations would be reached until after he was in office.

I finally proposed that I would recommend to the meeting of the Congressional leaders which had been called for tomorrow morning, either that Congress should authorize a delegation or that I would appoint it, including members from the Congress. The Governor undertook to express his public approval of this program in principle. I invited him to be present at the meeting of the heads of Congressional Committees which had been called for the following morning. He stated that he would prefer not to be present but that he would be seeing the Democratic members over night and would lay the foundations to what we had agreed upon; that I should elaborate in a formal memorandum the statement which I had made to him; that this statement should be issued the following day to the press to indicate both to the country and to the foreign governments the policies which we would follow; and that he would coincidentally issue a statement expressing his agreements to the principles laid down so that there could be no question of the solidarity of our national front. Governor Roosevelt proposed that Secretary Mills and Professor Moley should draft the form of the statement which he would issue and he asked them to meet with him the following morning at 9:00 o'clock.

Some other domestic matters were discussed. The interview lasted for over two hours.

[Herbert Hoover]

JOSLIN DIARY
November 22, 1932

Hoover's memorandum of his meeting with Roosevelt masked his doubts about Roosevelt's intelligence and stamina and his fears for the nation. Shortly after Roosevelt had left the White House, the president revealed his true feelings in a conversation with his press secretary, who recorded those feelings in his diary.

The historic conference over war debts was held today—the first time the President heading one political party and the President-elect of the opposition party have sat down together. The President was extremely nervous not so much because of meeting his opponent as because of the seriousness of the subject calling them together. Half an hour before the conference we got word Roosevelt had invited Garner to be present. This came from the V. P. The President could not believe Roosevelt would be so discourteous, but, to be prepared, notified Stimson to stand by if he should be needed. Garner did not show up so the only others present were Mills and Moley. It was a wholly courteous meeting and held in the Red Room for Roosevelt's convenience. Some progress was made during the two hours' discussion. But the President was downcast when it was over. He found Roosevelt affable, but woefully lacking in an understanding of the problems which threaten the welfare of the world. He was shocked by his physical condition. I shall not attempt to use his own words, but, briefly, he believes he is both physically and mentally unable to discharge the duties of the office he must so soon assume. He believes the country cannot but learn of his handicaps. He is surely disturbed more than I have ever seen him about anything, and, goodness knows, I have seen him worried about enough matters of the greatest possible consequences in the last year and a half. He believes the only hope for the new Administration is for Roosevelt to gather about him the strongest men the Democratic party has to offer.

ROOSEVELT STATEMENT
November 23, 1932

Following his meeting with the congressional leadership on the morning of November 23, the president released a detailed statement of his position on the debt question. He made no mention of his meeting with Roosevelt in the five-page statement. As agreed to in their meeting, Roosevelt also prepared a statement, released on the evening of the 23rd, that supported the principles behind Hoover's statement. No record of Hoover's reaction to Roosevelt's statement has been discovered.

My conferences with the President and with leaders of my party have been most illuminating and useful. I wish to express my appreciation of the opportunity, thus afforded me.

At this time I wish to reaffirm my position on the questions that have been the principal subjects of our discussions.

As to the debt payments due Dec. 15, I find no justification for modifying my statement to the President on Nov. 14, when I pointed out that "the immediate questions raised by the British, French and other notes create a responsibility which rests upon those now vested with executive and legislative authority."

With regard to general policies respecting these debts I firmly believe in the principle that an individual debtor should at all times have access to the creditor; that he should have opportunity to lay facts and representations before the creditor and that the creditor always should give courteous, sympathetic and thoughtful consideration to such facts and representations.

This is a rule essential to the preservation of the ordinary relationships of life. It is a basic obligation of civilization. It applies to nations as well as to individuals.

The principle calls for free access by the debtor to the creditor. Each case should be considered in the light of the conditions and necessities peculiar to the case of each nation concerned.

I find myself in complete accord with four principles discussed in the conference between the President and myself yesterday and set forth in a statement which the President has issued today.

These debts were actual loans made under the distinct understanding and with the intention that they would be repaid.

In dealing with the debts each government has been and is to be considered individually, and all dealings with each government are independent of dealings with any other debtor government. In no case should we deal with the debtor governments collectively.

Debt settlements made in each case take into consideration the capacity to pay of the individual debtor nations.

The indebtedness of the various European nations to our government has no relation whatsoever to reparation payments made or owed to them.

Once these principles of the debt relationships are established and recognized, the methods by which contacts between our government and the debtor nations may be provided are matters of secondary importance. My view is that the most convenient and effective contacts can be made through the existing agencies and constituted channels of diplomatic intercourse.

No action by the Congress has limited or can limit the constitutional power of the President to carry on diplomatic contacts or conversations with foreign governments. The advantage of this method of maintaining contacts with foreign governments is that any one of the debtor nations may at any time bring to the attention of the Government of the United States new conditions and facts affecting any phase of its indebtedness.

It is equally true that existing debt agreements are unalterable save by Congressional action.

JOSLIN DIARY
November 26, 1932

That Hoover was bitter about his election loss and his belief that the press had been too easy on Roosevelt was evident in a conversation he had with Ted Joslin on November 26. Joslin recorded Hoover's comments in his diary. "Perhaps it's a case of 'misery loves company,' " noted Joslin.

Saturday, November 26, 1932

The Scripps-Howard people are going after Roosevelt. The news for the third time this week carried an editorial today criticizing the President-elect, because of his attitude toward the war debts. I showed the President the editorial which was entitled "Roosevelt's Folly." Concluding reading it, he showed the "Indian" in him by remarking: "More power to their elbow. Let them go to it. The honeymoon seems to be over almost before it has started." It might seem he would want his successor spared from criticism so soon, especially when he has had to stand so much of it himself, but he doesn't. Perhaps it's a case of "misery loves company." ...

RICKARD DIARY
December 16, 1932

Edgar Rickard, one of Hoover's closest friends, recorded the president's fears about political appointments in the coming Roosevelt administration. For a man who prided himself on being a public servant rather than a politician, Hoover was offended by the Democratic plan to fill vacant offices.

Dec. 16, 1932

H. H. is sincerely desirous of securing Roosevelt's cooperation in handling Foreign Debt situation, and draft of message to Roosevelt is certainly gracious and should move most anyone. He fears the probity of the new administration, and evident that appointments will be made on strictly political record, and Farley has made it known that he will give consideration in the following order: (1) those prominent in supporting Roosevelt's pre-convention campaign, (2) those supporting Roosevelt's election, (3) contributors to Democratic campaign fund. Already all the telephone girls in [the] House [of Representatives] office have been let out and entire new lot, presumably selected by Tammany, have the jobs. Many members of new House are nonentities, as in some Republican strongholds Democrats put up merely to hold party organization were unexpectedly elected, an estimate states that there are 30 men previously convicted of crime, and one from Washington who only qualified as a citizen 10 days before elected. He [Hoover] plans to leave from New York immediately after March 4th by boat for Panama, stopping off there to fish for week or so and then proceeding to Palo Alto.

HOOVER TO ROOSEVELT
December 17, 1932

In an effort to reflect the views of both the outgoing and incoming administrations, Hoover telegraphed to Roosevelt to suggest that they jointly appoint delegates to the upcoming World Economic Conference. Hoover noted that the "urgency of the [economic] situation both at home and abroad" compelled him to move on the appointment of the delegation rather than waiting for the change of administrations. "I believe there would be no difficulty in agreeing upon an adequate representation for the purpose," Hoover added.

December 17, 1932

Gov. Franklin Roosevelt,
Hyde Park, New York.

My dear Governor:

As you have seen from the press the position of the debtor governments in respect to the December 15th payments is now largely determined. In accord with both your expressions and my own statements it is the duty of the United States to survey and exchange views on these questions individually with some of the debtor governments. It is necessary to consider the character of machinery to be erected for this purpose.

These problems cannot be disassociated from the problems which will come before the World Economic Conference and to some degree those before the Conference on World Disarmament. As the economic situation in foreign countries is one of the dominant depressants of prices and employment in the United States it is urgent that the World Economic Conference should assemble at as early a date as possible. The United States should be represented by a strong and effective delegation. This delegation should be chosen at an early moment in order that it may give necessary consideration and familiarize itself with the problems, and secure that such investigation and study is made as will be necessary for its use at the conference.

Beyond this such problems as the exchange of views in respect to debts cannot be accomplished in satisfactory manner through the ordinary routine of diplomatic contacts. Satisfactory conclusions can only be reached by free and direct round table discussion with each government separately where agreement may be had upon fact and where conclusions can be reached. It has been an almost universal practice in our government where unusual and vital questions are involved to appoint special delegations to undertake such discussions. The routine machinery of diplomacy neither affords the type of men required nor can they give the time from other duties which such discussions require.

While we must not change our established policy of dealing with each debtor separately, and indeed no other course could be entertained in view of the widely divergent conditions which exist in the different countries and the very different situations in which they find themselves, and while the decision heretofore reached not to consider the debt question at the coming World Economic Conference is a wise one, it seems clear that the successful outcome of the World Economic Conference will be greatly furthered if the debt problems can be satisfactorily advanced before that conference although final agreement in some cases may be contingent upon the satisfactory solution of certain economic questions in which our country has a direct interest and the final determination of which may well form a part of the matters coming before the Economic Conference.

It is desirable that such delegation should include members of the Congress in order that such intricate facts and circumstances can be effectively presented to the Congress. It is no derogation of executive authority to choose members from that quarter. It might be well to consider whether this delegation should also embrace in its membership some of the old or new members of the delegation to the Arms Conference in order that these three important questions should be given coordinate consideration.

If it were not for the urgency of the situation both at home and abroad and the possible great helpfulness to employment and agricultural prices and general restoration of confidence which could be brought about by successful issue of all these questions and the corresponding great dangers of inaction, it would be normal to allow the whole matter to rest until after the change of administration, but in the emergency such as exists at the moment I would be neglectful of my duty if I did not facilitate in every way the earliest possible dealing with these questions. It is obvious that no conclusions would be reached from such discussion prior to March 4th but a great deal of time could be saved if the machinery could be created at once by the appointment of the delegates as I have mentioned.

I shall be informing the Congress of the economic situation and of the desirability of the above proposed machinery for dealing with these conferences. I should be glad to know if you could join with me in the selection of such delegation at the present time or if you feel that the whole matter should be deferred until after March 4th. I believe there would be no difficulty in agreeing upon an adequate

representation for the purpose. In such selection the first concern
would be the selection of a Chairman for the Delegation.

Herbert Hoover

STIMSON DIARY
December 19, 1932

Stimson was very much involved soliciting Roosevelt's participation in issues
pending before the Administration. On December 19, Stimson met with Hoover
to discuss Roosevelt's delay in responding to the telegram of December 17.
Stimson sought the high ground in three press conferences later that day, but
he remained concerned about the "flavor of politics" that pervaded the press
accounts of the upcoming conference. [This document is from the Henry L.
Stimson Papers in the Department of Archives and Manuscripts at Yale University. It is used by permission.]

December 19, 1932

This time I felt that I was prepared for the President and that I
had some effect. He accepted some of my suggestions, more than
usual. I really think I helped his message. He and I worked over it
until about half past ten, and then Mills came in. Then after further
work, he pronounced it finished. I then suggested that we ought to
be careful about the publicity of it. I told the President that if it were
coming out from the State Department, I would have felt it worthy
of pulling a Woodley conference with the press on the subject. He
took my hint and asked me to help on it. I at once hurried back to
the Department; got hold of Regnier and McDermott; and after conference decided that we would have to have two. We wanted to get
the President's message into the afternoon papers so that Roosevelt
would get it. While I was over with the President, we had gotten a
message from Roosevelt's secretary that he had not gotten the message which the President had sent to him Saturday until last night;
but that he would try to get an answer back to the President by
Monday night. The telegram was sent to Hyde Park. We knew that
Roosevelt had been to Hyde Park, so it seemed that this was rather
a fishy story. Our inference was that Roosevelt was waiting to see
what the message was before he answered. He had learned from
Colonel House, of course, that there was going to be a message
because the President had told House so Saturday afternoon. So I
called in the three press agencies, the A. P., the U. P., and the
International News Service, and gave them a special talk first, at one
o'clock. Then after a hasty lunch, I hurried back and had a large
Press Conference with all the American press and the chiefs of

bureaus. At both these conferences I tried to stress the fact that we were trying to do what we would certainly do if there had been no interregnum. We were trying to put the two different administrations into as good a position [as] if they would have been had there been no break. The press took it pretty well, but I could see that there was a flavor of politics entering into it now which I had never had to bother [with] so much in the press conferences of my own at Woodley.

ROOSEVELT TO HOOVER
December 19, 1932

In a telegram to Hoover, Roosevelt rejected the premise that delegates to the World Economic Conference should address both debt and disarmament issues as Hoover proposed. "There appears to be a divergence of opinion between us in respect to the conference," noted Roosevelt. "I must respectfully suggest that the appointing of permanent delegates and the final determination of the program of the economic conference be held in abeyance until after March fourth." Based on advice of his advisers, Raymond Moley and Rexford Tugwell, Roosevelt resolved to go his own way on restructuring the debts of European nations.

Albany, N.Y. 850 P.M. Dec. 19th-1932.

The President:
The White House.

Dear Mr. President: I have given earnest consideration to your courteous telegram of December seventeenth and I want to assure you that I seek in every proper way to be of help.

It is my view that the questions of disarmament, intergovernmental debts and permanent economic arrangements will be found to require selective treatment even though this be with full recognition of the possibility that in the ultimate outcome a relationship of any two or of all three may become clear.

(1) As to Disarmament: Your policy is clear and satisfactory. Some time, however is required to bring it to fruition. Success in a practical program limiting armaments, abolishing certain instruments of warfare, and decreasing the offensive or attack power of all nations will in my judgment have a very positive and salutary influence on debt and economic discussions.

(2) As to the Debts: If any debtor nation desires to approach us such nation should be given the earliest opportunity so to do. Certainly in the preliminary conversations the Chief Executive has full authority either through the existing machinery of the Diplomatic

service or by supplementing it with specially appointed agents of the President himself, to conduct such preliminary investigations or inquiries without in any way seeking formal Congressional action. I am impelled to suggest however that these surveys should be limited to determining facts, and exploring possibilities rather than fixing policies binding on the incoming administration. I wholly approve and would in no way hinder such surveys.

(3) As to the Economic Conference: I am clear that a permanent economic program for the world should not be submerged in conversations relating to disarmament or debts. I recognize of course a relationship, but not an identity. Therefore I cannot go along with the thought that the personnel conducting the conversations should be identical.

By reason of the fact that under the constitution I am unable to assume the authority in the matter of the agenda of the economic conference until after March fourth next, and by reason of the fact that there appears to be a divergence of opinion between us in respect to the scope of the conference, and further by reason of the fact that time is required to conduct conversations relating to debts and disarmaments, I must respectfully suggest that the appointing of the permanent delegates and the final determination of the program of the economic conference be held in abeyance until after March fourth. In the meantime I can see no objection to further informal conferences with the agenda committee, or to the carrying on of preliminary economic studies which would serve an undoubtedly useful purpose.

I feel that it would be both improper for me and inadvisable for you, however much I appreciate the courtesy of your suggestion, for me to take part in naming representatives. From the necessity of the case, they could be responsible only and properly to you as President for the effective performance of their assignments particularly in matters calling for almost daily touch with and direction of the Executive. I would be in no position prior to March fourth to have this constant contact.

I think you will recognize that it would be unwise for me to accept an apparent joint responsibility with you when, as a matter of constitutional fact, I would be wholly lacking in any attendant authority.

Franklin D. Roosevelt.

STIMSON DIARY
December 20, 1932

Even though Stimson was not hostile toward Roosevelt, he did share Hoover's anger that the president-elect would not join in a common response to the debt and disarmament issues. Stimson, a man often given to understatement, confided to his diary that Roosevelt's telegram "showed a most laughable, if it were not so lamentable, ignorance of the situation in which Roosevelt is going to find himself when he gets in on March 4th." Yet Stimson was not willing to give up on FDR; he still believed that he could convince the president-elect "to yield on the main point." [This document is from the Henry L. Stimson Papers in the Department of Archives and Manuscripts at Yale University. It is used by permission.]

December 20, 1932

On my way to Cabinet I stopped in first to see the President. Mills was there, and the President showed me a little telegram which he had received from Roosevelt. It virtually declined to join in making the necessary appointments. It, however, left the door open for the President to go ahead and start on the necessary work of investigation and exploration on his own authority. The telegram showed a most laughable, if it were not so lamentable, ignorance of the situation in which Roosevelt is going to find himself when he gets in on March 4th. The President was drawing a telegram of his own in reply in an attempt to show how terribly off Roosevelt's message was, and it was a little bit combative and offensive. Mills and I, however, got him to tone down one or two sentences somewhat. Roosevelt had put himself terribly in the wrong, and I don't blame the President for wishing to show him up. His telegram was drafted for public consumption largely, but I cannot but believe that with a little tact we can get him to yield on the main point yet, and I was exercising my influence for that.

I went over to the Department and had a conference with Day and Williams, the two experts who saw Roosevelt at Hyde Park, or Albany, on Sunday. Their views rather corroborated the impression that we had gotten from Roosevelt's telegram. He really doesn't know what he is up against. Day thinks, however, that Roosevelt perhaps will go along further towards cooperation, corroborating what I thought, particularly if we convince him that we are in earnest, are playing fair, and are going to give him a free hand in the selection. So that when Mills and I went back to the White House after our talk with these men, we turned loose on the President on that line, and I got him to put in a sentence or two more in his proposed reply which carried it a little further that way. The telegram was then sent off. . . .

6

Crisis Before Christmas

The days before Christmas tend to be a time of good will and peace on earth. That was not the case in the week before Christmas, 1932. In spite of Hoover's efforts, Roosevelt refused to go beyond nominal cooperation on the growing financial crisis. Hoover was angry and frustrated. Congress ignored him and would not act on Hoover's legislation unless the president-elect gave his approval. Hoover tried intermediaries such as Henry Stimson, but to no avail.

Hoover was determined to lay the blame for the "Christmas crisis" on Roosevelt's door step by releasing a series of previously confidential documents to the press. In response, Roosevelt expressed shock and noted that he had cooperated with the president whenever he was asked. Efforts by intermediaries such as Secretary of State Henry Stimson and Felix Frankfurter came to naught. Neither man would budge from his position.

Perhaps the biggest crisis was over the definition of "cooperation." To Hoover, the term meant that he and Roosevelt would jointly govern the nation until Roosevelt was sworn in on March 4. But the Democrats—certainly Roosevelt—thought of cooperation as providing informal and ad hoc advice. Hoover was president and he alone should make the decisions.

Rexford Tugwell best captured the differences between the two men in his diary entry for December 23. "Governor Roosevelt is still puzzled to know why it is that Hoover insisted again and again on setting up a commission which would carry over from his term to another. . . . It is that Mr. Hoover is a different kind of man from Mr. Roosevelt. . . . The formal set up of governmental structure will never mean very much to Mr. Roosevelt. It means almost everything to Hoover.'' Whatever the explanation, Hoover and Roosevelt had reached an impasse and there seemed to be no solution.

HOOVER TO ROOSEVELT
December 20, 1932

Although angry and distrustful of Roosevelt, Hoover would not give up. "I am unwilling to admit," he telegraphed FDR, "that cooperation cannot be established between the outgoing and incoming administrations which will give earlier solution and recovery from these difficulties." He called on Roosevelt to select a group of his own advisers to work with the Hoover administration to "see what steps can be taken to avoid delays of precious time and the inevitable losses that will ensue from such delays."

December 20, 1932.

Governor Franklin D. Roosevelt,
Albany, New York.

My dear Governor,

I have your telegram expressing the difficulties which you find in cooperation at the present time. In the face of foreign conditions which are continually degenerating agricultural prices, increasing unemployment and creating economic difficulties for our people, I am unwilling to admit that cooperation cannot be established between the outgoing and incoming administrations which will give earlier solution and recovery from these difficulties.

If you will review my previous communications and conversations I think you will agree that while outlining the nature of the problems my proposals to you have been directed to the setting up not of solutions but of the machinery through which by preparedness the ultimate solution of these questions can be expedited and coordinated to the end that many months of delay and increasing losses to our people may be avoided.

I fully recognize that your solution of these questions of debt, the world economic problems and disarmament might vary from my own. These conclusions obviously cannot be attained in my administration and will lie entirely within your administration. I wish especially to avoid any embarrassment to your work and thus have no intention of committing the incoming administration to any particular policy prior to March 4. Even the exploratory work you suggest should be participated in by men in whom you have confidence, and I wish to facilitate it. What I deem of the utmost importance is that when you assume responsibility on March 4 machinery of your approval will be here, fully informed and ready to function according to the policies you may determine.

My frequent statements indicate agreement with you that debts, world economic problems and disarmament require selective treatment, but you will agree with me that they also require coordination and preparation either in the individual hands of the then President or in the hands of men selected to deal with them and advise him. There is thus no thought of submerging the World Economic Conference with other questions, but rather to remove the barriers from successful issue of that conference.

With view to again making an effort to secure cooperation and that solidarity of national action which the situation needs, I would be glad if you could designate Mr. Owen D. Young, Colonel House, or any other men of your party possessed of your views and your confidence and at the same time familiar with these problems, to sit with the principal officers of this administration in endeavor to see what steps can be taken to avoid delays of precious time and inevitable losses that will ensue from such delays.

Herbert Hoover

ROOSEVELT TO HOOVER
December 21, 1932

Roosevelt responded to Hoover's urgent appeal with a telegram of his own. The governor was blunt. The problem was not with the concept of cooperation, "but, rather, in defining clearly those things concerning which cooperation between us is possible." For Roosevelt, that list was very short and he was unwilling to appoint any advisors to work with the Hoover administration because "it would suggest the presumption that such representatives were empowered to exchange views on matters of large and binding policy." Roosevelt wanted nothing more from Hoover than to be kept informed of the president's actions.

Albany NY 9:14 PM Dec. 21st-1932.

The President:
The White House.

Dear Mr. President: I think perhaps the difficulties to which you refer are not in finding the means or the willingness for cooperation but, rather, in defining clearly those things concerning which cooperation between us is possible.

We are agreed that commitments to any particular policy prior to March fourth are not for many reasons inadvisable and indeed impossible. [sic] There remains therefore before that date only the possibility of exploratory work and preliminary surveys.

Please let me reiterate not only that I am glad to avoid the loss of precious time through delay in starting these preliminaries but also that I shall gladly receive such information and expression of opinion concerning all of those international questions which because of existing economic and other conditions must and will be among the first concerns of my administration.

However, for me to accept any joint responsibility in the work of exploration might well be construed by the debtor or other nations, collectively or individually, as a commitment—moral even though not legal, as to policies and courses of action.

The designation of a man or men of such eminence as your telegram suggests would not imply mere fact-finding; it would suggest the presumption that such representatives were empowered to exchange views on matters of large and binding policy.

Current press dispatches from abroad already indicate that the joint action which you propose would most certainly be interpreted there as much more of a policy commitment than either you or I actually contemplate.

May I respectfully suggest that you proceed with the selection of your representatives to conduct the preliminary exploration necessary with individual debtor nations and representatives to discuss the agenda of the World Economic Conference, making it clear that none of these representatives is authorized to bind this government as to any ultimate policy.

If this be done, let me repeat that I shall be happy to receive their information and their expressions of opinion.

To that I add the thought that between now and March fourth I shall be very glad if you will keep me advised as to the progress of the preliminary discussions, and I also shall be happy to consult with you freely during this period.

Franklin D. Roosevelt

STIMSON DIARY
December 21, 1932

Stimson refused to believe that the differences between the former and the future president could not be bridged. To Stimson's thinking, Roosevelt and his advisers failed to see the urgency of the situation. In conversations with Hoover, Stimson suggested that Lewis Douglas or some other Democrat be sent to FDR to raise his consciousness. Hoover was agreeable, but Roosevelt would not budge. [This document is from the Henry L. Stimson Papers in the Department of Archives and Manuscripts at Yale University. It is used by permission.]

We were all much troubled at the Department this morning by the failure of the President and Roosevelt to get together, and up to this morning there was no evidence of anything blocking it except the temperamental difficulties of the two men to get together. But Bundy came in with a story of having met Lew Douglas, of Arizona, last night. Douglas was with Governor Roosevelt when he was drafting his reply to the President. Douglas is a perfectly straight high-minded fellow, and the suggestion came up that we should use him to try to get the wires straightened out between the two men. I found on inquiry that Mills had the same idea, and that Douglas was on his way to see Mills. So I communicated with Mills and after Mills got through with him, he sent him over to me and I took him up to lunch. Douglas is very anxious about the delay and the hiatus in the international relations which the situation produces. He feels about it just as we do. After lunch I talked it over with him from my point of view; told him of all the difficulties that I saw in case the thing should be delayed until March 4th. He sympathized thoroughly. He thought it came from the failure of Roosevelt to appreciate the importance of the timetable just as we did; and he suggested various ways by which we could impress upon Roosevelt the danger he was running into. Douglas suggested that Mills call up Roosevelt directly. I rather questioned the wisdom of that, because I felt that the two men were not sufficiently en rapport [*sic*]. They didn't like and didn't trust each other. Finally, we telephoned to Mills and Mills telephoned the President and telephoned us back, saying that the President suggested that Douglas call up Roosevelt and make the direct suggestion that Roosevelt send down some men like Owen Young, or somebody else of that type, to confer with the President as to the timetable, not to go into the work of discussion with the British but just try to act as an explanatory liaison between Roosevelt and the President, so as to show Roosevelt what the situation was and what the limitations of time were. As a result Douglas called up Roosevelt from my house. I, of course, left him alone to talk with him, and he evidently had a very long talk. When he got through, he told me that he was going to hear again definitely at six o'clock from Roosevelt, and then he would be able to tell me what the situation was. He told me that he was a little disappointed with Roosevelt's position, but that it was better than it had been. He would not do what we wanted nor what Douglas wanted, he said, but that he would do something that he thought would help.

At six o'clock, he called me up again and said that he had his talk with Roosevelt and then gave me the outline of what he said would be Roosevelt's reply to the President's last telegram. He read me his note. It was not satisfactory. Roosevelt still declined to take any responsibility for the appointment of men to negotiate, but he said that he was willing to have the President appoint men, solely on his responsibility to explore the facts and the possibilities, and he said that he, Roosevelt, would keep in touch with the result of their work. I pointed out to Douglas that this still did not meet the essential difficulties, namely, that the British would not negotiate, or meet with, or discuss their views, with men in that limited light. They would not lay open their case before people who were going out of office on the Fourth of March, with no certainty that the views of these negotiators would have anything to do with the ultimate result, so that there would necessarily be just the same delay that we were afraid of. Douglas admitted that and said that he was disappointed, but that there was nothing else to be done.

At about eight o'clock I got the President on the telephone and told him what Douglas had told me. He asked me to come with Mills to the White House at about nine, which I did. There a new drama revealed itself, and we are able at last to put the real situation together as it now seems to be revealed. The President had some confidential news to the effect that Roosevelt was planning for a big dramatic meeting in March in which he would have MacDonald and perhaps some of the French Government come on to Washington and then settle the debt question. Colonel House is acting as gumshoe man apparently to make these arrangements and it has been done very confidentially, and Roosevelt has a banking house in New York from which he is getting confidential advice on exchange and the questions which are likely to come into the settlement. The President said that he has the word as to this direct, and it ties up with so many other things that we have been unable to understand before as to Roosevelt's attitude, and is on the whole such a natural thing for him to do, that I think it is probably the real solution. There are a lot of obstacles and dangers in it which probably Roosevelt does not see. In the first place, there is this loss of time, which we have been trying to avoid. In the second place, that is probably not the way to get a debt solution. It may be, but Mills with his experience and the President with his experience thought that it was not. A debt solution to be effective will probably have to be done with a lot of hard work in seclusion and silence and not before the brass bands of publicity; and, furthermore, in spite of his big success at Lausanne, I doubt if MacDonald is the kind of man to negotiate it, although his high-mindedness and conciliation will certainly help it. But if that is Roosevelt's plan, it very effectually shelves everything that we are trying to do and it leaves us with nothing except to show that we have done our best and to get out of it as diplomatically as possible. The President, Mills, and I had a long talk over the matter, one of the most satisfactory I have had with the President. He has shown up very well indeed in all of this negotiation with Roosevelt. His letters have been dignified and on a high plane of unselfishness. They made Roosevelt look like a peanut. Roosevelt's telegraphic answer, which he had discussed with Douglas, came into the White House while we were sitting together, and was even less satisfactory than Douglas had represented it to me. It confirmed the information that we had through the President in these other ways, and I guess that is the correct solution as to Roosevelt's plan. I brought Ogden Mills to his home in my car as we came home, and we both felt that it was pretty much the end of the era.

During the day at the Department, I took up the matter of arms limitation. The President, as I have said in my diary, has consented to send a message to Congress on the subject of getting authority to put an embargo of arms in the case of a war between nations.

HOOVER TO ROOSEVELT
December 22, 1932

If Roosevelt would not cooperate in this time of economic crisis, Hoover reasoned, then the world must know about it. A brief telegram was sent to Albany with the following press announcement from the President.

December 22, 1932

Hon. Franklin D. Roosevelt
Governor of New York
Albany, N. Y.

I wish to thank you for your telegram this morning and your views. There are so many garbled versions and so much speculation as to our recent communications being circulated that I am today releasing them to the press in order that there may be no misunderstandings.

Herbert Hoover

December 22, 1932

The President said:

"Governor Roosevelt considers that it is undesirable for him to assent to my suggestions for cooperative action on the foreign problems outlined in my recent message to Congress. I will respect his wishes.

"Situations will no doubt develop and will be dealt with by the

Administration as they arise, but of course no commitments will be made for the next administration.''

"The correspondence between myself and Governor Roosevelt is attached hereto.'' [The appended telegrams were HH to FDR Dec. 17; FDR to HH Dec. 19; HH to FDR Dec. 20; and FDR to HH Dec. 21, '32.]

ROOSEVELT PRESS RELEASE
December 22, 1932

Put on the defensive by the sudden White House announcement, Roosevelt denied that he would not cooperate with Hoover. Yet the governor was careful to define his ''cooperation'' in rather narrow terms.

Thurs. Dec. 22–10:30 p.m.

I am rather surprised at the White House statement issued this afternoon. It is a pity not only for this country, but for the solution of world problems that any statement or intimation should be given that I consider it undesirable to assent to co-operative action on foreign problems.

I have made to the President definite suggestion that he select his representatives to make preliminary studies. I have asked to be kept advised as to the progress of these preliminaries. I have offered to consult with the President freely between now and March 4th.

I hope that this practical program and definite offer of cooperation will be accepted.

Franklin D. Roosevelt

STIMSON DIARY
December 22, 1932

The growing hostility between Washington and Albany was evident to many Hoover and Roosevelt associates. In an effort to bridge the impasse, Roosevelt, through their mutual friend, Felix Frankfurter, invited Henry Stimson ''to come up here and settle this damn thing that nobody else seems to be able to do.'' Roosevelt seemed willing to trust Stimson because Stimson ''didn't play politics.'' [This document is from the Henry L. Stimson Papers in the Department of Archives and Manuscripts at Yale University. It is used by permission.]

December 22, 1932

. . . Frankfurter called me up from Albany. He was at the Executive Mansion spending the night with Roosevelt. He said that in the middle of their conversation, which lasted about two hours, Roosevelt suddenly out of a clear sky said, "Why doesn't Harry Stimson come up here and talk with me and settle this damn thing that nobody else seems to be able to." And on that basis Frankfurter called me up. He said that if I would call up Roosevelt and ask him if something couldn't be done, he would invite me up there the day after Christmas to spend the night and we could talk it over. Frankfurter and I had quite a long talk over the telephone. He thinks that there has been a terrible misunderstanding. He said that Roosevelt feels very badly that all cooperative efforts had been broken off. I told him that was the way we felt down here and that we had gotten the impression that Roosevelt had his own plans and didn't want any cooperation. Altogether it was a funny occurrence. I told Frankfurter that I would think it over. He is to be in New York tomorrow, and I told him I would telephone him there. Frankfurter told me that Roosevelt apparently had no acrimony against me at all even on the subject of my 1930 speech, which Frankfurter had specifically asked about, and Frankfurter told me that he had used the same words about me that had been reported to me by some of the newspaper men, namely, that I didn't play politics.

STIMSON DIARY
December 23, 1932

Stimson informed Hoover the next day of the offer from Roosevelt, via Frankfurter. As Stimson noted in his diary, Hoover "by that time was crystallized very strongly against going near Roosevelt. He said that the only way he would reopen the gate was to have Roosevelt send down two or three people of proper eminence to talk with Mills and myself." Hoover no longer trusted Roosevelt and would not lift a finger to reestablish contact with him. [This document is from the Henry L. Stimson Papers in the Department of Archives and Manuscripts at Yale University. It is used by permission.]

I went to the White House from Woodley, and then told the President about my talk with Frankfurter last night and the message from Roosevelt. He was against it I could see from the first. He asked me to tell Mills about it, and then Mills was to come in and talk with him about it, which we did. He by that time was crystallized very strongly against going near Roosevelt. He said that the only way that he would reopen the gate was to have Roosevelt send down two or three people of proper eminence to talk with Mills and myself. He felt that the situation was in a good political shape now so far as he was concerned, and he didn't care to reopen it. He was much influenced by the fact that every time he had any personal interviews with Roosevelt, there has been unfavorable propaganda evidently coming from Roosevelt through the press afterwards. Mills coincided with his views. I did not press the invitation at all. I simply told them the facts, because I was in a position where I could not press it, but I made very clear what I thought of Frankfurter and his personal devotion to me, and Mills coincided in my good opinion of Frankfurter.

HOOVER MEMORANDUM
December 23, 1932

Hoover's recollection of the meeting was more strident: Stimson was to have no contact with Roosevelt; "that so far as Frankfurter was concerned, he could be told that the President's last offer was still open." Hoover did allow Stimson the option of contacting Frankfurter if only to tell him that no one from the Hoover administration would contact Roosevelt for "private conversations."

December 23, 1932

The Secretary of State informed me this morning that at 11 o'clock last night Mr. Felix Frankfurter telephoned him from Governor Roosevelt's office in Albany, stating that the Governor was in a distressed state of mind over the result of communications on foreign policies; that the Governor had felt he was marching right along with everything the President wished to do and felt greatly hurt; that the Governor had expressed his high esteem for the Secretary of State and asked Frankfurter if it would be possible to have the Secretary of State call on him (without public notice of it) either in Albany or New York City, where he would be going in a few days, as he would like to have a confidential discussion with him alone.

The Secretary of State was anxious to go. I told him, after prolonged argument, that my instructions to him were that he should have no communication at all with Governor Roosevelt; that so far as Frankfurter was concerned he could be told that the President's last offer was still open; that if Roosevelt would send to Washington two or more eminent men of Democratic faith who understood the problems under discussion, and preferably three of them, to sit down with three Cabinet officers to discuss matters, with the firm intent of developing machinery by which these questions could be advanced, they would be welcome; that the purpose of such a conference should be to select delegates for the World Economic Conference and that these delegates should in the meantime carry on debt discussions; that they should neither commit this administration nor the next to any policy; that Mr. Frankfurter should be

informed that the interpretation of this last offer of the President by
Governor Roosevelt was only pretense because Lew Douglas in a
conversation with the Governor, urging him to accept the President's
offer to send men to Washington for such a conference, had been
informed by Roosevelt that he did not propose to send Ambassadors
to President Hoover.

I said that if the Secretary of State wanted to have any relations
with Frankfurter, who is an old friend, he should tell him the whole
story and inform him that no officer of this government is prepared
to call on Governor Roosevelt for private conversations; that in public interest we are prepared to go back to the only course out of
which practical results can be obtained is the above.

DIARY OF REXFORD G. TUGWELL
December 23, 1932

Rex Tugwell was one of the small coterie of Roosevelt advisors known as the
"Brains Trust." Like his colleagues, Tugwell had been a professor of economics
before he joined the Roosevelt team. In the diary entry below, Tugwell records
the genuine perplexity that Roosevelt and his advisers had over Hoover's insistence on a joint response to the economic crisis. "Mr. Hoover is a different
kind of man than Mr. Roosevelt," noted Tugwell, "he is a business executive
type . . . which is why he cannot grasp that the new administration will run
differently." The chasm between Hoover and Roosevelt was growing and there
were still more than nine weeks until the inauguration. [This document was
published in *The Diary of Rexford G. Tugwell: The New Deal, 1932–1935*
(Westport, CT, 1992), pp. 28–29. It is published by permission of Grace F.
Tugwell.]

December 23, 1932

I have been ill for two days and out of things. In the meantime
the exchange of telegrams between Hoover and Roosevelt has been
made public together with two supplementary telegrams in which I
had no part. It seems to me that these telegrams have made Roosevelt's situation perfectly clear and that for people who are new to
the formulation of public policy we have come off fairly well in this
exchange with a group who have been in charge of these matters
for the government for a good many years. Our position is more
clear-cut, the policy offers more hope of solution and our statement
is made with more clarity and candor than was theirs. Governor
Roosevelt is still puzzled to know why it is that Hoover insisted
again and again on the setting up of a commission which would
carry over from his term to another. I think my suggestion was the

only tenable one in the circumstances. It is that Mr. Hoover is a different kind of man than Mr. Roosevelt; he is a business executive type and feels he must delegate everything which is why he cannot grasp the notion that the new administration will be run differently. The formal set up of governmental structure will, I imagine, never mean very much to Roosevelt. It means almost everything to Hoover which makes it all the more surprising that so little in the way of functional reorganization has been accomplished in Washington during the last four years.

In this cartoon from October of 1932, artist Jay N. "Ding" Darling touched on the class distinctions between Hoover and Roosevelt. For "Ding" the choice for president was a clear one.

The hard-working president gets no help in this 1932 cartoon. "Ding" frequently depicted Roosevelt in a sailor suit, a reference to FDR's service as Assistant Secretary of the Navy in 1917–1918.

THAT WHITE HOUSE CONFERENCE.

Hoover and Roosevelt met on November 22, 1932, to discuss the problems that FDR would face when he became president. Cartoonist Clifford Berryman drew plenty of ghosts in the White House closets.

SHOULDER TO SHOULDER.

Hoover and Roosevelt never stood shoulder to shoulder on anything. From Berryman's perspective, there was a lot of talk on the European debt situation and no action.

FISHING DAYS ARE HERE!

This Berryman cartoon of May 9, 1933 touches on the popularity of the Roosevelt campaign song, "Happy Days Are Here Again." Clearly the song appealed to the voters.

Hoover supporters must have enjoyed this Berryman cartoon of January 9, 1938. A recession in late 1937 put FDR in the uncomfortable position of looking for economic solutions on "depression beach."

Berryman depicts Hoover with "tears" in his eyes but a smile on his lips over FDR's congressional defeats in 1939. In fact, Hoover never wrote to the White House when FDR was president.

In this cartoon of June 28, "Ding" shows Hoover knocking out Democrats right and left with his speech to the Republican National Convention of 1944. FDR had to clean up the mess.

7

Shuttle Diplomacy

Roosevelt's unwillingness to take action so infuriated Hoover that he saw no value in further communication. Making matters worse, Hoover believed that Roosevelt was untrustworthy and that every contact between the two men should be transcribed. Hoover was willing to let history judge the responsibility for the growing world economic crisis.

The one sliver of hope came from the presence of Henry Stimson, Hoover's Secretary of State, and a friend of Franklin Roosevelt. At Roosevelt's request, and with Hoover's somewhat reluctant approval, Stimson traveled to Hyde Park to convince the governor to take action. But Roosevelt remained skeptical of Hoover's plan for a joint commission to address the crisis. Roosevelt argued that Hoover's commissions were notoriously unpopular and any Roosevelt appointments would be thought of as potential cabinet officers. The president-elect was not willing to make that kind of commitment at that time.

Stimson countered by expressing Hoover's concern that action was needed immediately to shore up national and international confidence. Roosevelt responded by saying that he would be willing to meet informally with international representatives, but no more than that. Upon learning of the response, Hoover all but despaired. "The governor has not yet comprehended the problem with which the world is confronted and which we have tried to get before him," the president wrote to Stimson. "The question which we have to meet is: Will the United States take a courageous part in the stabilization of the world economic situation." It was an unanswered question.

JOSLIN DIARY
January 4, 1933

Hoover's continuing distrust of Roosevelt is evident in this entry from the diary of Theodore Joslin. Even incidental contacts, such as Roosevelt's phone call to set up an appointment with Hoover, were transcribed. Bitterness and cynicism are evident in Hoover's follow-up conversation with Joslin.

Wednesday, Jan. 4, 1933

Another contact today with Roosevelt. McIntyre called me and said the Governor wanted to talk with the President. I told him I would call back. I did so for two reasons. First I did not want him to think it too easy "to contact the President," but principally I wanted time to arrange for the conference set up. The President will not talk with Roosevelt if I know it without another party and a stenographer on the line. After arranging the hook up and hearing Miss Shankey in the Cabinet booth I had the call put through. Roosevelt, to our surprise, said he wanted to come here and talk with the President. The President said he thought it was a good idea. After hanging up, the President said: "I suppose he will tell the press I called him up and invited him to come here." That was too much for me. "If he does," I said, "I'll tell the truth, including the conference set up." The President laughed. It would be a good joke on the double crosser.

HOOVER TO STIMSON
January 4, 1933

Although doubtful that Stimson's meeting with Roosevelt would amount to much, Hoover sent detailed instructions to his Secretary of State. "I do not want any misunderstanding to occur about our relations with Governor Roosevelt on the debt question," he started his letter. What followed was a detailed repetition of Hoover's position on the issue. The bracketed sentence was deleted from the final draft. Stimson was well aware of Hoover's views; the letter was a reminder that Stimson was an emissary of the President of the United States.

Mon. Jan 4 [1933]

Dear Mr. Secretary:

I do not want any misunderstanding to occur about our relations with Governor Roosevelt on the debt question. I do not have the feeling that our attempts to communicate with him through a third party have turned wholly to the disadvantage of the cause which we represent and to our relations [and that there may be no mistake in the future I am not prepared to reopen this subject in any form unless Governor Roosevelt frankly accepts the last proposition which I made.] And he must accept it in even a wider form and that is that three, or a minimum of two, men of eminence with an understanding of these problems shall come to Washington and shall sit in with the responsible Cabinet officers for the formulation of a definite and positive organization of the machinery for handling the Arma [sic] Conference and the negotiation of the debt. Furthermore, such organization must take the form of the appointment now of some of the delegates to the Economic Conference, who should be empowered to carry on preliminary conversations with debtor countries, but shall not have the power to commit either this Administration or the next.

I again repeat that I take this attitude simply because I do not wish our efforts minimized down to mere conversations which are being misrepresented on every occasion to further disturb the public mind and our international relations. The only alternative is that he take over every responsibility after he takes office.

I realize Mr. Frankfurter's sincerity and his no doubt proper interpretation of Governor Roosevelt's chagrin, but the idea of any meetings between representatives of this Administration and Governor Roosevelt that are not public, in view of our experience lead us only into further difficulties as I have said above in our relations to our own people and our relations abroad. The above plan of handling our problem is public property and it is open to Governor Roosevelt to accept it at any time, but it will have to be a public acceptance and the men to be sent will have to be men whose own prestige, position and character will carry weight to the country. If you see him it must be public not secret as suggested.

Herbert Hoover

STIMSON MEMORANDUM
January 9, 1933

Stimson dutifully recorded the substance of his meeting with Roosevelt in the following memorandum. Roosevelt was critical of Hoover's approach to the debt crisis. In fact, Roosevelt would have nothing to do with Hoover's plan to appoint a debt commission; the governor believed that once he was president he could work out the matter directly with the Congress. In an effort to respond to urgency of the situation, Roosevelt offered to join with Hoover in a meeting with a representative of the British government. Stimson saw great difficulties with this plan, but promised to take it up with the president. [This document is from the Henry L. Stimson Papers in the Department of Archives and Manuscripts at Yale University. It is used by permission.]

MEMORANDUM OF CONVERSATION WITH FRANKLIN D. ROOSEVELT, MONDAY, JANUARY 9, AT HYDE PARK, NEW YORK.

(The talk began at 11 a.m., lasted through luncheon and on the drive down to New York City until about 5:30 p.m., there being no others present at any time.)

The conversation followed topics initiated by Governor Roosevelt. I confined myself to giving him the information he asked for. . . .

Roosevelt stated his objection to Hoover's proposal of appointing outstanding commissioners to begin promptly on any of these three matters: disarmament, Economic Conference, and debts. His reasons were twofold. First, because he was not ready yet to select his Cabinet and he felt that any such selections would be misinterpreted as Cabinet selections. Second, because his experience in the campaign had made him believe that he could get the necessarily unpopular debt settlement through Congress and through the country better if he did it himself rather than through a commission. He spoke of the unpopularity of Mr. Hoover's commissions as exemplified in the response to his speeches in the campaign. I emphasized the importance of the time schedule in these matters and the deterioration in the economic condition of the country which was now going on as I had learned it from Mr. Hoover on my way to Northampton. I explained to Roosevelt that Hoover's basic reason for prompt and dramatic action was to obtain the necessary psychological effect on the country to stop this deterioration. Roosevelt seemed to accept this. He then made a counter-proposal, in making which he said he was thinking aloud. In substance, it was to sound out the British and to get them to send over someone like Stanley Baldwin, who could talk, as he expressed it, with me and begin the necessary spade work on the debts, in which work he said that he would promise to take a personal part. In order to be perfectly sure I said, "In suggesting me you do not mean to keep out the President; this would have to be done by him substantially," and Roosevelt at once said, "Of course." I then pointed out certain weaknesses in this plan from what I knew of the British situation. I said I thought it would be very doubtful if Mr. Baldwin would come, certainly not alone, and described to him the cleavage in viewpoint that had developed during negotiations in the past between the British Treasury and others of the Cabinet, cautioning him as to the confidentiality of that information. We however talked out the plan and I told him that while I could see great difficulties, it might be possible to work something out of it and I promised him that I would take it up with that view and talk it over with the President. In one stage of the talk, Roosevelt dropped a remark indicating that these talks with the British might be taken up simultaneously with similar ones with France. I at once pointed out that we did not believe in such a policy of treating a government which had defaulted on even terms with one which had made its payment and he agreed with that distinction. He then asked me whether I had not heard that France intended to make her payment on March 5th. I told him I had not.

HOOVER TO STIMSON
January 15, 1933

Hoover was not impressed with Roosevelt's plan to meet with the British. "The Governor has not yet comprehended the problem with which the world is confronted," Hoover noted to Stimson in the following memorandum. To Hoover's thinking, any course of action short of sending a commission to Europe "might lead to actual disasters and disappointments which would make the situation even worse." But Hoover also was a realist. "If the Governor wants an Englishman to come over and if *he* will do all the negotiating," Hoover concluded, "we can facilitate it."

January 15, 1933

Memorandum for the Secretary of State

I have been thinking over your discussion with Governor Roosevelt and our conferences on the subject. I can express myself best on paper.

My understanding is that the Governor wishes us to invite some prominent British statesman to come to the United States for purposes of discussing the British debt. He proposes that we carry on the negotiations and he would be glad to see the representative and keep in communication with us.

This seems to me to disclose the fact that the Governor has not yet comprehended the problem with which the world is confronted and which we have tried to get before him. The question which we have to meet is: Will the United States take a courageous part in the stabilization of the world economic situation? The British debt question is but a small segment of this problem. It should not be discussed except where there is to be a full quid pro quo in effort on the part of Great Britain to bring economic remedy to the world which would alter the course of economic degeneration in the United States. One delegate from the British government, no matter how eminent, coming to the United States for the purpose of discussion of the debt, could only be disappointed. What is required is a group of the best brains of England, to sit down with a group of the best and most expert brains of the United States to work out a plan to reverse the economic forces now working in the world. This will be a discussion which will take weeks and months. No concession should be given to the British until that project is complete and then only if it shows results to the United States.

The United States and England should cooperate on this broad question. These two nations jointly could present a program to the world economic conference which would meet acceptance and remedy the destructive forces now operating. That can only be done through the collective thought of several Americans and several Englishmen who are going to devote themselves to the pursuit of this question from the day conversations are opened until the completion of the Economic Conference. All this will require preparation and study which will absorb all the time before March 4th. The announcement that this is in course is enough to aid the situation temporarily.

We therefore come back to the fact that if anything effective is to be done, Governor Roosevelt must designate three or more of the men he would like to undertake their own preparations for such negotiations. I would be glad to appoint them if they are men of understanding in these questions. I would be glad to give them every resource of the present administration, but they must negotiate on behalf of the incoming administration. Nothing else will carry confidence or effect results. Our original proposal did not contemplate any negotiation merely preparation and announcement.

If an English delegation is to come here they should not arrive before March 1st or until the new Secretaries of the Treasury and State are appointed. Otherwise a negotiation participated in by both administrations will result in the press and every politician trying to drive wedges between the incoming and outgoing administrations during the negotiations. It was for this reason that I proposed that the delegation should prepare and then go to Europe, not negotiate here.

It seems to me that any other course than the above is a futility and might lead to actual disasters and disappointments which would make the situation even worse.

If the Governor wants an Englishman to come over and if *he* will do all the negotiating we can facilitate it.

Yours faithfully,
Herbert Hoover

STIMSON DIARY
January 15, 1933

In the entry below, Stimson records his impressions of being in the middle between Hoover and Roosevelt on the debt crisis. He was "encouraged" by Hoover's response, but thought that he "was pretty rigid in some of the conditions he laid down." Stimson, nevertheless, discussed Hoover's proposal with Roosevelt, who agreed to travel to Washington to discuss the matter further directly with the president. Stimson reported to Hoover who agreed to the meeting. [This document is from the Henry L. Stimson Papers in the Department of Archives and Manuscripts at Yale University. It is used by permission.]

January 15, 1933 (Sunday)

. . . About lunch time the President sent over to me a memorandum giving his views on the discussion which I am having with Governor Roosevelt in trying to work out a way by which we can cooperate with him with respect to debts and the Economic Conference and prepare for that work. I was encouraged by the memorandum which showed progress by the President in coming to the idea of renewing cooperation with Roosevelt; although it was pretty rigid in some of the conditions that it laid down. I called up Mills right after lunch and read this over to him over the telephone and got his ideas about it. He has been coming around to it pretty well and then late in the afternoon Bundy and Feis came in and went over it with me and I wrote out myself as a result of these conferences notes for a talk with the Governor and then called him up. . . .

In my telephone conversation with the Governor, I said as follows, reading substantially from the notes I had before me: I told him that I had been working hard on the matter which I had discussed and that I would try to state to him the difficulties and dangers which we found in his plan, enumerating them at length and then give him the suggestions which we had to make in order to meet them. I said the difficulties were as follows:

First. Even if the debt negotiations were handled separately from the Economic Conference as Roosevelt in his conference with the President had previously suggested, nevertheless Mr. Roosevelt would want to be sure in advance of British cooperation in the conference before he would be willing to agree to a definite debt settlement. I pointed out, for example, that the United States would wish to secure the assurance of Great Britain that she would stabilize sterling as a means of raising world prices. This would be one of the parts of the Economic Conference. This would be a great advantage to us unless our nation proposed to join in the race for national inflation which is now going on among the nations, which, of course, I assumed Roosevelt would not want to do. He at once said that of course he did not want to join in such a race, and I then pointed out that unless we could be sure that Britain would agree to stabilize beforehand we would not want to give up our debts beforehand. He said he could see this perfectly and agreed with us. I pointed out that for this reason it would be necessary for the British representative who came over to discuss this matter with us to be prepared on this question and he would have to know this beforehand. Roosevelt agreed also on this. I pointed out also that unless we had a general British-American understanding before a conference the conference would be likely to fail. Cooperation between those two nations was virtually absolutely necessary for the success of the conference as a whole. On this point Roosevelt was very emphatic and cordial and agreed perfectly.

Then in the second place, I reminded him that I pointed out Monday when I was with him that it probably could not be a one man conference so far as Great Britain was concerned. They would probably want to send out several men and be prepared beforehand somewhat as to the line of discussion. He said he could see that, but he hoped we could try to keep the number of the British down. He did not want them to send too many. I told him we would do the best we could, but it would be pretty hard to control them on such a point as that.

Then in the third place, I told him that it would take time and continuous sessions; that we could not keep important British representatives who came here sitting around idle between intermittent discussions with him. We would have to have people on our part here ready to talk continuously. Roosevelt said he could see that and agreed to it.

In the fourth place, I said of course the Hoover representatives could not negotiate. All we could do was to do the preparatory work of investigation etc. to lay the foundations for his negotiations would be afterwards. This he agreed to at once. This has been his proposition, but I said that I was sure that very early in the meetings with the British negotiation was likely to crop up; at least very early there would be stated in the meeting the plan which each side might have and the American plan must be Roosevelt's plan, not Hoover's plan. This, of course, he agreed to do.

And finally in the fifth place, I said that if the conference were held in Washington there would surely be the danger of the press and members of Congress sniping at the conference just as soon as this stage of the negotiations and the disclosure of the respective plans was reached. Those plans would be sure to leak out and we would be sure to meet with Congressional and press opposition and be published. This also he said he could see.

Then I said that as a result of these difficulties which lay in the way and with a view to meeting his views as far as possible and yet avoid the dangers which were inherent in these conditions, I pointed out the following points:

In the first place, the British should not get here before March 1. If this was so, then by that time Roosevelt's Secretary of State and Secretary of Treasury would certainly be selected in his mind. He can't wait any longer than that and they would be the ones who could meet with the British. Before that time the Hoover Administration, principally Mills and myself could prepare and consult with Roosevelt and with his Secretary of State and Secretary of the Treasury if they were appointed before that time and get ready the data which the negotiators would use after the British got here. I pointed out that this would avoid as far as possible the idea of a commission by having the new Secretary of State and the Secretary of the Treasury act for Roosevelt. I pointed out also that by having an early announcement that there was to be a delegation of British coming over and that this matter was going to be taken up, we could get considerably before the actual meeting all of the advantage of the psychology for the benefit of the recovery of the country. Roosevelt took what I said pretty well and seemed to think that was the best thing that could be done. He offered no counter suggestion.

He told me that he had been having a conference with Russell Leffingwell and that Russell Leffingwell had pointed out substantially what I had said in my first point of the interconnection of debts and the problem of the Economic Conference. He said that Leffingwell had used the illustration that you couldn't tell which was the hen and which was the egg. It happened to be an illustration which I had used to Roosevelt last Monday. Then I asked him to take these suggestions which I was making into consideration and I was sure the President would be glad to talk to him when he came here next Thursday. Roosevelt said that he would arrive in the afternoon at about 3:30 and if the President desired he would come and see him at once on his way from the station, or he would drop in and see him the first thing the next morning whichever the President wished. He also asked if I would come and see him at the Mayflower. He said he would gladly come to the State Department, but unfortunately his lameness prevented him from getting up the small flight of steps before he entered that building. I said I appreciated this perfectly and I would come whenever and wherever he wishes.

I omitted to say above that I also told Roosevelt that it would be helpful to him to decide as early as possible the line of his policy in order to give the British some knowledge of the type of men they must send and the staff which those men should bring with them. He said he could understand that.

Bundy and Feis listened in on the auxiliary earpieces which I had in my study and were very much pleased with Roosevelt's attitude and with the success of the talk.

In the evening we had Frank McCoy and his wife and Jim Rogers and his wife to dinner and had a very pleasant evening.

I reported over the telephone to the President right after my talk with Roosevelt the substance of my talk with Roosevelt and what I had done and he asked me to make a careful memorandum of it.

HOOVER MEMORANDUM
January 15, 1933

In the following memorandum, the president records his frustration in dealing with Roosevelt on the debt crisis. He hoped to appeal to the governor's "vanity" in finding a solution to their impasse. The matter was in Stimson's hands; Hoover did not have the patience to deal with Roosevelt.

January 15, 1933:

In the afternoon I called the Secretary of State and suggested that in respect to my memorandum of that morning I felt there was another method by which we might advance the main issue of getting some indication to the American people of progress in the international situation and at the same time assure that debts would not be discussed separately from compensation and also possibly meet Governor Roosevelt's views as to methods. That inasmuch as early in March he would have his Secretary of State and Secretary of the Treasury appointed, and as he seemed to have a congenital objection to the appointment of anybody to prepare themselves for dealing with the debt questions and the compensations therefore, or the general foreign economic situation, we might simplify the business by Mr. Stimson suggesting in the proposed telephone conversation that whatever serious negotiations were undertaken would have to be undertaken by his Administration; that in any event, nothing could be accomplished before his inauguration except preparation that some time before that he would have his Secretary of State and Secretary of the Treasury appointed; that they could cooperate with the present Administration to prepare themselves; and that the British should be told that they could send a delegation here, to arrive

here as soon as the new Administration was installed and that the
new Administration could at once undertake negotiations; that our
big job was to give some satisfaction to the country that something
was going to be done about it; and that we had to assure that something was going to be done about it; [the] Governor agreed not to
discuss debts alone as he had proposed, but also compensations. That
by using his cabinet as a delegation it would avoid technically the
appointment of so-called commissions and save the Governor's face,
and that perhaps this suggestion might appeal to the Governor's
vanity and bring the matter to some advanced stage. The Secretary
agreed to put this altered proposal up to the Governor.

STIMSON MEMORANDUM
January 19, 1933

Stimson met with the British ambassador to clearly articulate Mr. Hoover's
policies on the monies owed to the U.S. government at the end of December.
Hoover and Stimson were in no mood to grant a moratorium to Britain when
they had already refused a similar request from France.

[Washington] January 19, 1933

Memorandum by the Secretary of State

The British Ambassador came in and said that he wanted some
time to have a long talk with me about the present situation respecting debts. I suggested that we begin with it now, although I told
him at the very start that I should perhaps be in a better situation to
discuss it twenty-four hours from now (by that referring to the coming meeting between Mr. Hoover and Mr. Roosevelt). We then reviewed the steps which had already been taken. I reminded him that
the last time we discussed this I had told him that this administration
was ready to keep its promise to appoint a commission to discuss
debts if the British desired, although we would not be at all surprised
if that offer were not accepted owing to the then deadlock between
Mr. Hoover and Mr. Roosevelt as to machinery for bridging over
the gap between the two administrations. I said I had taken the
ambassador's failure to bring up the subject again on any later occasion as an answer to my suggestion and an evidence that the British saw no reason for opening the subject with an administration
which was going out of existence so soon. He said yes, that was so.
I told him that since that time we had been trying to begin again
with efforts at cooperation between the two administrations and we
had been making some progress, as he could see from the newspa-

pers. I pointed out that Mr. Hoover's original proposal for bridging the transition period was to create a commission, which should represent Mr. Roosevelt's selections, which could take up the matter and actually negotiate even before March 4th, but that Mr. Roosevelt, for reasons which we could properly understand, had declined to accept that suggestion or to take any responsibility in negotiations before he actually became President. I said there remained then only the possibility of having the Hoover Administration confine itself to preparatory work with the idea that everything should be in as much readiness as possible by March 4th so that Mr. Roosevelt could begin the work of negotiation as quickly as possible. I told the Ambassador we were making some progress with this idea but nothing yet was settled. I asked him as a try-out whether it would be possible, in case we were successful with this new bridge between the two administrations, for the British to send over someone prepared and ready to begin negotiations by March 4th, and he replied that he did not think it would be out of the question. I said I would let him know if anything came of this effort.

During the course of our talk, he said that his Government faced the great difficulty of not knowing whether they could go ahead with any steps at all without offending France. He told me he said this not as a matter of legal possibility, for of course his Government could do it,—but as a political possibility as to whether they could do it without offending France, which they did not want to do. I replied that on our side he must realize that we could not in the light of our own public sentiment treat a nation which had defaulted on its debt in exactly the same way and in the same priority as we treated a nation which at great sacrifice had paid its installment. He answered yes, that he could also see that we could not, having refused to grant a moratorium to France for the December installment, without any further excuse or action by France reverse ourselves and discuss debts. I said of course that was so.

H[enry] L. S[timson]

JOSLIN DIARY
January 19, 1933

Hoover's frustration in dealing with Roosevelt left him in a bitter, angry mood. He took no action to prepare for Roosevelt's second visit to the White House and refused to allow photographers to record the visit. "I will never be photographed with [Roosevelt]," Hoover told Joslin. "I have too much respect for myself."

Thursday, Jan. 19, 1933

The Senate defeated the cloture resolution by one vote and, as planned, the regular Republicans divided their votes. The result was quite pleasing to the President.

Although Roosevelt is coming to the White House tomorrow, the President made no plans for the conference other than to arrange to have Stimson and Mills with him. The photographers were very insistent that they be permitted to make a photograph of the group, if not inside, then standing under the portico. I told them there would be no photographs. Later I advised the President of the action I had taken. He said: "That's right. I never will be photographed with him. I have too much respect for myself."

8

Face to Face

In spite of his frustration, and the failure of Henry Stimson to convince Roosevelt that he had to take action, Hoover agreed to meet with the president-elect a second time during the interregnum. So on January 20—the date that would become Inauguration Day in 1937—the two sides met in the Red Room at the White House.

Hoover was joined by Henry Stimson and Ogden Mills, the Secretary of the Treasury. Roosevelt brought with him advisors Raymond Moley and Norman Davis. Once again, the two sides reviewed their positions. Hoover, Stimson and Mills argued vigorously for Roosevelt to take action on the British debt crisis and the worldwide economic situation simultaneously; the two issues could not be separated.

But Roosevelt and Moley would hear none of it. The two issues must be separate and addressed in an orderly fashion. There would be time enough after March 4 for the new administration to take up these matters. The joint communique issued by the two sides after the meeting reflected Roosevelt's position on this matter.

Hoover had tried every tactic known to him to convince Roosevelt to take action before March 4, but to no avail. Yet Hoover could not, would not, give up. "I'll have my way with Roosevelt yet," he told Ted Joslin on February 1. Hoover never stopped trying, but never succeeded in this quest.

STIMSON DIARY
January 20, 1933

Stimson recorded all of the day's events in his diary. Roosevelt and his advisors, Norman Davis and Raymond Moley, arrived at the White House just before 11 a.m. and the meeting with Hoover, Stimson and Treasury Secretary Ogden Mills lasted until 12:15. Not much was accomplished. A joint communique was issued indicating that Roosevelt and his advisors would meet with the British in early March to discuss their war debts as well as the world economic situation. Roosevelt, Davis, and Moley departed and Stimson contacted the British with this news. [This document is from the Henry L. Stimson Papers in the Department of Archives and Manuscripts at Yale University. It is used by permission.]

January 20, 1933 (Friday)

I went to the White House direct from Woodley and told the President of my conference with Roosevelt last night. I spoke of the failure of the French proposition and urged him to begin his negotiations at eleven o'clock with the other one, viz., the British proposal, and get that clinched at any rate. Mills was already with him when I got there and heard the whole account. Mills had been in New York the day before and had gotten a pretty straight warning from Owen Young that the British were going to fight for independent settlement of the debts without making any promises to us in respect to the other elements of the world situation. Young had also commented to Mills on Roosevelt's lack of grasp of this whole situation and of his ignorance about it. This confirmed my observation of his wobbly attitude in the two interviews which I had just had on these matters, namely, the telephone talk Sunday and talk in the Mayflower yesterday.

Cabinet Meeting was curtailed and then Mills, the President and I went direct to the White House just in time to meet Roosevelt with Norman Davis and Moley in the Red Room. Ike Hoover arranged the seating. The President sat on the sofa with his back to the window; next on his right sat Mr. Roosevelt in a chair; then I and Moley on the next sofa and then Norman Davis and Mills on chairs, making a circle.

The President opened up his talk after some pleasant allusions between Roosevelt and himself about the success of the Far Eastern matter, in which both expressed themselves well satisfied with what had taken place. The President opened up then on the debt negotiations with Great Britain; and before he had gotten very far, Moley, to my surprise, jumped in as the opponent of any attempt to connect the debt negotiations with assurances as to the economic situation in general. It seemed to me such a reversal of Moley's attitude of the evening before, where he had been helpful on the subject, that I could not understand it. Roosevelt became rather wobbly again, and we all took a hand, principally myself. While we talked two cables came in from Geneva, No. 10 of January 20th, at 10:00 a.m., and No. 11, of the same day sent at noon, both from Sackett, confirming the report that Mills had from Young to the effect that the British were going to try to make a bargain without any compensation in regard to their attitude on the gold standard or other matters. I at once presented these cables to the meeting, reading pertinent extracts from them and making Moley read the whole of them, because they contained very express warnings from Sackett bearing directly upon what we were discussing.

Finally when we did not seem to get far with Roosevelt, I stood up in front of the mantelpiece and said that it was imperative that I, who had to conduct the negotiations with the British, should know where Mr. Roosevelt stood on this point, and whether he would or would not insist upon the importance of keeping open the opportunity and getting assurances from the British which would be a return for concessions which we might make on the debts. In reply to that I finally got what I considered such assurances. He spoke of the two subjects as being twins, but he and Moley seemed insistent that the negotiations on the subject of debts and the talk over these broader world conditions should be treated as physically two different discussions of which the results of one might be made conditional on the other. They spoke of having different representatives and holding the talks in different rooms; and in the communique, which Mr. Hoover drew up on the sofa while we were talking, they insisted on having language in it which would permit such an interpretation of the paper but would not make it too clear. (Copy of communique published after the White House conference follows.) Their conditions seemed to be based upon some relics of the campaign in the shape of positions which Roosevelt may have taken; but in the light of the fight which they are going to evidently have with the British, it seemed to the President, Mills, and myself to be a highly foolish position to take. In the argument over it, I was the principal protagonist. The President was tactful and conciliatory and finally drew the communique in a form which satisfied all. Mills, while making his position clear, very tactfully maintained a modest and aloof position, evidently on account of rumors that had been current about Roosevelt's personal dislike for him.

The conference lasted from eleven until about 12:15. Then we separated; Roosevelt and his followers going back to the Mayflower, while the President, Mills and I went back to the Executive Office and on the advice of Mills, I tried to draw up an aide memoire preparatory to the meeting which I was to have with the British Ambassador in the afternoon. I called up Roosevelt on the telephone and read it to him. He had just been on the point of leaving for the train, but he made two criticisms of his own, one, the old one arising out of the argument that the two discussions be kept separate with the British as he wanted them, and the other being that he feared my language implied commitment to the reduction of debts. He suggested that Moley come to the Department to help me with it in the afternoon, and I agreed. During the time I was with the President, he wrote out a memorandum of the White House talk, a copy of which I shall annex to this diary.

I went out to Woodley for a hurried lunch, thinking over the aide memoire again; and at Woodley I drafted a new paragraph which avoided any possible suggestion or commitment on reducing the debts. I then hurried back to the Department and met Moley at two thirty and after a while I got in Bundy and Feis, and Professor Tugwell also joined us. Then we had a battle royal again over the separation of the two discussions. They never gave us any clear reason as to why they wanted the separation, but they were insistent on it as Roosevelt's wish. Probably it was because they did not want to follow the President, who has always insisted that there must be a quid pro quo for what they gave up. I warned them again and again that they were riding for trouble when they met the British here. I told them that I felt so strongly about it that in order to protect myself I would have to leave a memorandum showing that I had brought this warning to them. Finally, I drew up an aide memoire for my talk with the British Ambassador which they accepted quite satisfactory to them. It made the two discussions concurrent and conditional upon each other. But it did not mention that we should demand assurances in the one field as compensations for concessions in the debts. I read the final aide memoire to both the President and Mills over the telephone, telling them that it was the best I could do under the circumstances and they accepted it as satisfactory in the light of the difficulties. . . .

We then separated and I sent for the British Ambassador and told him that I was authorized by Mr. Roosevelt to invite them to send representatives and handed him the aide memoire as the content of my message. I pointed out to him the second paragraph with emphasis, telling him that I felt responsible that there should be no misunderstanding as to Mr. Roosevelt's desires to have the two discussions take place simultaneously and conditioned one upon the other. He asked if that meant "gold." I said, "Yes, I thought it would but I could not define it further." He evidently was very much gratified at our success in getting forward on this matter and told me he was very grateful for what I had done.

After he left I had the press in for a background conference. I had heard they were disappointed with the meager character of what had been given out in the communique, and I pointed out to them that this step meant a saving of a month or six weeks, and showed them how it meant this. I also pointed out, however, that the proposal first made by the President did mean an earlier beginning of not only preparatory work but of negotiations prior to the Fourth of March; but that Mr. Roosevelt's rejection of that limited the prior work to preparation only and that negotiations would not begin until after the Fourth of March. I, however, said that Mr. Roosevelt's position was quite comprehensible and that I made no criticism of it.

WHITE HOUSE STATEMENT
January 20, 1933

The joint communique offered little hope for a quick resolution to the debt crisis. Roosevelt would do nothing until he was president.

January 20, 1933.

The following is a White House statement.

The Conference between the President and the President-elect this morning was attended by Secretaries Stimson and Mills and Messrs. Norman Davis and Moley. The discussions were devoted mainly to a canvass of the foreign situation and the following statement covering the procedure to be followed was agreed upon:

"The British Government has asked for a discussion of the debts. The incoming Administration will be glad to receive their representative early in March for this purpose. It is, of course, necessary to discuss at the same time the world economic problems in which the United States and Great Britain are mutually interested, and therefore that representatives should also be sent to discuss ways and means for improving the world situation."

It was settled that these arrangements will be taken up by the Secretary of State with the British Government.

STIMSON MEMORANDUM
January 20, 1933

Stimson met with the British ambassador shortly before six p.m. to inform him of Roosevelt's plans. Stimson would go no further than the language of the communique. When asked for more information, Stimson told the ambassador to use their own interpretation: "I said that he could understand my reluctance to assume to interpret Mr. Roosevelt's words any further."

January 20, 1933

MEMORANDUM OF CONVERSATION BETWEEN
SECRETARY STIMSON AND THE BRITISH AMBASSADOR,
SIR RONALD LINDSAY.

I sent for the British Ambassador and he came at 5:45 p.m. I told him that I was authorized by Mr. Roosevelt to extend through him to Great Britain an invitation to send representatives here by the fourth of March to take up the discussion of the debt between our two countries as soon as possible after Mr. Roosevelt's inauguration. I handed the Ambassador a memorandum, a copy of which is attached. I told him that memorandum contained about all I had to say. But I called his especial attention to the second paragraph, saying I felt responsible that there should be no misunderstanding on the part of the British as to Mr. Roosevelt's expectation that they should send, at the same time, representatives prepared to discuss the other matters mentioned therein besides debts. Sir Ronald asked me what was defined by these other matters and whether they included "gold." I said that I would not try to give the full content of what had been expressed in the memorandum in general language, but would leave that to their own interpretation or to further inquiries, and I said that he could understand my reluctance to assume to interpret Mr. Roosevelt's words any further. The Ambassador went away expressing great gratitude for what he asserted I had done in the matter.

H. L. S.

COPY OF AIDE MEMOIRE HANDED TO THE BRITISH
AMBASSADOR, SIR RONALD LINDSAY, BY SECRETARY
OF STATE STIMSON, JANUARY 20, 1933.

In our previous correspondence on this subject the British Government has expressed a desire for a discussion in the near future of the debts owed by that government to the United States. I am authorized by Mr. Roosevelt, the President-elect, to say that he will be glad to receive at Washington a representative or representatives of the British Government for that purpose early in March, as soon as possible after his inauguration.

Mr. Roosevelt wishes it to be understood that any discussion of the debts which the British Government may wish to bring up must be concurrent with and conditioned upon a discussion of the world economic problems in which the two Governments are mutually interested, and therefore that representatives should also be sent at the same time to discuss the ways and means for improving the world situation.

HOOVER MEMORANDUM
January 20, 1933

As his dismay with Roosevelt grew, Hoover kept a detailed record of his conversations with the governor. Hoover solicited Stimson's advice on this draft.

Conference on January 20, 1933 Between President Hoover and Governor Roosevelt

At the conference at eleven o'clock this morning were Mr. Roosevelt, Secretary Stimson, Secretary Mills, Norman Davis, and Mr. Moley. I outlined again briefly the necessity of some indicated course of action or program by the American government in connection with the International economic situation, first, in order that this vital relief should be put in course of accomplishment, and second, that some hope of stability should be given to the world by the indication of a definite purpose on the part of the American government at the earliest moment.

I reviewed the subject shortly and stated that I understood the Governor wished that the British Government, having asked to take up debt questions, should be informed that the new Administration would be prepared to receive their representatives early in March to discuss the debt question. The Governor agreed that this was his idea and that it should not be confused with the questions before the Economic Conference. I stated that I was convinced that the debt question was but a segment of the whole international economic problem, and that if we were to make any sacrifice in connection with debt it must be made in exchange for positive quid pro quo to the American people of positive and definite order; that the debt question could not be separated without sacrifice of American interests; that the indication to the British to send a representative on debts alone, as he proposed, would lead simply to discussion of reduction of debt, out of which the British had everything to gain and we had everything to lose.

I reiterated that it was absolutely vital that the American people should receive definite and positive quid pro quo (and I repeated this several times) for any adjustments or concessions made in respect to the debt; that it was impracticable to discuss the debt without discussing these compensations; that among these compensations were many of the problems which were before the World Economic Conference; that it was vitally necessary for us to have agreement as to what line the British would take. I stated there were other forms of compensations which should be required.

I also suggested that united of [sic] action between Great Britain and the United States as the two greatest commercial countries in the world, in a program to be laid before the Economic Conference for the rehabilitation of the situation, would make the conference a success. I pointed out that such leadership would be followed by the entire world, and that it was the only road to stability, the only way to turn the tide in price levels and thus halt the degeneration now going on.

There were other questions of compensation besides those at the Economic Conference that might well be raised in such a discussion, and I do not see how debt questions could be separated from the compensations.

Governor Roosevelt again stated that he felt that the debts and the Economic Conference that [sic] should be kept separate. His view was that a British representative should come to the United States for the purpose of discussion of debts, and that the other questions might arise naturally in the course of such discussion.

Secretary Stimson pointed out with emphasis that it could not be indicated to the British that we would receive their representative to discuss debts and then later raise these vital questions; that the British would at once take advantage of the situation that they had not been forewarned, that other collateral questions would be raised; that if he intended to raise such questions, the British must be informed of it before starting and that if he did not intend to raise them he would find himself and the United States simply losing the debts with nothing to come to the American people.

Secretary Mills pointed out the propaganda being issued from the British Treasury to the effect that they were not prepared to give any compensations, and that they had only one view—cancellation or major reduction. He reiterated that the debts were our only weapon to secure safety and compensations that no debt settlement ever ought to be made until all these were absolutely secured.

I pointed out again that no single man could represent all these questions; that the British Government should be notified so that they could bring a number of men adapted to the problems which would come up; and that the United States should be prepared to meet them with effective personnel.

I felt that it would be very desirable for some man of the stature of Mr. Baldwin or Mr. MacDonald to come, but he would have to be accompanied by others if they were going to compass the problem which really confronted us; that it would be a long and tedious negotiation and I pointed out the history of the Arms Conference.

Professor Moley kept insisting that the two things must be kept separate. He admitted that perhaps if two separate representatives were sent on the two subjects at the same time they could be discussed separately. He stated that if one representative came on debts and another on economic questions, they could discuss the different questions in different rooms and thus maintain the separation.

Governor Roosevelt suggested that he personally would discuss the debt questions, and that naturally the departmental officials would discuss the economic question, but that there ought to be a separation in the matter.

The Secretary of State reaffirmed that no concessions on the debts should be made until he had secured a quid pro quo in forms which would compensate the American people, and that thus both subjects should be dealt with together, whether by separate delegations or by one. I pointed out that if we had separate delegations they would coordinate themselves even if the Americans did not do so.

Mr. Mills stated again that he could not then separate the discussions.

Norman Davis agreed that they could not be separated.

I realized it was now a question of saving the Governor's face in view of his public statements, and I stated that often enough these were questions of a formula, and that we might try to arrive at a formula. I suggested that we could split the formula into two parts, but that they should run coincidently; that the British should be informed that the Administration would be glad to receive their representatives to discuss the international economic situation in which the debts and their collateral questions would be considered.

Professor Moley and Governor Roosevelt objected to this as being too obvious a connection of the debt question with other economic questions; that it might involve us in determining the agenda and purpose of the Economic Conference. They wish to keep these matters entirely separate. Davis pointed out that the agenda was merely a menu and meant nothing. I stated that the big thing was the quid pro quo.

During the conversation, some cables from Ambassador Sackett at Geneva had been brought to Secretary Stimson. The Secretary read portions of them aloud and pointed out that in these cables we were now warned that the British intended to insist that the British debt must be settled before and as a separate matter from the consideration of any of these other economic questions; that, therefore, unless we gave notice that we held a contrary view and should insist on it, the British were likely to refuse to discuss these economic matters when they were here for the debts. Secretary Stimson showed these cables in their entirety during the conference to Professor Moley and to Mr. Davis, beside reading portions of them aloud at the conference. (The cables thus read were Geneva cables, N. 10 of Jan. 20, 10 a.m. and No. 11 of Jan. 20, noon)

We again went over the ground that these things could not be separated, pointing out this was a drive to get debt reductions without a quid pro quo and that it was sacrificing our interests.

Finally I suggested the following formula:

"The British Government has asked for a discussion of the debts. The incoming administration will be glad to receive their representative early in March for this purpose. It is, of course, necessary to discuss at the same time the world economic problems in which the United States and Great Britain are mutually interested, and therefore that representatives should also be sent to discuss ways and means for improving the world situation."

This seemed to meet the Governor's desires. He pointed out that the two sentences showed that the two subjects were separate.

Secretary Mills pointed out that the British Government must be informed that the two subjects were indissolvable and they would have to send representatives on both subjects and not upon one alone.

The Governor suggested that the Secretary of State should so inform the British Government of this verbally.

The Secretary of State then insisted upon having concrete instructions as to what he was to say to the British Ambassador. The Governor and Mr. Moley agreed that he was to insist verbally to the ambassador that the two subjects in the two different sentences were indissolvable, that one purpose could not be accepted without the other.

In order that there should be no misunderstanding, the Secretary of State repeated that it was his instructions that he should inform the British Ambassador that in reply to their request for discussion of the debt, President Roosevelt would receive their representative early in March for such discussion, but at the same time the whole compensations must be discussed and considered at that time; that the British were to be clearly informed that we expect in this discussion that there should be a compensation that is a quid pro quo to the American people in any adjustment, and that they should not send representatives to the United States under any misapprehension as to our purposes.

Finally, the formula was agreed to. The result is to state our appearance of separation to the public, but a consolidation of them in fact in British delegations.

Governor Roosevelt asked how the Far Eastern situation was proceeding, and I told him that the evident unity of action between the two Administrations had greatly stiffened it, and from our point of view it was having a good effect.

I took up with him the question of confirmation of Chairman Pomerene and President Miller of the Reconstruction Corporation, pointing out that this, the most gigantic financial institution in the world, would be left completely at sea on March 4th, without direction and in the midst of a national crisis. I asked if he would secure that his colleagues in Congress would act upon their confirmations. I informed him that the three Republican members would want to retire and that he would have to be prepared to find new members.

I also suggested that the bill before Congress providing seed loans through the Department of Agriculture should be amended so that these loans could be made through the new agricultural banks instead of the departmental officials. I asked if he would make this suggestion to his colleagues, that it was very much in his interest as their administration through the Department agents and local voluntary committees led to great wastes, and that there was already a duplication of effort between these two institutions. I pointed out that the bill was in conference and that it would be desirable to have early action.

JOSLIN DIARY
January 23, 1933

Once again, the president confided to his press secretary his unvarnished views of the president-elect. Hoover, frustrated at his inability to convince Roosevelt to take action, suffered as the country suffered.

Monday, Jan. 23, 1933

Roosevelt is doing everything wrong so far as the international situation is concerned in the President's opinion. Also party leaders here are putting the cart before the horse. The President said today:

"Neither Roosevelt nor his party sees the international problem in the right light. Anyone who will read my correspondence with Roosevelt should see what I was trying to do was to get him to appoint the economic conferees before taking up the debt matter. We didn't want to say it, but that would have given the country the debts as a club. Now the British have done just what Mills and I thought they would do. But it is Roosevelt's funeral not mine. Nevertheless our country will have to suffer."

NOTES BY MILDRED HALL
[January 29, 1933]

On January 28, Eleanor Roosevelt visited to the White House in anticipation of the coming inauguration of FDR. She arrived at 11 a.m. and received a cordial tour from Lou Henry Hoover. The visit was faithfully recorded by Mrs. Hoover's secretary, Mildred Hall.

After some correspondence had "filtered" back and forth, eleven o'clock on January 28th, '33 was the time set for Mrs. R to come to the WH to see just what she would need to add the living touches to the furnishings there.

A few minutes before eleven, LHH and MH went down to the Green Room to await the arrival of Mrs. R.   LHH was explaining to MH about the small set of books on the table in the Green Room being the only "library" in the WH on the day HH became President. In the midst of this explanation, The Chief Usher announced Mrs. R., who was rather breathless from her walk down from her hotel. Mrs. H, after greeting Mrs. R, continued her explanation, and went further into the library situation, telling Mrs. R. that the Library of Congress had books on a WH deposit—enough to fill the shelves on the second floor—and that the American Booksellers books were already on the shelves.

LHH asked Mrs. R if she would like to look at the house now, because she realized Mrs. R was quite busy. Mrs. R protested that it was most kind of LHH but she really shouldn't take LHH's time. However, we started out, through the Blue Room, the Red Room, the Dining Room—LHH saying that of course she had changed nothing except the picture over the fireplace and the one of President Lincoln. Mrs. R was interested in the Private Dining Room, and we looked in there.

The Usher [Irwin H. Hoover] took us to the second floor and left us. We walked up the hall, to the Oval Room door, LHH pointing out the pieces of furniture that belonged to her, and saying that there were really only the beds and chairs and tables in the WH, but none of the little things one wanted around to make it livable. As we entered the Oval Room, Mrs. R broke in to ask what belonged to LHH. The piano and two sofas and pictures and ornaments were hers, LHH said.

From the Oval Room to the Monroe Room, we went, this piano and these chairs, the stands holding the vases, etc. belonged to the WH. LHH told the story of the Monroe Room, with the furniture which belonged to Monroe, or which was copied from that which used to belong to Monroe, the pictures given to go with the room, the ones loaned from the National Gallery of Art. The rose sofas and chairs had belonged to the house at time of Monroe's occupancy.

Then to the study, where only a few things belonged to LHH. The Rose Bedroom came next, and that was as it had always been. As we were leaving that room, MH reminded LHH about the curtains in the Oval Room, and LHH said that she wanted to explain about the curtains in the Study, which belonged to her. So we went back to look at the red curtains. The collection of prints belonged to the President, LHH said, on being asked.

Down the steps, to the Oval Room again, where Mrs. R admired the curtains very much. LHH said that they partly belonged to her, and if Mrs. R very particularly wanted them, she (LHH) would leave them. Apparently Mrs. R very particularly wanted them!

Mrs. R led the way over to the hallway over the north portico, and walked into the Yellow Bedroom, where DSM [Dare Stark McMullin] was working. Everything except the little things there belonged in the WH.

Through the Blue Bedroom, into the hall. A quick look at the Lincoln Room and the little Northwest bedroom.

An explanation of the palm room and the birds. LHH wondered if Mrs. R would like the bird cage dismantled. Mrs. R said no.

Down the little hallway to the President's bathroom and dressing room, through the bedroom, where Mrs. H was so horrified at the bright blue coverlet that she forgot to tell Mrs. R that the bed belonged to LHH. Through the little closet hallway into LHH's dressing room, with its bathroom.

Out into the hall, where Mrs. R was asked if she would like to see the third floor, which had been put on during the time Mr. Coolidge was in office. She would, in order to see what servants quarters there were, but she didn't want to take LHH's time.

Again we went up in the elevator. She was told that these rooms (PHB's [Phillipi Harding Butler], MH's [Mildred Hall] and 33 [sic]) had very nice cottage bedroom furniture, but at present were being used for offices. A look in at the sun porch, where DG [Doris Goss] was. A glance in the sewing room, and [Kosta] Boris' rooms, which once had been used as a nursery for the grandchildren. An indication of the pressing room and Nora [Mannix]'s room, from the hallway. She was told that the housekeeper had two rooms and bath, similar to Boris' suite, but she did not seem inclined to look at them nor when asked if she would like to see the housekeeper, did she want to do that. She had pointed out to her from the first arch, the cedar room, the linen closet and the storerooms, etc. She glanced at the closets on both sides of the archway. More carefully she inspected the servants quarters on the West end.

Then, just as we were stepping into the elevator, LHH said she thought if Mrs. R wanted to see the kitchens, the housekeeper had better show them to her, as she (LHH) didn't know much about them. MH went back for Ava Long and then ran down the steps, arriving at the basement floor almost as soon as the elevator did. Mrs. Long was introduced and took Mrs. R into the kitchen, the ice boxes, the storerooms, the servants dining rooms, and brought her back to the doctor's office where LHH was waiting. JTB [Joel T. Boone, M.D.] told of his department, and the number of patients he took care of. Mrs. R smiled and went out.

LHH, Mrs. R and MH then went to the Red Room to see if there were any more explanations or anything Mrs. R. wished done. They were served orange juice. The Usher came in, Mrs. R shook hands, thanked LHH and took leave. LHH and MH went upstairs. Shortly thereafter, LHH remembered the bed and upon calling the Usher found that Mrs. R was still in the house. She was brought back to the second floor and shown the large bed. She said she would like the room LHH used for a dressing room for Mr. R's bedroom, and that the brass bed (which LHH explained had been in there when she came) could be put back there, with the twin beds, one of which was used in LHH's study, were to be set up in the large bedroom for Mrs. R.

Appreciation was expressed all over again and goodbyes said, and Mrs. R departed, about an hour after she arrived.

JOSLIN DIARY
February 1, 1933

If Stimson could not persuade Roosevelt to take action, perhaps the U.S. Senate could. Hoover met with Senator David A. Reed, Republican of Pennsylvania, to press his case. The president told Reed that Congress best be wary of Roosevelt or it would be cut out of any debt negotiations. Reed and a colleague attacked Roosevelt in the Senate on January 31 and Hoover admitted to being the progenitor of the attack. "I'll have my way with Roosevelt yet," Hoover told Joslin.

Wednesday, Feb. 1, 1933

Senator Jim Ham [James Hamilton] Lewis and Senator Reed went after Roosevelt in the Senate yesterday, saying in effect that he apparently was going to make the same mistake that Wilson did in dealing with the European powers. When I mentioned it to the President he said:

"I had Reed down here and pumped him full for half an hour. I told him that we were in a fair way to have the mistakes of the Versailles Treaty made all over again. I have made three debt proposals to Roosevelt and he won't accept any of them. He wants to deal directly with MacDonald. That's his great ambition. Now if he does, and tells the British for instance that for certain considerations we will cut the debt 50 percent, the British won't pay anymore than fifty percent whatever attitude Congress takes. It has the President's word and will ignore Congress. [sic] This is something I have always steered clear of. Congress should be kept in the picture. I intend it will be. I'll have my way with Roosevelt yet."

9

End of Our String

The last two weeks of the Hoover presidency were pure hell. As the economic crisis worsened, Hoover was powerless to coerce Congress into action. No one would act without Roosevelt's authority and the president-elect was silent. Hoover felt compelled to appeal to Roosevelt once again, in the strongest terms, to take action.

On February 18, Hoover sent a desperate, handwritten appeal to Roosevelt to take action for the good of the country. Only Roosevelt could calm the nation's jitters. Something must be done. But no response was forthcoming from Hyde Park.

Hoover came to believe that Roosevelt's refusal to act was purely political. If the banks failed before March 4, the American people would blame Hoover. Even though millions of Americans were suffering, Roosevelt would do nothing. Hoover received a piece of intelligence documenting this strategy on February 25, in a memo passed from James Rand to Ted Joslin.

Hoover fumed until the 28th when he sent another letter to Roosevelt; but this time he had it hand carried by a secret service agent. Roosevelt responded on March 1, saying that his response to the letter of the 18th had been misplaced. It did not matter, though, because Roosevelt had not changed his mind about taking action.

But Hoover would not give up. Day and night from March first to the third, Hoover tried to find a way to end the crisis. All to no avail. Finally, on March

3, even Herbert Hoover had to admit defeat. "Ted," he told his press secretary, "we are at the end of our string."

HOOVER TO ROOSEVELT
February 18, 1933

As the country's economic crisis worsened, Hoover became more concerned. On February 18, he penned a long letter to Roosevelt urging him in the strongest terms to speak out on his economic plans. Hoover noted that a "tremendous lift" would come to the nation "by the removal of fear," a theme that Roosevelt would echo in his inaugural address. But action was needed now. "I am taking the liberty of addressing you," Hoover wrote, "because both of my anxiety over the situation and my confidence that from four years of experience that such tides as are now running can be moderated."

February 18, 1933

/s/ My dear Mr. President Elect:

A most critical situation has arisen in the country of which I feel it is my duty to advise you confidentially. I am therefore taking this course of writing you myself and sending it to you through the Secret Service for your hand direct as obviously its misplacement would only feed the fire and increase the dangers.

The major difficulty is the state of public mind, for there is a steadily degenerating confidence in the future which has reached the height of general alarm. I am convinced that a very early statement by you upon two or three policies of your administration would serve greatly to restore confidence and cause a resumption of the march of recovery.

The large part which fear and apprehension play in the situation can be well demonstrated by repeated experience in the past few years and the tremendous lift which has come at times by the removal of fear can be easily demonstrated.

One of the major underlying elements in the broad problem of recovery is the reexpansion of credit so critically and abruptly deflated by the shocks from Europe during the last half of 1931. The visible results were public fear, hoarding, bank failures, withdrawal of gold, flight of capital, falling prices, increased unemployment, etc. Early in 1932 we created the agencies which have steadily expanded available credit ever since that time and continue to expand it today. But confidence must run parallel with expanding credit and the instances where confidence has been injured run precisely with the lagging or halting of recovery. There are, of course, other factors but I am only illustrating certain high lights.

Within the last twelve months we have had two profound exam-
ples of the effect of restoration of confidence. Immediately after the
passage of the measures for [the] credit expansion act early in 1932
there was a prompt response in public confidence with expression
in rising prices, employment, decrease in bank failures, hoarding,
etc. even before the actual agencies were in action. This continued
until it was interrupted by the aggregate of actions starting in the
House of Representatives last spring again spread fear and practical
panic across the country. This interruption brought back all the dis-
astrous phenomena that I have mentioned but near the end of the
session when it became clear to the country that the revenue bill
would be passed, that inflation of the currency and bonus were defeated, that the government credit would be maintained, that the gold
standard would be held, etc. Promptly for a second time confidence
returned and ran parallel with the expansion and reconstruction
measures. The country resumed the march of recovery. At once there
was a rise in farm, commodity and security prices; production, industry and employment. There was a practical cessation of bank
failures and hoarding, and gold returned from abroad. This continued
during the summer and fall when again there began another era of
interruptions to public confidence which have finally culminated in
the present state of alarm and it has transformed an upward movement into a distinct downward movement.

The facts about this last interruption are simple and they are pertinent to the action needed. With the election, there came the natural
and inevitable hesitation all along the economic line pending the
demonstration of the policies of the new administration. But a number of very discouraging things have happened on top of this natural
hesitation. The breakdown in balancing the budget by the House of
Representatives; the proposals for inflation of the currency and the
wide spread discussion of it; the publication of R.F.C. loans and the
bank runs, hoarding and bank failures from this cause; increase in
unemployment due to imports from depreciated currency countries;
failure of the Congress to enact banking, bankruptcy and other vital
legislation; unwillingness of the Congress to face reduction in expenditures; proposals to abrogate constitutional responsibility by the
Congress with all the chatter about dictatorship, and other discouraging effects upon the public mind. They have now culminated to
a state of alarm which is rapidly reaching the dimensions of a crisis.
Hoarding has risen to a new high level; the bank structure is weakened as witness Detroit and increased failures in other localities.
There are evidences of flight of capital and foreign withdrawals of
gold. In other words we are confronted with precisely the same
phenomena we experienced late in 1931 and again in the spring of

1932. The whole has its final expression in the increase of unemployment, suffering and general alarm.

During all this time the means of available credit expansion has been in progress but neither borrowers nor lenders are willing to act in the [interest] of business. While the financial agencies of the government can do much to stem the tide and to localize fires, and while there are institutions and situations that must be liquidated, these things can only be successfully attained in an atmosphere of general confidence. Otherwise the fire will spread.

I therefore return to my suggestion at the beginning as to the desirability of clarifying the public mind on certain essentials which will give renewed confidence. It is obvious that as you will shortly be in position to make whatever policies you wish effective, you are the only one who can give these assurances. Both the nature of the cause of public alarm and experience give such an action the prospect of success in turning the tide. I do not refer to action on all the causes of alarm but it would steady the country greatly if there could be prompt assurance that there will be no tampering or inflation of the currency; that the budget will be unquestionably balanced even if further taxation is necessary; that the government credit will be maintained by refusal to exhaust it in issue of securities. The course you have adopted in inquiring into the problems of world stabilization are already known and helpful. It would be of further help if the leaders were advised to cease publication of R.F.C. business.

I am taking the liberty of addressing you because both of my anxiety over the situation and my confidence that from four years of experience that such tides as are now running can be moderated and the processes of regeneration which are always running can be released.

Incidentally, I will welcome the announcement of the new Secretary of the Treasury as that would enable us to direct activities to one point of action and communication with your good self.

I wish again to express my satisfaction at your escape and to wish you good health.

Yours sincerely,
Herbert Hoover

The President Elect
Franklin Roosevelt

JOSLIN TO HOOVER
February 25, 1933

Hoover's anger at Roosevelt and his "Brains Trust" was compounded by the news that these "new dealers" would take no action to prevent the collapse of the banking industry. In fact, they wanted the banks to fail before March 4 so that Hoover would get the blame. Word of this scheme came to Hoover from James H. Rand, Jr., President of Remington-Rand, who had lunched with Rex Tugwell. Rand called Ted Joslin who passed on the information to the president. Hoover thanked Rand in a letter dated February 28. "I can say emphatically," Hoover wrote, "that [Tugwell] breathes with infamous politics devoid of every atom of patriotism. Mr. Tugwell would project millions of people into hideous losses for a Roman holiday." [This document was published in *Public Papers of the Presidents: Herbert Hoover, 1932–33* (Washington, D.C., 1974), pp. 1056–57.]

James Rand telephoned the following message to me at 3:49 p.m., Feb. 25, 1933, from Room 2808, Pierre Hotel, N.Y.C. (Regent 4–5901)

"Prof. Tugwell, advisor to F.R., had lunch with me. He said they were fully aware of the bank situation and that it undoubtedly would collapse within a few days, which would thus place the responsibility in the lap of President Hoover. He said we should not worry about anything excepting rehabilitating the country after March 4th. Then there will be several moves: No. 1, an embargo on the exportation of yellow chips. No. 2, suspension of specie payments. No. 3, reflation, if necessary, after Nos. 1 and 2.

"After that arrangement to be made for the so-called business men's committee of sixty-odd prominent manufacturers, who have been invited to spend half a day with the new Secretary of the Treasury, Mr. Woodin, on Tuesday in an attempt to gain the support of the business interests for a program.

"My suggestion is that the collapse be not allowed to happen before March 4th. Taxpayers are all bank depositors. If banks are allowed to freeze under State legislation they will all freeze in the next two weeks. The State legislation and the bill passed today in the House inspire much greater fear and have accelerated withdrawals of gold and currency.

"The Ohio situation will break on Monday. One large Cleveland bank refused withdrawal of $100,000 to our company today. Withdrawals throughout leading cities yesterday and today were terrific. The only thing that will save the situation in the opinion of our committee is the guarantee of bank deposits for two years, effective on Monday. That is the opinion of bankers who dare tell the truth, including Melvin Traylor of Chicago.

"My suggestion, which I am conveying for the committee, is that the President send a special message to Congress today asking for this guarantee of bank deposits for two years under certain conditions of supervision by Federal Reserve Banks in their respective districts—limitation of dividends and interest and making insurance of bank deposits optional with any banks on payment of one-eighth of one percent of its deposits. If this is done the President will get the credit by all thinking citizens for having saved the day. If nothing is done and collapse happens before March 4th, it will be a calamity and will be blamed on the Administration by Republicans and Democrats alike.''

T. G. Joslin

HOOVER TO ROOSEVELT
February 28, 1933

By February 28, Hoover had yet to receive any reply to his handwritten letter of February 18. The Secret Service confirmed in writing that Operative John West had hand delivered the letter to Roosevelt. Unwilling to wait any longer, Hoover wrote again on February 28.

Feb. 28, 1933

/s/ Dear Mr. President Elect

It is my duty to inform you that the financial situation has become even more grave and the lack of confidence extended further than when I wrote to you on February 18th. I am confident that a declaration even now on the line I suggested at that time would contribute greatly to restore confidence and would save losses and hardships to millions of people.

My purpose however is to urge you—upon the basis of evident facts—that the gravity of the situation is such that it is desirable that the co-ordinate arm of the government should be in session quickly after March 4th. There is much legislation urgently needed but will not be completed by the present session. The new Congress being in majority with the administration is capable of expeditious action.

But beyond that, it would make for stability in public mind and there are contingencies in which immediate action may be absolutely essential in the next few days.

I am at your disposal to discuss the situation upon your arrival here or otherwise. I wish to assure you of the deep desire of my colleagues and myself to co-operate with you in every way.

Yours sincerely,
Herbert Hoover

The President Elect
Franklin Roosevelt
New York

ROOSEVELT TO HOOVER
March 1, 1933

Roosevelt responded the next day with a letter of apology and dismay. He had been surprised to learn that his letter of February 20 had not been mailed to Hoover. He assured Hoover that he was very concerned about the bank crisis and would take action as soon as possible.

Hyde Park
March 1, 1933

The President
The White House

/s/ Dear Mr. President:

I am dismayed to find that the enclosed which I wrote in N.Y. a week ago did not go to you, through an assumption by my secretary that it was only a draft of a letter.

Now I have yours of yesterday and can only tell you that I appreciate your fine spirit of co-operation and that I am in constant touch with the situation through Mr. Woodin, who is conferring with Ogden and with various people in N.Y. I am inclined to agree that a very early special session will be necessary—and by tonight or tomorrow I hope to settle on a definite time—I will let you know— you doubtless know of the proposal to give authority to the Treasury to deposit funds directly in any bank.

I get to Washington late tomorrow night and will look forward to seeing you on Friday.

Sincerely yours,
Franklin D. Roosevelt

* * *

49 East 65th Street
Feb. 20, 1933

/s/ Dear Mr. President;

I am equally concerned with you in regard to the gravity of the present banking situation—but my thought is that it is so very deep-seated that the fire is bound to spread in spite of anything that is done by way of mere statements. The real trouble is that on present values very few financial [institutions] anywhere in the country are actually able to pay off their deposits in full, and the knowledge of this fact is widely held—Bankers with the narrower viewpoint have urged me to make a general statement but even they seriously doubt if it would have a definite effect.

I had hoped to have Senator Glass' acceptance of the Treasury post—but he has definitely said no this afternoon—I am asking Mr. Woodin tomorrow—if he accepts I propose to announce it tomorrow together with Senator Hull for the State Department. These announcements may have some effect on the banking situation, but frankly I doubt if anything short of a fairly general withdrawal of deposits can be prevented now.

In any event Mr. Woodin, if he accepts will get into immediate touch with Mills and the bankers.

Very sincerely yours,
Franklin D. Roosevelt

The President
The White House

JOSLIN DIARY
March 1, 1933

With less than four days left in his administration, Hoover gave up any hope of convincing Roosevelt or the Congress to take any action on the banking crisis. The president confided to Joslin that Roosevelt would have to take "responsibility for the current critical situation."

Wednesday, March 1, 1933

The President advised Mills by letter this afternoon that his appointment with Woodin tonight was to advise him that this Administration would forward any legislation on the banking crisis that the incoming Administration would care to sponsor. He said it would be futile with the session almost over to proceed in any other way as it long since has been demonstrated this Congress was responsive only to the incoming Administration. If Roosevelt will indicate his pleasure, the President will incorporate his wishes in a message. The President said that all the protestations Roosevelt may make between now and Mar. 4 or thereafter will not save him from responsibility for the current critical situation. The President thinks the responsibility is absolutely his and thus puts it equally up to him.

Government reports are as bad as ever. Two hundred million more went into hoarding today. More banks closed or went on a five percent basis. At this rate every bank in the country will be frozen in a fortnight.

DIARY OF JOEL T. BOONE
March 3, 1933

Joel T. Boone was the White House physician during the Coolidge and Hoover years. His recently opened diary provides researchers with some extraordinary glimpses into the presidency. He recorded this particularly tense moment when the president was first confronted with Roosevelt's plan for a general bank "holiday." [This document is from the Joel T. Boone papers in the Manuscript Division of the Library of Congress. It is used by permission.]

... (The President) seemed to feel positively that he could solve this economic problem now had he been given a chance; that it (the way out) was all very clear to him. The telephone on his study desk rang, which he answered. A heated conversation with Mills occurred. Finally the President said, "God, a proposition of that sort is diabolical; it is cruel to put me in such a position the last few remaining hours of my Presidency: I will not do it unless Governor Roosevelt personally asks me as an executive act to do it; I could not live it down for thirty years."

It seemed to be a general bank moratorium. After emphasizing his points of argument, his voice broke and then he said, "Mills, can you give me one single valid reason why I should do it?" There was silence from the other end. The President waited; then hung up the telephone.

I was sitting in a rocker facing the fire place which bore the marker that in this room President Lincoln had signed the proclamation freeing the slaves. History was being reenacted. Over the mantle was the picture of Lincoln with his cabinet—a cabinet that was not harmonious or always loyal. He had to take a position in opposition to them repeatedly. Lincoln lives as the dominating spirit.

Tonight the President and I were the sole figures in the room.

When the President pushed back his chair, I arose and was tempted to commiserate with him, but stood silent. He paced the floor kicking his toe against the carpet as he walked, head down, hands in pockets. I felt he needed his own thoughts uninterrupted by foreign and probably unbefitting ones from me. ...

HOOVER MEMORANDUM
March 3, 1933

The banking crisis continued to worsen during the waning days of the Hoover Administration. The president met with his successor on the afternoon of March 3 in yet another attempt to develop a common response to the crisis. At 8:30 p.m., Roosevelt asked Hoover what he thought of a national bank holiday. Hoo-

ver was firmly negative. Bank moratoriums should be authorized by state governors; the federal government should limit its efforts to hoarding and foreign
exchange. The two men talked again at 11:15 and agreed not to proclaim a
national bank holiday, but the crisis continued. [This document is printed in
Public Papers of the Presidents: Herbert Hoover, 1932–33 (Washington, DC,
1974), pp. 1076–1084.]

Friday, March 3, 1933

At 9:30 in the morning Secretary Mills came to see me and stated
that he felt the New York banks had taken action which he believed
would enable them to get over the weekend. I stated that it seemed
to me the intermediate stage here had not yet been undertaken—that
was the declaration of any needed day to day holidays by the Governor of New York. All the other States had acted on their own
authority to protect themselves and to bring the Federal Government
into it merely because New York was in trouble should be put up
to Governor [Herbert] Lehman, who had power to take action. Secretary Mills informed me that when he found Mr. Woodin was taking the matter up with Roosevelt he sent for Senator [James F.]
Byrnes and explained the situation, feeling that Byrnes went to Roosevelt and told him Woodin's difficulties. Byrnes indicated his great
distress at the situation but said he could not do anything further. I
showed Mr. Mills Governor Roosevelt's letter of March 1, in which
he used the expression ''You doubtless know of the proposal to give
authority to the Treasury to deposit funds directly in any bank.'' I
told him I did not understand what this meant, but it indicated he
had something in his mind. Mills explained to me that [Russell]
Leffingwell and [S. Parker] Gilbert of J. P. Morgan & Co., had de-
vised a plan which the Federal Government was to deposit currency
as an ordinary depositor in any bank up to the full demands of any
of the bank's depositors; that Mr. Leffingwell had presented the plan
to Roosevelt. He also knew he had presented it to Mr. Woodin, but
Woodin had rejected it as impossible. It represented a 100 percent
guarantee of all deposits irrespective of assets of the bank; that it
would be a most gigantic inflationary scheme and, of course, meant
going off the gold standard. I asked what he thought would happen
to Government bonds. He said it was obscure, but, of course, everyone would run for gold if they could get it. He did not think there
was any likelihood of getting it in view of Woodin's attitude.

I expressed amazement that men of their presumed financial experience would propose such a plan, and could not believe that it
was without limitations, and stated that the bank guarantee plan as
I had worked it out was dangerous enough but that it had within it

enough restrictions to limit the dangers to a microscopic amount compared with this plan. I told him, however, that Tugwell's statement and others that had come to me, would check up fairly well with the plan, as indicating that the President-elect was seriously entertaining such ideas. He expressed his belief that it was so fantastic that it could not be possibly adopted; that they would have to come to the bank guarantee or to the clearinghouse scrip.

At 12 o'clock, Secretary Stimson called me to say that he had just had a conversation with Senator [Cordell] Hull, who stated that he had been with Roosevelt last night when they were endeavoring to get him to join in declaring a bank holiday; that Hull had strongly urged it on the Governor and was much disappointed that it had not been done but that there were "too damned many people about." He said he had taken the Governor into a separate room but there were still too many people; that Hull was much upset by developments of the previous evening.

Secretary Stimson asked if he was acting as Secretary of the Treasury and of State, and he said he guessed so, as he was trying to help out.

At 3:30, Secretary Mills called and stated that the situation in New York and Chicago during the day had been bad; that it was necessary that we have suspension of banking until legislation could be taken care of. He wanted me to at once send up and ask for a joint resolution calling for a 3-days' holiday and wished to take it up with Roosevelt when he called at 4 o'clock. I arranged for Secretary Mills and [Federal Reserve Board] Governor [Eugene] Meyer to be at the White House to take part in the discussion with Roosevelt. In the meantime, I told Mills that the Governors of all the other States had taken the initiative in protecting banking systems so as to meet local requirements; that I felt our effort should be to keep banks open, not closed. I said I was confident that no resolution could be passed by Congress; that it was not necessary; that it would destroy banking, which was going all right in certain localities; that I did not care to have my name on a message asking for a general moratorium in the United States until a plan for action under such a moratorium had been worked out; that I felt it inescapable that the banks should have local holidays by Governors to enable them to issue scrip, and that our proclamation should be limited to control of hoarding and exchange, thus keeping the banks open in many localities. A moratorium could not pass Congress in any event, as there would [be] at this late hour nothing but debate from refractory persons in the Senate. I stated I would do anything of the kind on the request of Governor Roosevelt and not otherwise.

After the social formalities of tea I told Governor Roosevelt that

the situation had been very bad during the day and that Governor
Meyer and Secretary Mills were waiting and I would like him to
hear their statement. They were brought in, and Roosevelt asked to
bring in Moley, which was done. I asked Governor Meyer to tell
the Governor what the situation was in New York, which he did.
Meyer made rather a rambling discussion of the whole situation, but
finally drew up to the point that he felt there was no solution except
national legislation; that Congress would have to meet quickly. He
wanted a national moratorium in the meantime. Secretary Mills re-
inforced these ideas, and I intervened stating that the situation varied
in each State as to the measures to be taken; that Governor Lehman
had the same authority as every other Governor; that it would strike
me that Roosevelt could quite well talk to Governor Lehman, who
would no doubt act on his recommendation and could by acting with
local authorities better adapt it to local needs than national action,
which would embarrass many localities. Roosevelt stated that he had
an appointment to talk with Governor Lehman at 6 o'clock for other
purposes, and it would make a convenient time to talk with him.

Some conversation arose as to whether State holidays could be
applied to Federal Reserve banks, and it was suggested that they
had closed the Federal Reserve bank on Columbus Day, which was
not a legal holiday in many States; that they did not seem to have
to stick to national holidays on other occasions. I saw no reason why
they needed a national holiday at the moment, especially as many
States were comfortable and it was a pity to close their banks.

Mills told the Governor that national legislation was necessary
and that it would be desirable to call in the leading men of the
country and get it into a concrete plan. I assured the Governor that
I would cooperate in any fashion he wanted to hold the situation
during the next 24 hours, and to solve the national situation. To this
he made no response. I stated we had gone through four such periods
in this administration and we were getting used to such critical times
and had given much thought to the immediate steps and future steps
and would be glad to contribute.

I asked Secretary Mills to come to the office following the interview, and suggested that he get Harrison to consult Governor Lehman. He told me that Harrison told him Lehman would act in any
way that Harrison recommended. I asked him why they did not do
that last night instead of spending the night working on Roosevelt.
They thought it would be better to close the banks nationally, but I
suggested that this was not essential if steps were taken to stop
hoarding and foreign exchange, and that we should work to keep
every possible banking facility alive.

I then suggested to Mills that it seemed to me we were deficient in our relations to the new administration and the public in one particular; that we had 4 years experience dealing with these problems; that had we been met with this situation we would have had solution. We have alternative solutions, either clearinghouse or guarantee, which we know perfectly well is the only way out, dangerous as it may be, and I felt it desirable for me to transmit them personally to Roosevelt and tell him it was the sum of our opinion. Mills objected strongly and said he was not satisfied with it, although he agreed we would not get far away from them in any solution. I pointed out that in this crisis some solution would be produced, and that when it is produced we would get behind it as good citizens and it would be better if we registered our view on twice as sound a proposition as was possible in advance. He felt we should not take this responsibility but should insist that men be brought to Washington to formulate a plan in which they would take responsibility for final conclusion. I said this was all right, but that our views would help any such group. I felt certain that the next administration would say we had left the crisis to them without a suggestion as to method of solution, despite their repeated failure to cooperate with us.

At 7:45 Secretary Mills rang me up, and again stated that the New York situation had been very bad during the day; that there has been a loss of 110 millions of gold to foreigners; 20 millions to others, 200 million currency to the interior; that we could not go on for another day without getting under water in the Federal Reserve bank; that it was absolutely necessary, in his view, to issue a proclamation of a national banking holiday, to last until Tuesday night. He said that he had been with Mr. Woodin, and they were both urgent that I should sign it at once. I told him that I did not like the idea at all; that I could not entertain it unless it was directly asked for by Governor Roosevelt, and that if I signed it I should issue it as a ministerial act on behalf of the President-elect; that I believed the situation could be much better handled by a control of hoarding and exchange and possible clearinghouse scrip, together with local action by Governors and cooperation with State bankers; that the agreement with Governor Roosevelt at 5 o'clock had been that he would take up the matter with Governor Lehman, as we were all agreed that the Governors having started these moratoriums should carry them through where it was necessary and should adapt each moratorium to their own State requirements, but that my ideas of control and clearinghouse action, instead of closing, should be put forward. Mills was very urgent, and I became equally resistant. I stated the object of my life had been to keep banks open, not to close them, and I proposed to fight on that line to the end.

I rang up the Attorney General, and asked what his views of it was [sic] and told him that I was very much opposed to a moratorium as a matter of public policy; that to impose a moratorium on 10 or 12 States which had been proceeding with normal business, in order to take care of New York State interests, seemed to me to be a crime; that in any event the situation in New York could only mean the shifting of business in 3 hours on Saturday, and that it was not a loss of values; that no such sum would compensate for the enormous losses caused in areas which were not yet affected; that controls could be established which would keep the banks open in New York. Mitchell stated that he was very much opposed to general closing as a matter of public policy, and very doubtful about its being valid, and that he would call Mills up and caution him.

At 8:30, Governor Roosevelt rang me up and asked me what I thought of issuing the proclamation declaring a national holiday. I told him I had been thinking the matter over; that I hadn't changed my view from that expressed at our 5 o'clock conference, that this matter should be taken care of by the Governors of the States, with a national control limited to hoarding and foreign exchange. I told him if he would only believe me in giving him this advice that he should continue with Lehman and not project a national closing until he had his bearings. I told him there were forces of selfishness moving, but in any event I felt sure that the safest ground was to proceed in the manner indicated. He informed me that he had not been able to get hold of Lehman but that he agreed with me.

At 9 o'clock, Mark Sullivan came in, and I told him the circumstance. He advised strongly against taking the action, especially after Governor Roosevelt had refused to go along the day before on a hoarding and exchange control, when we could have saved the situation which developed during the day in New York and Chicago; that it would be to take a responsibility which I had no right to take, because I had no powers of correction of the wrong which might arise but should hold to my constructive program.

Being unable to get Mills on the telephone at the moment, I called up [Under secretary of the Treasury Arthur] Ballantine and expressed to him my conviction that we should stop the movement for a national closing and concentrate on Lehman and the Governor of Illinois for local action with national control of hoarding, etc. Ballantine was very strong for national closing. I told him that I did not believe our officials had a right to put me in that position. I felt it was forcing my hand against my own conviction as to what was best for the country.

At 9:30, I asked Mills and the Attorney General to come to the Executive Offices. With [Henry M.] Robinson and Sullivan we discussed the matter at length. Mills was bitterly disappointed at my attitude and would not give way on any proposition. He wanted me to call Governor Harrison on the telephone, which I did. I asked Harrison if they had approached Lehman for New York State action. Harrison argued at great length that a holiday in New York and Illinois would not answer the question and admitted that he had made no presentation to Lehman. I quoted to him the statement from Mills that Lehman had agreed to put in the holiday if Harrison asked for it in the name of the Federal Reserve bank. He did not deny it but said that Lehman was a weak reed to lean upon; that we had no time; that the proclamation must be issued at once. I told him he had better pursue the matter with Lehman giving local authority and raised the questions of control of hoarding and foreign exchange by national proclamation; that I was informed that Lehman had come out with a statement at 3 o'clock in the afternoon saying that there was no occasion for closing banks, that he had not been requested to by anybody, and that he did not propose to do it. I pointed out to Harrison the position that this placed me in of doing something which the Governor of New York State said was entirely uncalled for. He evaded the question of limiting national proclamation to hoarding and exchange control, but said this would leave some Federal Reserve banks in difficulties if State Governors did not act. Harrison endeavored to argue the question on the basis of the probable debacle the next day, and intimated that mine would be the personal responsibility. This I resented greatly and told him so, that it could be remedied by control of exchange and local action by the Governor.

Eugene Meyer then rang me up and was extremely discourteous in his threats. He then put me on the telephone to Adolph Miller to reinforce his statements. I asked Miller what would be the effect if I gave the authority to the Federal Reserve Board to control the hoarding of currency and gold, putting in such regulations as would control the foreign exchange. Miller said it could be managed without going off the gold standard and would save the situation. Meyer again interposed with the statement that this would not do at all, that he had discharged his duty by informing me of the situation, and that he proposed to hold me accountable for the national debacle, that nothing would save the situation but a national moratorium. He said controls were nonsense; we must close all the banks. I pointed out the great evils this would bring, especially as the Board had opposed all my efforts at clearinghouse set-ups, and they would have to be installed instantly and were not ready.

He rang up Mills and wanted Mills to repeat to me a letter which he had written in an endeavor to pass the responsibility from the

Federal Reserve Board over to me. Mills very properly refused to repeat the letter, and told Meyer such a document had never been passed by the Board. Meyer said it had been. Mills pointed out there could be no quorum unless he, Mills, had been present, and that he had not been present. Mills told him he could put nothing of the kind over on us, and rang off.

At 11:15, I rang up Governor Roosevelt. I told him we were still considering the problem and that we were at work on it. He said that he was at work on it also. I asked him what his views would be of a joint request from himself and myself to the Governors of New York and Illinois to put in one day's holiday in order to give time to turn around and that we by proclamation should organize a control of exchange and hoarding that would allow the banks to open on Monday. He said that might answer, but went on to say that he had now talked to Lehman; that Lehman informed him that as late as 7 o'clock the Chairman of the New York Clearing House, Mr. J. P. Morgan, Thomas W. Lamont, and others had told him there was no occasion to close banks on Saturday; that it was simply panic on the part of Federal Reserve officials. I told him that I thought the situation was serious, but that the only way to get at it was through the authority of the Governor in State institutions and our control of hoarding and exchange. He said that Lehman was within a few minutes having a meeting with both of these groups together; that he had no doubt that they would settle it. I asked him if he agreed with my view that there should be no national proclamation closing all the banks. He said he did not want it and would not support it as he wanted to consider the whole question. He told me that he had been talking with Senator Glass for an hour. Glass was opposed to a national closing; that he was opposed to national legislation; that he considered the whole business to be cleaned up through a series of clearinghouses if the bankers of the country would stand up and change their attitude; and that he, Roosevelt, was taking that view. I asked him if I might repeat to my colleagues his statement while he held on to the line. He did so. I told him that I thought that ended all question of national proclamation and he agreed.

Robinson then at once rang up Chicago and asked them how they were coming on. They expressed the view that the President should not under any circumstances issue a proclamation; that they had the Governor of Illinois in a meeting at that moment with the Federal Reserve and representative banking officials, together with the clearinghouse people; that the Governor was perfectly prepared to put in the holiday if the banks asked for it and that a national closing might do much harm.

At 12 o'clock, Dawes rang me up and asked what the situation was, I told him the situation.

I then went to bed.

JOSLIN DIARY
March 3, 1933

Joslin records a brief and somewhat partisan view of the day's events in his diary. Joslin portrays Hoover as the activist imploring Roosevelt to join in a plan of action. In truth, the Hoover and Roosevelt camps were wary of one another and unwilling to take unilateral action. The failure of this last effort left Hoover "both angry and depressed," noted Joslin. "Ted," Hoover sighed, "we are at the end of our string."

A last effort to join forces for the common welfare before the Congress ends tomorrow failed as have all the others. The president said this morning: "We were up until after one o'clock trying to induce Roosevelt into entering a holiday agreement that would take care of this situation. I was here and Mills and the Federal Reserve were at the Treasury. We were in frequent communication through the night. As a result of the conferences, Woodin implored Roosevelt to take action, but he refused point blank. (He had party leaders from Congress with him.) Then we tried to get Woodin's permission to use his name so that we could go through with the plan. This he said that he could not do. So we told them to go to hell."

I asked him what I should say about the A[ssociated] P[ress] report that the President would issue a statement or send a message to Congress on the banking crisis.

"I know where that originated," he replied. "It came from the other camp. They want to jockey me into proceeding. But I won't go it alone. Say only 'there is no expectation of doing anything of the kind' and stick to it. Don't go any further for there is still a last chance."

The "last chance" was his conference with Roosevelt at 4 [o'clock] after his customary request call with Mills, Meyer, Robinson, and Moley present. They argued for an hour but to no avail. The president wouldn't let me say anything to the press. At 6 [o'clock] I asked him if there was anything further. He was leaning [against] his desk, both angry and depressed. "No, Ted, we are at the end of our string."

STIMSON DIARY
March 4, 1933

Stimson and his wife joined Secretary of the Treasury Ogden Mills for the Inaugural Day activities. On the ride to the Capitol, Mills briefed Stimson on the last-minute efforts to find a compromise. "It looks to me," Stimson noted, "as if there had been a little too much politics on both sides." [This document is from the Henry L. Stimson Papers in the Department of Archives and Manuscripts at Yale University. It is used by permission.]

March 4, 1933 (Saturday)

A dreary day but it did not rain, and sometimes there was a ray of sunshine. Charlie Gamble had come down last night and got here this morning in order to see the sights. Gene took him in hand and was very helpful and made it possible for him to see about everything there was to see during the day.

Mabel and I drove down to the White House shortly after ten, arriving there before anybody else. It had been arranged that Mills and I would be in the same car, and Mrs. Mills with Mabel in her car, and so the other members of the Cabinet, two by two, divided up, the ladies going up first and getting their seats in the Senate Chamber. After the Cabinet had arrived, the Inauguration Committee came in and escorted the President out to the automobile in which Roosevelt had arrived, an open car; and then we followed in our cars in the procession up Pennsylvania Avenue to the capital[*sic*]. On the way Mills told me of the events of last night. He had been up until three thirty a.m. in the Treasury with Ballantine and others and with Woodin, and he was very critical of the President's attitude last night. Apparently after long argument Roosevelt had at last come around and asked the President to declare a holiday. This was much the same proposition that the President had been asking him to do two or three days before. Friday, yesterday, had been a terrific day, and the reserves in gold had been practically all drawn out, some $300,000,000, but when Roosevelt finally came to the point, the President thought it was too late to have him do it as a national matter and insisted that it be done by the principal states concerned such as New York and Illinois, which had refused to declare a holiday. Finally, after extended argument pressure was brought on Lehman, the Governor of New York, and he declared a holiday in New York early in the morning; and that with Illinois and other states practically produced a moratorium over the whole United States. But as Mills said, in case Lehman had not yielded and the banks had opened on Saturday, they on Sunday would have gone bust, and the fault would have been lain at the President's door. Afterwards I told the President that he had pulled out pretty safely; that the Democrats had been trying to make him signalize the last acts of his administration by an admission of bankruptcy. It looked to me as if there had been a little bit too much politics on both sides. Roosevelt was originally at fault because he refused to help at a time when it would have done some good and would have saved that last day, Friday. But when it came to the last minute and he had consented to do it, the President himself was actuated by personal interests.

10

Political Intrigue

His inglorious departure from the presidency did not mean that Herbert Hoover was about to leave politics or public life. Hoover had fought against the odds all of his life and he was not about to give up because of a political defeat. As the titular head of the Republican Party, it was Hoover's nominal responsibility to marshal the troops and rebuild the party for the 1936 elections. As his train chugged west to California, Hoover gave these matters considerable thought.

The first six months after his departure from Washington were filled with rumors. The most popular story was that Hoover and Andrew Mellon, the former Secretary of the Treasury, had been arrested in New York, caught in the act of sailing to Europe with gold bullion stolen from Fort Knox. Such stories left Hoover bitter; he was certain that Roosevelt's henchmen—Stephen Early, Charles Michelson and Louis Howe—were behind these stories.

Hoover vowed to devote as much time as possible to exposing and defeating Roosevelt and his New Deal programs. Yet Hoover was no down-and-dirty politician. He generally remained aloof and confined his attacks to rather dry speeches and books such as *Challenge to Liberty* published in November of 1934.

And the New Dealers were not above paranoia. Throughout the 1930s, various Democratic operatives speculated on the movement of various Hoover men such as Lawrence Richey, Hugh Gibson and Jay Darling. What were they up to? More important, what was Hoover up to?

The end of the decade shifted the nation's attention to the threat of a new

war in Europe. Roosevelt edged the United States closer and closer to our tra-
ditional allies, the British and the French. Hoover and many other Republicans
urged caution. There was no need for young Americans to fight and die yet
again on European soil.

H. E. NEGLEY TO STEPHEN T. EARLY
March 11, 1933

Rumors about Herbert Hoover absconding with large sums of gold notes spread
throughout the country during the week after he left office. Was there any truth
to these stories? H.E. Negley wrote to Stephen T. Early, Assistant to the President. Early responded on March 25 with a denunciation of the rumors. ''I wish
I knew who the responsible scandalmongers were,'' he wrote to Negley. ''I
would certainly tell them what I think. I have always admired Mr. Hoover and
still do.'' That last statement would have surprised Hoover. [This document is
from the Stephen T. Early Papers at the Franklin D. Roosevelt Library.]

Mar. 11th, 1933.

Mr. Stephen T. Early
Secretary to his Excellency,
The President of the United States,
White House, Washington, D. C.

Dear Sir:

In politics, as in private life, I feel a strong desire for fairness so
when a man has achieved a goal and afterwards loses, because a
better man shows up, I do not think it fair to trounce on him when
he is down.

In substance, that is what is happening to Herbert C. Hoover. The
day will come when another man will also take the place of President Roosevelt and he also should not be trounced on simply because it was impossible to please every one.

In view of the above statements, I will quote a rumor circulating
here to the effect that Mr. Hoover was caught with a passport to
England and $4,500,000.00 in gold notes in his possession. Also
that the U. S. Treasury proved to be short $200,000,000.00 that Mr.
Hoover could not explain to the new administration.

Please do not place me as some crank, but I would be very much
pleased if you would tell me if there is the slightest chance that any
part of this could be true. I believe this started as a joke, but some
people expect to see it in the papers momentarily now. Thanking
you very much for your reply, I am,

Yours very truly,
H. E. Negley

HOOVER TO JOHN C. O'LAUGHLIN
March 25, 1933

That Hoover was no fan of the first hundred days of the Roosevelt administration goes without saying. In fact, Hoover had his own name for the period—"the winter of the Roosevelt hysteria." Although Hoover did not criticize the new administration in public, he did vent his feelings in letters to friends such as John "Cal" O'Laughlin, a local Washington newspaper publisher. [This document is from the John Callan O'Laughlin Papers in the Library of Congress.]

March 25, 1933

AIRMAIL   /s/ Personal

My dear O'Laughlin:

Many thanks for your letters. They are most helpful and I trust you will keep them up. Washington news has gone onto the third page here, and there is mighty little of it.

February, March, and April, 1933, will someday be known as the winter of the Roosevelt hysteria. The panic over the possibilities of the New Deal (and those fears seem in a fair way to be justified); the unnecessary closing of the Banks for dramatic purposes; the program for opening them by killing off 5,000 Country Banks; the passage of fiscal measures which increased and did not decrease government expenditures; the authorization of white rabbits by Congress in a spirit of total abandonment of responsibility for the first time in 150 years—are but part of what we shall see. But until the hysteria begins to pass we can do little else than show that the Republican Party kept its head.

Larry will be in Washington by Monday and will be helpful to you.

Sincerely,
/s/Herbert Hoover

Mr. J. C. O'Laughlin
Army & Navy Journal
1701 Connecticut Ave., N.W.
Washington, D. C.

DIARY OF HAROLD L. ICKES
May 2, 1933

A touch of paranoia rippled through the Roosevelt cabinet on May 2, 1933. Attorney General Homer S. Cummings warned his colleagues and their families against the nefarious plots of Hoover aide Lawrence Richey. There is, however, no evidence to indicate that Hoover, Richey, or the Republican Party were spying on the Roosevelt cabinet. [This document is from *The Secret Diary of Harold L. Ickes*, edited by Jane Ickes (New York, 1953), I:30.]

May 2, 1933

. . . The Attorney General said at the Cabinet meeting today that he was informed that a strict espionage was being maintained of Cabinet members and other officials high in the Government Service. This work is under the charge of Lawrence Richey, one of the secretaries to former President Hoover, and is supposed to be in the interest of Hoover particularly, and of the Republican party in general. Richey is maintaining elaborate offices in the Shoreham Building. He warned all of us to be on our guard against people who might thrust themselves upon our notice and he said that the same precaution should be taken by our wives and members of our families. His information is that some women are being employed to worm themselves into the confidence of our wives.

ICKES DIARY
May 17, 1933

Ickes, a self-described "curmudgeon" and Secretary of the Interior, unilaterally decided to change the name of Hoover Dam to "Boulder Dam," and so it was dedicated by Franklin Roosevelt on September 30, 1935. In his diary entry for May 17, 1933, Ickes rationalized his action, but many Americans saw the change as mean-spirited and partisan. Hoover said nothing, but keenly felt the injustice. President Harry Truman and the 80th Congress restored the name Hoover Dam on April 30, 1947. [This document is from *The Secret Diary of Harold L. Ickes*, edited by Jane Ickes (New York, 1953), I:37–38.]

Wednesday, May 17, 1933

A number of insulting letters, some of them anonymous, have been coming in attacking me for changing the name of Hoover Dam to Boulder Dam. Some time ago Dr. Mead, Commissioner of Reclamation, asked me how I wanted this project designated, and I said that I wanted it called Boulder Dam. On Saturday when I went out of Washington somebody apparently gave a story to the Associated Press that I had issued an order changing the name. The story carried a quotation from me which I never gave and which was very unconvincing. This is what started the criticism. As a matter of fact, I never issued any formal order. I have always called this Boulder Dam myself, as do many people, and I have continued that usage since I came to Washington. I consider it very unfair to call it Hoover Dam. Hoover had very little to do with the dam and in fact was supposed to be opposed to it. To call it Hoover Dam is to give him credit for something for which he is not entitled to credit, and ignore those who dreamed of this proposition and brought it to a successful conclusion after years of effort. The dam never was officially named Hoover. My predecessor ordered it named Hoover Dam, but my understanding is that when a bill was introduced in Congress to name it Hoover Dam, the bill could not pass and the proposition was dropped until Wilbur, an appointee of Hoover's, named it after Hoover.

W. H. GARRETT TO LOUIS HOWE
June 7, 1933

A second letter regarding Mr. Hoover and the nation's gold supply reached the White House on June 7. This time, the writer speculated that Hoover was in league with his former secretary of the treasury, Andrew Mellon, and that both men were under house arrest. Louis Howe, one of Roosevelt's closest advisers, responded bluntly: "Of course there is no truth in the statement, and I do not know how such a story was ever started." [This document is from the Louis McHenry Howe Papers in the Franklin D. Roosevelt Library.]

June 7, 1933

Hon. Lewis McHenry Howe,
Secretary to the President,
Washington, D. C.

Dear Sir:

Since March 4th there has been a current report that immediately after March 4th President Roosevelt ordered the arrest of Ex President Hoover and that Mr. Hoover was detained in his Hotel at New York by order of the President; that the occasion was that Mr. Hoover and Mr. Mellon were detected in trying to escape to England with two hundred million in gold; that the ship on which Mr. Hoover intended to go to Panama was found to have $26,000,000 in gold; that no publicity was made on this matter by order of the President.

Now, Mr. Howe, I have tried from many sources to get the facts about this. If it happened you are bound to know it. Won't you please give me the facts and state that it is true or that it is not true?

Thank you in advance for a reply,

Yours truly,
/s/ W. H. Garrett

EDWARD E. HUNT MEMORANDUM
August 8–9, 1933

In this long, rambling memorandum of conversations held over several days, Hunt and Hoover reflect on a range of political issues, the majority focusing on the ineptitude of Franklin Roosevelt and his administration. Hunt and Hoover scheme to publish an article on the last 100 days of the Hoover administration, an article showing FDR to be the tool of his nearest adviser. Hoover also confided to Hunt that he believed that Louis Howe was the man responsible for the gold-hoarding stories. Even though five months had passed since he had left office, Hoover remained a bitter man.

August 8, 1933

. . . I remarked that I should like to be a "brain trust buster." H. H. warmly approved. He thought Roosevelt completely dominated by some of his "brain trust." Chester Rowell who had sat next [to] Roosevelt at the San Francisco Club meeting last Fall, remarked that [Roosevelt told him that] he hadn't looked at a word of his speech but "hoped it was a good one. Moley wrote it." This was the speech which aroused such enthusiasm amongst the "liberals."

He wanted me to go through the confidential record from November 8 to March 4. No one else had seen it. He won't publish it against Roosevelt now, because he wants him to have a chance. But the record damns Roosevelt completely.

Vox populi, vox Dei has often proved false in our history. . . .

August 9, 1933.

I read the record of the "last 100 days" of the Hoover Regime. Garet Garrett's article in the Saturday Evening Post called "The First Hundred Days" (of Roosevelt) had just appeared and both H. H. and I were enthusiastic. The confidential record is amazing and disheartening. It shows up FDR as the tool of the nearest advisers, ignorant and flippant and incalculable. H. H. is steady, dignified, indefatigable in the task of devising ways to help the country no matter what it might mean to him personally . . . I am to use this and any other material in the Washington archives. Miss McGrath will give it to me.

H. H. will get Garet Garrett to do the article on "The Last Hundred Days." It should begin with the speech in Madison Square Garden which is strangely accurate in its prophecies.

Some question of mine led him to the days just after the inauguration. He said Louie Howe had spread the slanderous story of his gold hoarding and that he was under arrest in his New York hotel. Moran had called up Larry Richey to say that he had been ordered from Washington to send up two operatives. Richey said they weren't wanted; that no one was needed but a uniformed policeman to stand in the corridor and keep out "nuts." H. H. wanted no protection and needed none. Moran said that he must send them up. Richey said he would throw them out if they came . . . The point was that Howe wished to make it look as if there were restraint. It was a strange exhibition of petty vindictiveness towards a great public servant. . . .

JAMES A. FARLEY TO ROOSEVELT
October 12, 1933

What was Hoover up to? That question came to Roosevelt's attention in communiques such as the following note and letter from James A. Farley. Appointed postmaster general by FDR, Farley had been the president's campaign manager. More important, Farley had political connections all over the country. [This document is from the Franklin D. Roosevelt Papers in the Franklin D. Roosevelt Library.]

October 12th, 1933

Honorable Franklin D. Roosevelt,
The White House,
Washington, D. C.

Dear Mr. President:

Attached hereto is a copy of a letter I received from Fred Davis, a very good friend of mine from Sioux City, Iowa.

Fred was very active in both the pre-convention and fall campaigns in your behalf, and I really think he knows what he is talking about.

Sincerely yours,
/s/ Jim

Attachment.

Sioux City, Iowa
September 29, 1933

Hon. James A Farley, Chairman
Democratic National Committee
Hotel Biltmore
New York City

Dear Jim:

You may have noticed in the news that ex-President Hoover was in Des Moines yesterday. But the press stories did not tell why he was there. I'll give you the low-down: He came to Iowa expressly to have a talk on politics with Jay N. Darling, cartoonist of the Des Moines Register and the New York Herald-Tribune. Darling, the son of a Congregationalist minister, was raised in Sioux City. He did his first reporting under me on the Sioux City Journal. His first political cartoons were drawn at a congressional nominating convention which I was covering. So, you can see, I know him pretty well. We are very good friends—always have been. I see him once in a while, at which times he talks to me quite freely regarding his personal affairs, his ambitions, his hopes. He is politically ambitious. Recently he has been giving considerable thought to his becoming a candidate for the Republican nomination for the United States Senate. My opinion is that he could win such nomination over anybody—even Dickinson. I might say in passing that Darling owns about half the stock of the Des Moines Register and Tribune publishing company, which is worth a lot of money.

Hoover frequently entertained Darling, both at the White House and at the Rapidan Camp, as well as having him along for a companion on deep sea fishing trips. Naturally, Darling looks upon Hoover as a man of excellent judgment; still regards him as a sort of super man.

So Hoover, through with his visit at the Century of Progress, motored from Chicago to Des Moines yesterday and visited a few hours with Darling. It no doubt was a communion of congenial souls. Under the softening influence of a harvest moon, they conversed with each other, perhaps they dreamed together. Anyhow, a few hours later, during the midnight lunch recess in the plants of the Des Moines Register and the Sioux City Journal, when the mergenthalers were silent and the copy desks had a breathing spell, there was an exchange of gossip between the two friendly editorial rooms, over long distance. The gist of the confidential talk from the Des Moines end of the line was that Hoover, in his conversation alone with Darling, dwelled at length upon the possibilities of 1936, his probable control of the Republican National Committee at that time, etc., and, in the course of outlining some of his plans, suggested to Darling that he thought Hoover and Darling would make a good Republican ticket with which to go before the country.

The Register boys said that every one in their office was sworn to secrecy, so I was more or less surprised today to see the following paragraph in Harlan Miller's independent column in the Register. I cannot figure out how that happened to be printed. It surely will be embarrassing to Darling, in view of the ban of absolute secrecy which was placed upon the conversation between the two in the privacy of the Darling home.

The Paragraph:

Quotation from Des Moines Register

"Over The Coffee"
by H. S. M.

"They say Mr. Hoover's visit to Des Moines was motivated by a desire to urge Jay (Ding) Darling to run for vice-president with him in 1936 . . . My guess is that he was also drawn by a fond desire to revisit the place where, for a brief moment last October, our hospitable Iowans gave him the illusion that there was still hope for him in November."

Faithfully yours,
/s/ Fred Davis

ROOSEVELT TO HOOVER
November, 1933

Herbert Hoover left the White House on March 4, 1933, not to return until after Roosevelt's death. This was a self-imposed exile. In fact, Hoover received his first White House invitation after leaving the presidency in early December, 1933. He and Mrs. Hoover were in California and did not attend the reception on December 7.

The President and Mrs. Roosevelt
request the pleasure of the company of

Mr. and Mrs. Hoover

at a reception to be held at
The White House
Thursday evening, December the seventh
nineteen hundred and thirty-three
at nine o'clock

HOOVER TO STIMSON
July 9, 1934

Some sixteen months after leaving office, a wistful and somewhat disillusioned Herbert Hoover shared his views on the so-called "New Deal" with his former secretary of state. "My feelings on the New Deal are benumbed most of the time," Hoover wrote. "Some time I shall break loose, but I haven't the remotest idea that it will do any good." Hoover did indeed "break loose" with the publication of *Challenge to Liberty*, his critique of the New Deal published in the early fall of 1934.

July 9, 1934

My dear Friend:

I have your inquiry as to my doings and feelings. I am engaged part time in making a living in farming and mining on such moderate scale as keeps me out of the haunts of capital and enables me to reject offers of corporations and of radio and press or platform stuff for cash. So far the living for my many dependents seems assured and I feel better than I did when I contemplated the alternatives. It would not support a Long Island establishment, but it does all right for Palo Alto, and I can enjoy the superior scenery and climate as a part compensation. The fishing, except when I can borrow a sea-going yacht, is no good.

My feelings on the New Deal are benumbed most of the time. Some time I shall break loose, but I haven't the remotest idea it will do any good. I have long since resolved that just one final blast from me will register my concluding contribution to American life. After we have gone a ways further the only alternative will be action from the economic middle class in pure Fascism, and that will probably cover your and my span. I don't know what comes after that but I assume the cycle of the old Roman Empire probably holds good when people start away from the fundamental distinction between Liberalism and all other forms of government—i.e., on one hand that men are endowed with certain rights from the Creator, and on the other that they get them from the Sheriff, or Bureaucracy, or "Presidents," or "Leaders," "Commissars," or kings, or in any event you get them only partly and spasmodically if and when. You can put it down that November 8, 1932, was the date that the American people after an experiment with this philosophy for 150 years concluded to go over to this well known theory of the Middle Ages (now revamped in new slogans) because the price of stocks and what did not suit them and because New York produced an unusual crop of scalawags.

I believe that true Liberalism will survive in England, and with this lamp still a light in the world our children may come back to it. You might philosophize upon an unwritten versus a written Bill of Rights. In the one case a people are daily alive to its guardianship; in the other they think it is part of the things old and worn out.

I am thankful for the book. It is a contribution to the thoughtful. I envy your ability to go where you please without being plagued to death with suspicions and people.

Please give my respects to Mrs. Stimson and remind her that we can provide every [form] of European scenery, tranquility, noise, and nastiness within [a] hundred miles of Palo Alto, and there is free board, lodging, and conversation besides.

Yours faithfully,
Herbert Hoover

Honorable Henry L. Stimson
32 Liberty Street
New York City

EARLY TO CHARLES MICHELSON
January 14, 1936

As the election season of 1936 approached, the White House staff became increasingly concerned about Hoover and his views. Steve Early wrote to political operative Charles Michelson asking that he find a way to discredit Hoover. "Hoover is most vulnerable on agriculture," Early wrote, "and here is a chance to bowl him over." [This document is from the Stephen T. Early Papers in the Franklin D. Roosevelt Library.]

January 14, 1936

PERSONAL
Memorandum For Mr. Charles Michelson.

Dear Charlie:

I get it from good authority that Herbert Hoover is to make a speech on January sixteenth and that it will deal with agriculture. I am told, also, he is spending considerable time in preparing this address and it will be a real effort on his part.

Of course, I know some answer will be made; that you will see to this.

I wonder if some Senator should not be looking up Hoover's perfectly terrible farm record and preparing to expose this record when Hoover has spoken. It has been suggested that some of the Democratic Senators might ask their Republican colleagues whether they believe in Hoover's agricultural philosophy. Hoover is most vulnerable on agriculture and here is a chance to bowl him over.

Stephen Early
Assistant Secretary to the
President

ELEANOR ROOSEVELT TO LOU HENRY HOOVER
May 7, 1936

Lou Henry Hoover and Eleanor Roosevelt shared a common faith in the value of scouting as a positive force in the lives of young girls. In fact, Mrs. Roosevelt was so committed to the idea that she wrote to Mrs. Hoover, then GSA president, to promote a plan to establish girl scout troops in correctional facilities. Mrs. Roosevelt also raised the question of a portrait of Mrs. Hoover for the White House. [This document is from the Eleanor Roosevelt Papers in the Franklin D. Roosevelt Library.]

May 7, 1936

My dear Mrs. Herbert Hoover:

I know that while you were here you took up with the Board of the Girl Scouts the question of the possibility of having Girl Scout Troops in the training schools for delinquent girls in the different states. I visited the one here yesterday, and had a long talk with Dr. Smith who has just come to take it over. She told me she felt that there was nothing that would change people's attitude toward these schools and these girls more than to have the Girl Scouts allow them to start Troops. I realize how unfortunate it was when the girl on parole was taken in her uniform in a raid, but it seems to me we could guard against this by saying no girl in a correctional school could wear her uniform except on the campus, and she would have to be free or paroled, and a member of an outside Troop, before she could again gain the privilege of wearing her uniform in the way any other member of the Troop would wear it.

I wonder if you could again take up this whole question in the next Board meeting. It would mean a great deal I think here in this school and in many other similar schools I have visited. After all, the Girl Scouts should be of use to the least-privileged children as well as to those who have homes and greater opportunities. I shall be most grateful if you will let me know what you think and if you would be willing to bring the matter up for discussion.

To turn to an entirely different subject, are you ever going to let us have your portrait to hang with the others here in the White House? I am most anxious to see it in place before I leave and understand that there is one but I have never been able to get hold of it.

Very cordially yours,
Eleanor Roosevelt

Mrs. Herbert Hoover
Palo Alto, California

WILLIAM C. BULLITT TO ROOSEVELT
July 23, 1937

Roosevelt's man in Paris, William C. Bullitt, wrote to the president with news of the comings and goings of Hugh Gibson, a friend and advisor to Herbert Hoover. Like all Roosevelt associates, Bullitt was suspicious. But the president was not and dismissed the matter in his response to Bullitt on August 5. [This document is from William C. Bullitt, *For the President: Personal and Secret* (Boston, 1972), p. 244.]

Paris
July 23, 1937

Personal and Confidential
Dear Mr. President:

. . . What the devil is Mr. Hoover's Ambassador to Brussels up to [Hugh Gibson, former Ambassador to Brussels and then Ambassador to Brazil]? He has now passed through Paris three times and has carefully avoided seeing me each time and his Belgian wife has been announcing to all and sundry that he is now to take up again his duties under the Hoover regime, which consisted of running the entire diplomatic service of the United States of America on the continent of Europe, representing the President at all conferences, etc.

You may or may not remember that it was your humble servant who, when everybody else wanted Gibson kicked out of the Service because he was Hoover's best friend, stood up for him and advised you to keep him in the Service. I have nothing personal against him but it seems to me bad ball when an Ambassador straight from headquarters does not cooperate to the extent of coming in even for a conversation. Gibson, of course, loves you, myself and all other Democrats in the same manner that Mr. Hoover does and I think that whoever sold you that baby as an ambassador in Europe was not especially wise.

I don't want you to do anything about this except to be damned careful not to put Brother Hoover in charge of the conduct of our relations with the European continent.

Blessing and good luck.

Yours affectionately,
Bill

LOU HENRY HOOVER TO ELEANOR ROOSEVELT
August 7, 1937

Mrs. Hoover extended to the First Lady a second invitation to attend the annual Girl Scout Convention, but for a second time in as many years Mrs. Roosevelt had an engagement that prevented her from attending. ''I was tremendously impressed by my visit to the Twenty-Fifth Anniversary celebration,'' she wrote to Mrs. Hoover on August 19 about a visit several years previous. ''I came away feeling that we were preparing a fine group of young women to take their places in the world.'' [This document is from the Eleanor Roosevelt Papers in the Franklin D. Roosevelt Library.]

August 7, 1937

My dear Mrs. Roosevelt:

The Call to the Girl Scout Convention to be held in Savannah on October thirteenth to fifteenth has no doubt reached you.

As President of the organization, I wish to extend you a more formal invitation than that implied by this Call, which of course is also an invitation to you as one of the members of the Girl Scouts.

The occasion is always an inspiring one to those who are able to attend, and they would naturally feel especially honored if you could join them for a few hours.

If you can do so, will you examine the tentative program as published in The Call, and in accepting let us know at what time you can be present? Of course we should anticipate an address from you at that time, and would wish to have it duly included on the program, which should go to the printer early in September.

With the Girl Scouts' optimistic hope that you will be able and willing to accept, I am,

Yours sincerely,
/s/Lou Henry Hoover
President of the Girl Scouts

STIMSON DIARY
November 1, 1937

The depth of Hoover's bitterness over his election loss is evident in these passages from Stimson's diary. Even though he was in relatively good humor during his brief stay at the Stimson estate, Hoover could not lay to rest his anger at Ogden Mills and at Roosevelt in the waning days of his administration. In fact, the criticism was so forceful that Stimson felt compelled to defend his own meetings with FDR. Five years had not closed the wound of election day, 1932.

[This document is from the Henry L. Stimson Papers in the Department of Archives and Manuscripts at Yale University. It is used with permission.]

November 1, 1937

I called at the Waldorf Astoria Hotel last evening for Mr. Hoover and drove him out to Highhold where he spent the night with us, I driving him back again this morning. Only Mabel and Nan were present at Highhold. He chatted in a most humorous and friendly way, entirely different from his manner in the White House. Mabel, who had looked forward to the interview with much dread, was much surprised and called him a transformed man. He told story after story in the evening, all of them with their quaint touch of humor and delightful character sketching. But even now when he turned to political matters he fell back into the same appearance of strain and pessimism. The fate of the country and party hung over him like a cloud and rendered him extremely pessimistic.

Again and again it crept out in his talk that he felt that the United States was pursuing a course under FDR now which would lead to the end and destruction of democracy; and again and again he emphasized the impossibility of checking such a course until it had brought such disaster and misery that it would change our government to autocracy in getting relief. . . .

HOOVER TO MARK SULLIVAN
September 18, 1938

In spite of his criticism of Roosevelt and his policies, Hoover had never rejected the New Deal in its entirety. In the following letter to his friend Mark Sullivan, Hoover suggests that many New Deal programs traced their origins to Republican administrations. Hoover thought that it might be "entertaining to the public" if Sullivan were to do a newspaper column on the subject. [This document is from the Mark Sullivan Papers in the Hoover Institution at Stanford University.]

The Waldorf Astoria,
New York City,
September 18, 1938.

My dear Mark:

I read your piece in the Tribune this morning with a good deal of interest.

The only reason that I drop you this note is that it seems to me a pity that it should appear to the country that support to certain New Deal measures has been suddenly discovered by the Republicans. Many of these measures are the direct outcome of previous Republican Administrations. For instance, my Administration proposed a much more drastic reform of banking [than] that finally enacted by the New Dealers. We created the Power Commission in its present form and proposed extension of its authorities, which was defeated by the Democrats. We proposed a public health bill, which was passed by the lower House and defeated by a Democratic filibuster in the Senate.

Generally, I think it might be entertaining to the public to trace out the origins of a large number of these New Deal things which we can properly support if they are well founded as to method. For instance, old age pensions had been enacted by Republican administrations in 16 states. I had the subject thoroughly investigated for federal action, but could not undertake such a measure in the midst of depression. The whole housing business goes back ten years before the New Deal. Its foundations were laid by Republicans, culminating in the Housing Conference in Washington and the Home Loan Banks. Much the same could be said as to the development of relief for agriculture. Whether it is wicked or not, it was my administration that established the scheme of loaning money to farmers on their crops to cushion fall of prices. Etc, etc.

With kind regards,
Yours faithfully,
Herbert Hoover

ELEANOR ROOSEVELT TO LAWRENCE RICHEY
February 9, 1939

Relations between Eleanor Roosevelt and the Hoovers were altered by Mrs. Roosevelt's newspaper column of February 3, syndicated to hundreds of papers across the country. ''My Day'' was Eleanor Roosevelt's effort to keep the public informed of her work as First Lady. As she noted on February 3, she rarely used her column to talk about partisan politics, but a headline noting Mr. Hoover's concern about war, set her off on a tangent. She was particularly critical of a Hoover speech delivered on September 28, the eve of the Munich conference between English Prime Minister Neville Chamberlain and German Chancellor Adolf Hitler. When Hoover assistant Lawrence Richey wrote to complain and asked her to retract her criticism, she responded as follows.

February 9, 1939

My dear Mr. Ritchey [sic]:

I am in receipt of your letter of February seventh.

In reply, may I invite your attention to the sequence of events, to the implications and to the general significance of the timing of these events. To me, they are most interesting and very enlightening.

First, the President addressed his peace message on September twenty-sixth.

Second, Mr. Hoover delivered his address in Kansas City on September twenty-eighth—the eve of the Munich Conference.

Third, the Munich Conference met and adjourned on September twenty-ninth and the world breathed a sigh of relief.

It is true that Mr. Hoover, in the beginning of his Kansas City address, expressed approval of "the efforts of our Government to maintain peace." Mr. Hoover was kind enough to say, in the same paragraph, that "the President has rightly urged negotiation as the way out."

The address of the former President in Kansas City was delivered within the twenty-four hours preceding the meeting of Mr. Chamberlain with Herr Hitler in Munich. At that time, ours was an anxious world. The threat of war was imminent.

Mr. Hoover, following the reading of the one paragraph to which I have referred, comprising all of sixty-one words, continued to the extent of some five and a half printed columns and speaking as our only living ex-President, proceeded to criticize the President and the policies of our Government. He said "hate is preached from the White House for the first time." Obviously, although not by name, Mr. Hoover charged the President with preaching hate, with stirring up ill-will; with setting worker against employer, employer against worker, worker against worker.

Let me remind you again that this was the former President of the United States attacking the President of the United States and doing so at a time when the peace of the world hung in the balance—when our country should have been revealed to the other Nations of the world as one great and united democracy rather than as the scene of conflict between the President of the United States and his predecessor in office.

I cannot help but wonder what encouragement Mr. Hoover's remarks that evening in Kansas City gave to the forces responsible at that time for conditions which threatened the peace of the world.

Neither can I help but wonder how the man charged with preaching hate could, at the same time, be praised by the man who spoke in Kansas City for his advocacy of peace. To me, the whole thing seems so paradoxical, so inconsistent. In the circumstances, I see no obligation to make the correction you request.

Very sincerely,
Eleanor Roosevelt

Mr. Lawrence Richey,
The Waldorf-Astoria,
New York City, N.Y.

HOOVER TO O'LAUGHLIN
April 14, 1939

Hoover expressed the hope that the United States could stay out of war to his good friend "Cal" O'Laughlin. Hoover was critical of Roosevelt for not making it clear that the United States would remain neutral in any European conflict. Roosevelt, however, would take no such stand. [This document is from the John Callan O'Laughlin Papers in the Manuscript Division of the Library of Congress.]

April 14, 1939

Mr. J. C. O'Laughlin
1701 Connecticut Avenue, N. W.
Washington, D. C.

My dear Cal:

As usual, that was a most hopeful letter. And probably the only thing that will keep us out of war is the British. They have sanity. They do not want to go to war. And they are today the only outstanding skillful group of world diplomats.

If Roosevelt had maintained at least the tone of voice of Chamberlain in this situation, he might have been in a position, at the proper moment, to have been of great service to the world in bringing these people around a council table. It appears that the situation is rapidly drawing to a stalemate that will break in that direction, or some incident that will provoke war. There is however, no public official in the world today, who could act as a catalyst in this situation.

I was glad to see Republicans breaking out in the Senate. The idea that Republicans ought not to protest over such wickedness as this because they belong to the opposition party is a trial to my soul.

There is one thing certain, and that is, that if Roosevelt had taken a resolute attitude from the beginning that we were not going to be involved in Europe, there would have been a million more men employed today.

Yours faithfully,
Herbert Hoover

HOOVER TO O'LAUGHLIN
July 18, 1939

In mid-summer, little more than six weeks before the Germans would roll through Poland and start World War II, Hoover provided O'Laughlin with his thinking on neutrality, appeasement, and Roosevelt's actions toward the European powers. By offering sympathy to the British and the French and insulting the Germans and the Italians, Roosevelt had pushed the entire world closer to war. And Hoover was deeply concerned about the consequences of another world war. [This document is from the John Callan O'Laughlin Papers in the Manuscript Division of the Library of Congress.]

July 18, 1939
/s/Personal

Mr. John C. O'Laughlin
1701 Connecticut Avenue, N.W.
Washington, D. C.

My dear Cal:

Many thanks indeed for your letter of the 15th.

The neutrality action which Hull outlined has plenty of sense about it. The difficulty rests in the total lack of confidence in what the President's intentions are. These powers in the hands of a President who is determined not to get the American people into war is one thing, but in the hands of a President who has shown every indication that he wants to join in the mess is another.

My recollection is that the President's original plan was that he should have the authority to determine who was the aggressor and then to put the neutrality bill in action, on this basis. I cannot make out from the press despatches whether this phase of the matter has been dropped or not.

There is one thing that is looming up between the lines, and that is, that the western democracies, if they thought they had the full support of the United States, would attack at once in order to avoid the strain of waiting two or three years until these totalitarian states are alleviated of some internal pressures. Moreover, in order to put the indelible stamp of ownership of their territorial possessions for the next generation, they may determine to go to war and wipe out all opposition. In other words, if Roosevelt gives such support to the western democracies, they may precipitate a world war instead of some sort of accommodation to get the world through until it obtains more or less stability.

It seems to me vital that these western democracies should be possessed of the fact that the American people are not going to war and that they should not predicate their policies on that basis.

I do not believe for one moment that these democracies are in any danger of attack from Germany or Italy. They can, of course, always find plenty of question on which they can raise the question of defense. I am convinced it is Roosevelt's action which has stirred public opinion in France and England into the abandonment of the appeasement policy and into aggressive lines. How much further this will go, no one can tell; but it has measurably advanced the possibilities of war in the world, and the end of that war to save democracy will be that there will be no democracy left.

Yours faithfully,
/s/Herbert Hoover

11

Loyal Opposition

Throughout the last thirty years of his life, Herbert Hoover remained unalterably opposed to Franklin Roosevelt and everything that he stood for. Efforts on Roosevelt's part to bridge the chasm between himself and Hoover were met with silence from Hoover. The Hoovers were invited to at least two social occasions at the White House and both invitations were refused. Efforts by Eleanor Roosevelt to acquire a portrait of Mrs. Hoover to hang in the White House were thwarted by Mrs. Hoover. Neither Hoover would have anything to do with the President and First Lady.

Perhaps the most telling evidence of Hoover's opposition to Roosevelt was the former president's refusal of the president's request for assistance with food relief in Europe in the years before the United States entered the war. It is the only time in his life that Herbert Hoover ever refused a direct request for assistance from a president of the United States. Hoover had helped Wilson, Harding and Coolidge before his presidency. And later in life, he would help Truman, Eisenhower, Kennedy and Johnson. But not Roosevelt; not ever. The anger was too deep.

Roosevelt had approached Hoover about taking on the role of food relief administrator. There was no one else in the world with as much experience with famine relief, and those in need were the small countries of Europe whose people so revered Hoover. But Hoover refused two official emissaries from the White House in September of 1939. Hoover would later refer to his food relief work during the war as "four years of frustration." Frustrating they may have been, but they were not linked in any way to Roosevelt.

ELEANOR ROOSEVELT TO MARIE MELONEY
September 10, 1939

Marie Meloney, editor of *This Week* magazine, ardently admired both Herbert Hoover and Franklin Roosevelt. With the outbreak of war across Europe, "Missy" Meloney quietly campaigned to have Herbert Hoover take over the government's relief enterprises. Meloney wrote the First Lady promoting Hoover for this job and received an open-minded response. Apparently, the idea appealed to the president, because he sent Myron Taylor to speak with Hoover about the matter. For her part, Mrs. Roosevelt was ready to convene a conference of "leading women" to assist Mr. Hoover. [This document is from the Eleanor Roosevelt Papers in the Franklin D. Roosevelt Library.]

> Hyde Park, N. Y.
> Sept. 10, 1939.
>
> Dear Mrs. Meloney:
>
> I have talked to the President and I think Mr. Myron Taylor who happens to be lunching with Mr. Hoover today, will sound him out as to his willingness to undertake a major relief job. The President has told Mr. Taylor that if Mr. Hoover is willing to undertake it, he will be glad to talk it over with him.
>
> He has suggested that Mr. Hoover would of course be free to develop his own ideas.
>
> After this meeting and by the time I get back in Washington next Saturday, [and] the President tells me the results, he will then be willing to consider what you have suggested, namely, the calling of a conference of leading women from all over the country and the young people at the White House to assist Mr. Hoover.
>
> If he is unwilling to talk to the President, I think it will be done in any case with the idea of developing later a wider plan.
>
> I would like to have from you a list of people whom you feel should be called to this conference. I am asking Mrs. Reid to dine with us on Monday in Washington and I shall talk to her about it also.
>
> I will not go beyond calling this initial conference. At this conference those present after the presentation of the general idea, will be asked to nominate and vote for a chairman and officers who will undertake to carry out the organization. The conference will not be called until early October.
>
> Affectionately,
> [Eleanor Roosevelt]

HOOVER MEMORANDUM
September 11, 1939

In spite of Taylor's appeals, Hoover was reluctant to be drawn into the Roosevelt administration. Indeed, Hoover even turned aside a personal request from FDR to meet with him on food relief issues. "I felt that to come down to the White House would only create speculation and unnecessary discussion in the country," Hoover recorded in the memorandum that follows. Hoover saw himself as the leader of the Republican Party and a potential candidate for the 1940 presidential nomination. He would not compromise his role as leader of the loyal opposition by meeting with the president.

New York City,
September 11, 1939

Mr. Myron Taylor called upon me at eleven o'clock this morning and stated that he had been in conversation with President Roosevelt, and the President had expressed a desire for me to come down to see him on Wednesday afternoon, the 13th; that he wished to consult me on the organization of relief measures for European countries.

I told Mr. Taylor that I could give him my advice right away, which I hoped he would transmit to the President. That was that the American Red Cross had a staff fully trained in relief work and of large dimensions, that it had engaged in the relief of Japan and China and of American disasters over the last twenty years, that it had committees and organizations in every city, town, and village in the country, that it would be able to start on a moment's notice at recruiting food and supplies, that if some capable administrator were set up as the head of their European division they could get under way at any time on an hour's notice, and that I certainly thought it was desirable from the President's point of view that all relief measures should be concentrated under this one heading.

Mr. Taylor stated that the President felt that the Red Cross should stay within its much narrower field as an adjunct to military activities. I reminded him that the Red Cross had long since been organized far beyond this narrow field and had the complete confidence and esteem of the country; that any new relief mechanism would have to parallel it over the entire country; that it would take a long time and be very difficult to secure an equal mechanism. I told him that I would be glad if he would transmit this to the

President and said that I felt that to come down to the White House would only create speculation and unnecessary discussion in the country.

Furthermore, I told him that I would be delighted to advise the President further on this subject if he would address any questions to me on this or any other subject. I told him he could tell the President that I had some responsibility in the Republican Party, and that on a policy of keeping the United States out of war I felt sure that he would have the support of the party; that there would be natural differences of opinion on methods but that I hoped that Republican opposition, if there were such, would be entirely constructive opposition.

RICKARD DIARY
September 14, 1939

Roosevelt refused to take no for an answer. The president sent Norman Davis, president of the American Red Cross, to meet with Hoover. In this following entry from the diary of Edgar Rickard, Davis reiterates Roosevelt's offer to have Hoover take over European relief issues. Davis also refers to a real or perceived slight involving Hoover and the Secret Service.

Thursday, September 14

. . . Dine at Waldorf—H. H., Arch Shaw, Norman Davis and most interesting evening. Davis came direct from F.D.R. with request that H. H. take over entire Relief problem, also said F.D.R. could not understand why H. H. not friendly with F.D.R. and had never heard of withdrawal of Secret Service men at Inaugural. H. H. accepted place on Red Cross. Committee, but no contact with F.D.R.

EDWIN M. WATSON TO ROOSEVELT
September 15, 1939

Davis left his dinner with Hoover with a sense of optimism, or so it seems from the note below. However, in spite of what the note says, Hoover never agreed to meet with Davis on Monday, September 18. Davis did brief the president on his dinner meeting with Hoover having set up the appointment through Roosevelt's military aide, Edwin M. Watson. [This document is from the Franklin D. Roosevelt Papers in the Franklin D. Roosevelt Library.]

The White House
Washington
September 15, 1939.

MEMORANDUM FOR THE PRESIDENT:

Norman Davis says that Hoover is coming Monday. He thinks it most important that he report what Hoover said yesterday to him (Norman Davis) before Hoover gets here.

E. M. W.

ELEANOR ROOSEVELT TO MARIE MELONEY
September 17, 1939

The First Lady quickly concluded that Hoover's reluctance to join with the Roosevelt administration had more to do with politics than anything else. She confided her feelings in the following letter to Missy Meloney. Meloney's undated response questioned whether Davis had accurately conveyed the former president's thinking. "I cannot believe that he would refuse to help in a work which he is best fitted to do," Meloney wrote. [This document is from the Eleanor Roosevelt Papers at the Franklin D. Roosevelt Library.]

Sept. 17, 1939.

My dear Missy:

I have been over all this very carefully and have it well in mind, but I think it is not the kind of organization we could hope to have unless the government would really request us to do it and it was evident to most of our citizens that there was a real war menace. Otherwise we could never organize so systematically, so I am therefore returning it to you. I think we could do this very successfully when the need arose but at the moment I can not use it.

Mr. Hoover as I fear, succeeded in making Mr. Norman Davis feel that he is only interested in relief as a secondary matter because he told him that while he would be willing to consult with the Red Cross, he did not think he could set anything up because next year he might be directing a political campaign.

I am still trying to induce them to do something on a fairly comprehensive scale and I think after the Red Cross meeting tomorrow and by the time I get back on the 26th, the gentlemen may have straightened out their thinking on this subject. I think men are slower than women under certain circumstances.

It was very nice to see Helen Reid last night. She was as she always is, a dear and I hope she got something out of her visit. Take care of yourself. With much love,

Affectionately,
[Eleanor Roosevelt]

HOOVER MEMORANDUM
September 18, 1939

Hoover summarized and reiterated his views on European relief in the memorandum that follows. As he had to Myron Taylor and Norman Davis, Hoover underscored his belief that the American Red Cross was the most appropriate organization to handle international relief. The former president agreed to join in the Red Cross effort, and "would be delighted to take part in their councils or assist in any way possible."

September 18, 1939

A gentleman [Myron Taylor] called upon me a week ago Monday and said that President Roosevelt wished me to consider the organization of the country to support distressed civilians in Europe. I replied that I felt that my greater service would be to devote my whole energies to keeping the United States out of this war. But beyond that I had already been surveying the relief problem, that my recommendation in any event was that the American Red Cross should at once undertake the leadership in all such movements. I stated that the Red Cross had long since been converted from a purely military adjunct into a great civilian relief institution; that it had an able Chairman and a fully trained staff with large experience; that it had committees of the best citizens in every town and village of the country; that it could start on 24 hours [sic] notice to recruiting money and supplies; that it had working arrangements with the European Red Cross societies by which on a day's notice they could set up an effective distribution agency at any part of Poland or other point in Europe. I stated that to duplicate this organization would involve duplication waste and bring less results. I stated that if the President agreed with this advice and would put the Red Cross officials in communication with me I would give them every possible cooperation and plans of organization.

On Wednesday, Mr. Norman Davis, Chairman of the Red Cross, called me up and we arranged a meeting in New York. On Thursday we spent four hours in discussion of means and methods. Mr. Davis wished a memorandum of my plan that he might present to his Executive Committee, which I at once made and which he approved. I informed Mr. Davis I would be delighted to take part in their councils or assist in any way possible.

RICKARD DIARY
September 19, 1939

Hoover was suspicious of Roosevelt's motives in asking him to head relief efforts. In fact, he came to believe that Davis was a well-intentioned dupe of Roosevelt's efforts to "sidetrack" the former president into relief work. Hoover wanted to be free to criticize the White House if it did anything to compromise U.S. neutrality.

Tuesday, September 19, 1939

Dine with H. H. He concerned over Norman Davis change of front re Red Cross, and evident that while Norman may be trying to give square deal that White House trying to sidetrack H. H. into relief work. Mrs. Roosevelt has injected herself into this business and has talked with Marie Meloney, trying to get Marie to persuade H. H. he must take over European Relief problem. Senator LaFollette calls H. H. on phone and asks him to support the retention of present embargo legislation. H. H. will not enter controversy at this time.

HOOVER TO O'LAUGHLIN
September 24, 1939

By mid-September, Hoover was convinced that Roosevelt was playing a game of power politics in Europe. It would, Hoover thought, inevitably lead the United States down a path to war. He confided his thoughts to Cal O'Laughlin in the letter below. [This document is from the John Callan O'Laughlin Papers in the Manuscript Division of the Library of Congress.]

> The Waldorf Astoria,
> New York City,
> September 24, 1939.

My dear Cal:

Many thanks for yours of the 23rd, which as usual is illuminating.

It becomes clearer day by day that the crux of this situation is the profound public distrust of the President. For two years he has been moving step by step into power politics. My own early interpretations in a public address and now the general acceptance of the public is that these steps if continued will lead us into war or at least great embarrassment. The very contention he makes as to the reaction from the failure of Congress to repeal the embargo early in the summer is certain proof as to how far at least he thinks he had already gotten the weight of America into power politics in Europe. I am convinced if any other one of our 31 presidents had made the address which he made Thursday to the Congress on the Neutrality Bill it would be passed immediately.

It would, of course, seem useless to present a new course for action at the present stage of the debate. I hope you will keep me advised as you think the situation arises where I could inject it with any hope that would be of public service.

Yours faithfully,
/s/Herbert Hoover

Mr. John Callan O'Laughlin
Army Navy Journal
1701 Connecticut Avenue,
Washington, D. C.

ELEANOR ROOSEVELT TO MARIE MELONEY
October 8, 1939

In her letter of October 8, the First Lady all but admitted that there was little chance that Hoover would head up the food relief effort. In fact, Mrs. Roosevelt had serious doubts that the Red Cross could handle the job. Most interesting is her speculation that Hoover's response might have been different had the request come directly from the president. In her response to Mrs. Roosevelt, Meloney again reiterated her belief that Mr. Hoover was committed to help through the Red Cross. [This document is from the Eleanor Roosevelt Papers in the Franklin D. Roosevelt Library.]

October 8, 1939.

Dear Missy:

Thank you very much for the list. It hasn't come as yet, but I will let nobody know who has sent it and I will keep it under lock and key for use if the time comes when we may organize. I am deeply grateful to you and I can assure you that I will only use it for this purpose.

After talking again to Mr. Norman Davis, I gather that Mr. Hoover feels that the Red Cross should do this relief job and that he will help the Red Cross, but he does not think it should be a separate agency.

This is rather a difficult thing because the executive committee of the Red Cross feels that they are an emergency agency and should not be called upon to do a long rehabilitation job. They also feel that this type of job will eventually require government money as it did when Mr. Hoover did it before, and that the Red Cross should not break its rule of taking voluntary contributions which do not come from the government.

I also heard from someone else that Mr. Hoover felt a little hurt that Franklin had not talked to him himself. I think he has a right to feel that way because I think Franklin should have talked to him, but many of the men around Franklin felt it was wiser to sound Mr. Hoover out first.

I have no idea what has happened since I have been away, but I will ask the President in a day or two. It seems to be impossible to get anything done until the neutrality question is settled. All I can get is that no one can reach Poland and that none of the other nations would take help. I feel sure that China would, but can get very little at present from them.

I will let you know what I can find out from the FHA as soon as possible.

I do hope you continue to be careful of yourself. I enjoyed the novel you sent me very much.

Affectionately,
[Eleanor Roosevelt]

HERBERT HOOVER TO SAM PRYOR
October 27, 1939

In the following letter to Sam Pryor, Hoover articulated his opposition to Roosevelt's pro-war policies. With forthright candor, Hoover called on Roosevelt to explain the motives behind his recent actions. ''Surely there is ample cause for Americans being filled with anxiety as to our future,'' concluded Hoover. Pryor was the Eastern Manager of the Republican National Committee and a Hoover confidante. A notation on this document indicates it was sent to Pryor on October 27, but no copy of the letter is retained in the Hoover papers.

[Draft]

The President last night expressed great indignation that anyone should challenge the idea that we might send our sons to war in Europe. He had very rough statements to make about all of those who have raised their voices in protest.

In view of this indignation the President should at once explain certain matters to the American people which have caused the greatest of uneasiness and distrust in the minds of every thinking person.

He should explain to the nation at once what he meant when he proclaimed that America will join with other nations to quarantine dictatorships. He should inform the American people how he proposed to proceed in doing this.

He should explain what he means by national policies of involving us in Europe with more than words and less than war.

He should explain what he meant by his statement to the Senate Military Affairs Committee that the American frontiers were in France.

He should explain why he proposed a few years ago to abolish poison gas and bombing planes and why he protested so vigorously at their barbarous use in China and Spain and Ethiopia and Poland and at the same time he proposes now that America shall sell these things. He should explain why he now attacks those who protest that we should not be engaged in these barbarities.

He should explain why if America is in no danger of sending its sons to this war or, as he says, becoming involved in this war, did he declare a national emergency.

He should explain why he searched for guns on the ''Bremen'' before the war broke out and now allows armed merchant ships to come into our harbors freely.

He should explain why daily from the White House there has been a constant emanation of statements and news that would create a war psychosis in the United States, and then berates all of those who protest at our being drawn into the war.

It is these things that make us fearful that we may be involved in this war. To them is added the constant deluge of propaganda from the other side that would induce us to get into this war. Surely there is here ample cause for Americans being filled with anxiety as to our future.

DIARY OF STEPHEN T. EARLY
December 14, 1939

Hoover had established the Finnish Relief Fund on December 6 to raise money to aid the embattled Finns. Hoover's visibility on the issue caused the press to ask why Hoover was not leading the government's effort to provide European relief. In an effort to clear the air, Steve Early briefed the press on December 14. He noted that the president had sent Myron Taylor and then Norman Davis to invite Hoover to head up European relief. ''Nothing came of the effort,'' Early recorded in his diary, ''it appears that Mr. Hoover did not accept the offer.'' [This document is from the Stephen T. Early Papers at the Franklin D. Roosevelt Library.]

DECEMBER 14, 1939
THURSDAY

. . . Three subjects were discussed at my press conference today: Belair's story on Joe Davies; Mr. Hoover's refusal to take over the directorial work of relief in Europe; and Wallace's taking over of the Farm Credit Administration.

In the Times this morning there was a story that told the world that the Ambassador's resignation was on the President's desk. I had denied that story the night before but apparently the Times thought they knew something that neither the State Department nor the White House knew. I told Belair that the Times was looking so far into the future that it had an advantage over the White House.

In order to straighten the boys out on the second story I told them that at about the time—and slightly before—Germany moved into Poland the President and his advisors here were doing their best to prepare for the emergency they felt would come—by "emergency," I mean war in Europe and its effect upon the U. S. The President was trying to get the neutrality laws revised; tightening up and strengthening the national defenses. Not only were they working on ways and means of protecting the neutrality and studying the language of the proclamations that the President issued later but they were also thinking of the question of relief in Europe in the event of war. As a preparatory step or measure he asked Mr. Norman Davis, Chairman of the American Red Cross, to see Mr. Hoover and ascertain from Mr. Hoover whether he would accept a post, the title of which might have been sort of "General Manager of Relief." Apparently Mr. Davis saw Mr. Hoover and since nothing came of the effort, it appears that Mr. Hoover did not accept the offer. . . .

ICKES DIARY
December 24, 1939

When the Soviet Union attacked Finland on November 30, Hoover swung into action. Within a week he had marshaled his friends to raise money for food and other supplies. The humanitarian effort received widespread praise from the American press as well as the Finnish people. The failure of the American Red Cross to subsume this Finnish relief effort angered Harold Ickes, who confided his complaint to his diary. [This document is from *The Secret Diary of Harold L. Ickes*, edited by Jane Ickes (New York, 1953), III:95–96.]

December 24, 1939

. . . Herbert Hoover has been making quite a play of marshaling relief for Finland, and, of course, the newspapers have all fallen for it. The President remarked at Cabinet that Norman Davis had let Hoover get away with this. Norman Davis is president of the Red

Cross and the Red Cross has been supplying all of the civilian needs in Finland since the invasion of that country by Russia. Chatfield Taylor was in Poland when the war broke out in Finland and he flew at once to the latter country and has been there ever since as the representative of the Red Cross. Nevertheless, Hoover is getting all the headlines on Finnish relief. Naturally the Administration does not like this but it has not been able to counteract it so far. The President said that what Norman Davis needed was a good publicity man and that he was trying to find one for him. . . .

HOOVER TO WILLIAM R. CASTLE
August 21, 1940

During the summer of 1940, Hoover and his associates lobbied the British government to allow humanitarian shipments to reach the starving people of Norway, Holland, Belgium, and Poland. In a speech before the House of Commons on August 20, Prime Minister Winston Churchill vigorously opposed the plan. Hoover saw the diabolical workings of the "New Dealers" behind this opposition. He confided his frustration to his good friend Bill Castle. Castle responded with a supportive letter on September 4.

August 21, 1940

Mr. William R. Castle
2200 S Street
Washington, D. C.

My dear Bill:

I am greatly obliged for your letter of the 19th.

Hugh [Gibson] cables that it is impossible to do anything in London unless we have the prior approval of the Administration, and I gather from in between the lines that Churchill's attitude was either approved or coached on by Washington. Our New York office suggests that we should get ourselves in line with the Administration by asking you to discuss the matter.

I am entirely against this. The New Dealers would rather see the people of Central Europe starve than to see the opposition have anything to do with any kind of constructive or humanitarian action. In any event, pressures to a death point will not become violently dangerous until after the election. If we win this election we will make short and swift work of these attitudes in Washington.

Just to give you my ideas on this subject, I am sending you herewith a copy of a letter I wrote to Gram Swing, who has been loyally supporting the matter.

I have not thought it wise to say anything about Churchill's state-

ment. I am sorry the whole subject came up for public discussion
at the time it did—right in the middle of the "Battle of England"
when everybody's nerves are tense. It arose from a UP statement
from London which needed to be clarified, and in addition I had a
cable from Hugh asking for a statement of clarification of our proposal.

My own thought is that we will need to take the matter up a little
later on.

I think you might consider whether there is not an essence for a
public speech or statement by yourself in my letter to Swing.

I agree with you about Buell and all of the advisers on foreign
affairs. Anne O'Hare is the only hope of sanity.

I hope to be in the east sometime early in September and will
then have an opportunity for full discussion with you.

Yours faithfully,
Herbert Hoover

HOOVER ADDRESS
October 24, 1940

Hoover was among many Republicans—and not a few Democrats—who questioned Franklin Roosevelt's decision to seek a third term as president. Hoover
couched his criticism as a concern about the rise of personal power, and how
that power was being used to push the nation toward war. Just as important,
Hoover noted, Roosevelt's personal power was stifling the economic progress
of the nation. He delivered these remarks in a radio address from Columbus,
Ohio. [This address is printed in *Herbert Hoover Addresses Upon the American
Road, 1940–1941* (New York, 1941), pp. 224, 238.]

. . . I do not suggest that Mr. Roosevelt aspires to be a dictator.
It is however understatement to say that he has builded [*sic*] personal
power to a dangerous point in this Republic. Moreover, there are
forces and men around him who are implacably pushing further and
further in that direction. The exact reason that this tradition has been
a living force over all these years is to meet just such a situation as
this. The reasons why that rampart of freedom should be maintained
are far higher than partisanship. They reach to the foundations of
free men and women.

. . . It is not only a tradition against a third term about which we
are concerned. We are concerned with a vital check upon the rise
of personal power in the Republic. There has been a gigantic and
insidious building up of personal power of the President during these

two terms. The President himself admits these powers provide shackles upon liberty which may be dangerous. Many of these extraordinary powers have been obtained under claims of emergencies which proved not to exist or to have expired. Despite many promises, there has been no return of these dangerous powers or the unused powers, or those which proved futile or for which emergencies have passed.

. . . Under assumptions of personal power we are steadily drifting toward war. And one result of the use of these powers has been to stifle the restoration of productive employment, and a prosperous agriculture, and to involve the peace of the American people. . . .

HOOVER MEMORANDUM
November 16, 1940

On November 16, Hoover had lunch with Wendell Willkie, the recently defeated Republican presidential candidate. Willkie noted that Roosevelt was trying to get him to "come down to Washington" and discuss world affairs first with Henry Stimson and Frank Knox and later Roosevelt himself. Hoover advised Willkie to stay away from Roosevelt, because the president and his men could not be trusted. "He seemed to agree with this," Hoover noted.

. . . He [Willke] said that Roosevelt was trying to get him to come down to Washington; that Stimson and Knox had sent word to him that he should come down and discuss matters with them and Hull, and intimated that Roosevelt probably could be brought into the conversations a little later. I told him that I never would discuss things with No. 2 men in any event, and that I would not discuss things with Roosevelt unless such discussions could have two or three honest men present with him who knew the subject well in order that he should have protection for himself against a mass of smearing liars, and that the subject should be discussed by men who had a larger background in foreign affairs than he could expect to command. He seemed to agree with this.

We discussed the election shortly. I pointed out that the mysterious thing about the election was the fact that obviously the regular Republicans went into the ballot boxes and voted local Republican tickets, and therefore they must have been Republicans, and yet at the same time did not vote for him. He asserted that it was because they wanted to go to war and they believed Roosevelt was a liar in his public assertions and would take them to war, and that therefore they preferred Roosevelt as being the more likely avenue to get in the war than himself. I did not dispute this with him as my only object was to call his attention to the fact that he had run far behind the regular Republican ticket. . . .

ICKES DIARY
December 1, 1940

On November 18, Herbert Hoover launched "The National Committee on Food For the Small Democracies" to provide food and other supplies to Finland, Norway, Holland, Belgium and Poland. The Committee hoped to save millions from "the inevitable famine and pestilence which confront them." Roosevelt took note of Hoover's efforts at a cabinet meeting on December 1. Ickes recorded the president's irritation with Hoover and his new committee. [This document is from *The Secret Diary of Harold L. Ickes*, edited by Jane Ickes (New York, 1953), III:385–86.]

. . . The President expressed concern over Herbert Hoover's persistence in working up public sentiment here to feed the people in the occupied countries of Europe. Before he came into the Cabinet room, the President had a conference with Davis, of the Red Cross, and Thomas Lamont, of Morgan and Company. Lamont had promised that he would do whatever he could to keep Hoover in control. This would make a very unpleasant issue in this country and would complicate the foreign situation badly. Of course, in the final analysis, England will not permit supplies to be sent into the countries that have been occupied by Germany. But if England persists in this blockade, it will have the effect of creating anti-English sentiment in this country and we ought to avoid that if we can. Hoover pretends to believe that supplies sent over from this country to the occupied countries can be restricted to those who need them. However, few agree with him.

Of course the Germans would take what they wanted, or at least their equivalent, which would have the same effect. Harsh and cruel as is the policy of withholding food from starving people, to do otherwise would be to strengthen Germany in its assault upon civilization. It is incomprehensible to me that a man who has been President of the United States should be deliberately throwing himself into an enterprise which has the disapproval of the Government of the United States. There must be something to the report that Hoover has always hated England. This act on his part, while humanitarian on the surface, would, in effect, be an underhanded blow struck at England and therefore at the United States.

ROOSEVELT TO HOOVER
December 17, 1940

A second invitation to socialize at the White House came to the Hoovers in the middle of December. Given his distrust of Roosevelt, Hoover could not bring himself to attend even so perfunctory a reception at the White House.

> The President and Mrs. Roosevelt
> request the pleasure of the company of
> Mr. and Mrs. Hoover
> at a reception to be held at
> The White House
> Tuesday evening, December the seventeenth
> nineteen hundred and forty
> at nine o'clock

HOOVER TO CASTLE
March 1, 1941

Hoover saw Roosevelt's lend-lease program as another step closer to war. "Whether it is the beginning of our military participation in the war or not," he wrote to Castle, "it substantially projects the American people further out into the emotional rapids which lead to the cataract of war." He concluded that all the Republicans could do was "to hold the President to his promise not to spill blood."

> The Waldorf–Astoria
> New York City
> March 1, 1941

My dear Bill,

I have been thinking over our telephone conversation on the Lend-Lease Bill.

The American people have been so fooled as to the purpose and character of this bill that there remains no hope of adequately amending it. It is a war bill, yet 95 per cent of the people think it is only aid to Britain.

The bill (a) surrenders to the President the power to make war, any subsequent action by Congress will be rubber stamp work; (b) empowers the President to drive the country still further toward a national socialist state; (c) empowers the President to become real dictator of opposition policies to the Axis. He can determine who, in what way and how much aid any nation may receive from the United States.

Obviously the bill as it stands is not in the greatest interest of Britain. The fullest help to the British to defend themselves would be an authority to give to them all of our accumulated defense material which we could spare; to give them an appropriation of anywhere from two to three billions with which to buy other things; to allow them to spend the money directly themselves and to conduct their own war in the way that seems to them to be the wisest. The whole of these sums should be secured upon such collateral or such properties as they possess irrespective of whether it is enough to cover these sums.

How the President uses these powers remains to be seen. Whether it is the beginning of our military participation in the war or not it substantially projects the American people further out into the emotional rapids which lead to the cataract of war.

There is a point in these emotional rapids where even Boatman Roosevelt will have gone so far out into the stream that he cannot control the boat, even though he will be so inclined. That current is strong enough from our natural sympathies and our hates of the whole Hitler thesis. Already the real interest of America and the long-view interest of the world are being drowned by foreign propaganda, the suppression of truth, the beating down of every warning voice, with no restraints from the Administration. The very existence of these powers will actuate war psychosis. For instance, soon after the bill passes we shall hear the cry, ''Why provide all this material and have it sunk in the Atlantic? We should convoy it with our navy!'' Then we will have American boys torpedoed and war is on. Next we will have an agitation to send an expeditionary force to Africa.

All that we can hope to do is to use our energies and influence to keep down emotions and to hold the President to his promises not to spill American blood. So long as we do not enter armed conflict we are not in a technical state of war. So long as we are not in a technical state of war we still have a chance. It is a thin chance to save this nation from 20 years of war and total destruction of liberty on the earth.

Yours faithfully,
Herbert Hoover

Mr. William R. Castle
2200 S Street, N.W.
Washington, D. C.

SUMNER WELLES TO ROOSEVELT
June 24, 1941

The State Department kept itself informed on any and all Hoover statements, especially those related to war and peace in Europe. In the cover memo and the memorandum that follows, Under Secretary of State Sumner Welles briefed the president on what he had learned from Lord Halifax about Hoover's recent activities. [This document is from the Franklin D. Roosevelt Papers in the Franklin D. Roosevelt Library.]

June 24, 1941

My dear Mr. President:

I am enclosing herewith a copy of a portion of a memorandum of conversation which I had with Lord Halifax on Sunday. It is possible that you may feel it desirable to have some steps taken in order to deal with the reports which Mr. Hoover is circulating. Believe me

Faithfully yours,
Sumner Welles

Enc.
Memo. of conversation
with Lord Halifax,
June 22, 1941.

The President,
The White House.

DEPARTMENT OF STATE

Memorandum of Conversation
Date: June 22, 1941

Subject: Statements of Mr. Herbert Hoover regarding alleged German peace proposals

Participants: British Ambassador, Lord Halifax; Under Secretary, Mr. Welles

Lord Halifax called to see me this morning at his request.

The Ambassador brought up the subject of information which had reached him to the effect that Mr. Herbert Hoover was busily engaged in spreading the report in many circles in the United States that Hess had brought to Great Britain specific and concrete German peace proposals. The reports emanating from Mr. Hoover further allege that when the leaders of the Conservative Party in England learned of this fact, they called upon Mr. Churchill and demanded that he give these proposals full consideration, with the threat that, in as much as the Conservative Party constituted the chief support of Mr. Churchill in the House of Commons, such support would be withdrawn unless Mr. Churchill agreed to discuss these peace proposals; furthermore, that it was for this reason that Mr. Churchill had urged Ambassador Winant to return to Washington by air immediately in order to lay these facts before the President and obtain the President's acquiescence to consideration by the British Government of these peace proposals. Mr. Hoover further was claiming that Hess was the seventh peace emissary sent to England since the outbreak of the war and that the other emissaries had been sent from Germany to Dublin in a German plane and returned in a British plane. Mr. Hoover was maintaining that he was absolutely positive that these facts were correct as he set them forth since he obtained his information from Hugh Gibson who is now in London and who got them from reliable inside sources.

Lord Halifax said he merely wished me to know of the information he had obtained in this regard in order that the Administration might be able to deal with these reports in any way it saw fit. He said that it was unnecessary for him to say that the reports were entirely untrue and that, of course, this Government was aware of the general nature of the statements that Hess had made upon his arrival in Scotland.

ROOSEVELT TO WELLES
June 25, 1941

Roosevelt was clearly concerned about Hoover and the reports he was spreading about German peace initiatives. But what could be done without giving publicity to the issue? Clearly Roosevelt was perplexed, and neither he nor Welles had any ideas on what should be done to isolate Hoover.

June 25, 1941.

MEMORANDUM FOR THE UNDER SECRETARY OF STATE

I agree with you that steps are necessary to deal with these reports circulated by former President Herbert Hoover—but what steps? This does not merit a Government statement but I do think it merits a communication to Mr. Hoover.

F.D.R.

HOOVER TO CASTLE
September 4, 1941

Hoover was eerily prescient in his prediction that the United States would enter the war "through the Japanese back door." Three months and three days after this letter was written, the Japanese attacked Pearl Harbor and the United States entered the war.

September 4, 1941

My dear Bill:

I am just wondering how you are getting along.

I am convinced from traveling around over the West that the country is getting more and more opposed, even bitter, against this war movement. I think this accounts for the rabidness of Roosevelt's talking. In the meantime, they certainly are doing everything they can to get us into war through the Japanese back door.

Sincerely yours,
Herbert Hoover

Mr. William R. Castle
2200 S Street, N. W.
Washington, D. C.

HOOVER TO ROOSEVELT
September 8, 1941

His distrust of the president and his unwillingness to set foot in the White House, did not mean that Hoover was unsympathetic to Roosevelt in time of tragedy. He sent the following telegram to the Roosevelts upon the death of the president's mother. The telegram was acknowledged with a printed card from the White House.

September 8, 1941

President Franklin D. Roosevelt
Hyde Park, New York

Mrs. Hoover and I wish to extend to you and Mrs. Roosevelt our deepest sympathy in the loss of your mother, and to join you in your personal grief in a time of heavy burdens.

Herbert Hoover

12

War Years

The attack of the Japanese navy on Pearl Harbor and the United States' declaration of war on Germany and Japan altered the rivalry between Hoover and Roosevelt. An ardent patriot, Hoover supported the president in his efforts to control the economy and marshal supplies to win the war. He had done the same for Wilson and he would not change his position because of his personal distrust of Roosevelt.

Hoover devoted himself to the eventual end of the war. In their 1942 book, *The Problems of Lasting Peace*, Hoover and co-author Hugh Gibson developed many of the principles that would be incorporated into the charter of the United Nations. The positive response to the book also led a number of Americans to suggest that Roosevelt ask Hoover once again to become famine relief administrator.

Roosevelt would have none of that. In fact, he set James Rowe and Robert Patterson on a mission to discredit Hoover. Using confidential documents from the papers of Edward House at Yale University, Patterson claimed that Hoover had advocated shipping food supplies rather than troops during the first war. The report was leaked to Vice President Henry Wallace and Senator Theodore Green, who lambasted Hoover. The documents, however, were misdated and the claims were false.

Hoover was livid at this latest "dirty trick" from Roosevelt's henchmen. Through Perrin Galpin, Hoover pestered both Yale and the War Department for the names of those involved. It would finally take a letter of apology from

Hoover's old friend Henry Stimson, now Roosevelt's Secretary of War, to mollify the former president.

In the midst of all this nastiness, the Hoovers and the Roosevelts exchanged notes at the sudden and sorrowful passing of Sara Delano Roosevelt, Lou Henry Hoover, and Franklin Roosevelt himself. Both families were to suffer through great grief during the war years.

With Roosevelt's death on April 12, 1945, Hoover began to look to the future. Within a matter of six weeks he would be back in the White House and working with the new president, Harry Truman. Hoover had finally escaped from under the shadow of Franklin D. Roosevelt.

HOOVER ADDRESS
May 20, 1942

In an address before the 26th Annual Assembly of the National Industrial Conference Board, Hoover commented on the limitations of freedom in time of war. Indeed, Hoover said the all but unthinkable—that the president must have dictatorial economic powers and must have the support of the American people in regulating the economy. A Democrat could not have said it better. Much to Hoover's dismay, the press emphasized his recommendation to give FDR more power.

> . . . We may first contemplate the limitations on economic freedom, for here are the maximum restrictions. To win total war President Roosevelt must have many dictatorial economic powers. There must be no hesitation in giving them to him and upholding him in them. Moreover, we must expect a steady decrease in economic freedom as the war goes on. . . .
>
> The President has unbelievable burdens in war; he deserves every support in this task. We cannot expect him to watch and direct the host of war agencies and officials that we must have to make war. The Congress and the people have to watch them. . . .

ROOSEVELT TO WELLES
July 20, 1942

Not widely known as a man who carried grudges, the president did, nonetheless, have a long memory. When Henry Stimson recommended the appointment of James Grafton Rogers to handle bacteriological warfare, Roosevelt said no. The president remembered Rogers as the Assistant Secretary of State in the Hoover Administration who blocked his efforts to participate in negotiations for the St. Lawrence Seaway in October 1931.

July 20, 1942

Memorandum for Sumner Welles:

Please let me have your confidential slant on James Grafton Rogers. My impression is to say no. I have a dim recollection that he did not do anything except to block the initiation of state and federal control over the St. Lawrence River when I was Governor.

What do you think?

F. D. R.

[Enclosed]: Confidential letter from the Secretary of War, 7/16/42, to the President, recommending appt. of James Grafton Rogers to handle the project of bacteriological warfare, about which the Secretary of War and Paul McNutt talked with the President.

HOOVER TO WILLIAM ALLEN WHITE
October 16, 1942

In the following letter to his old friend, Hoover predicts that Roosevelt's influence is on the wane and that the Republican Party "will necessarily ride the reaction which is inevitable from the war." The challenge, as Hoover correctly observed, was in establishing sound policies prior to governing. Hoover hoped that his new book, *The Problems of Lasting Peace*, would serve as the blueprint for those policies.

The Waldorf–Astoria
New York, New York
October 16, 1942

Mr. William Allen White
Emporia Gazette
Emporia, Kansas

Dear W. A.:

Many thanks for your letter.

The Republicans are likely to carry the House at this moment. I am appalled at the problems that may be present with our supply of statesmanship.

Certain the President is slipping. The fact that high qualities as a politician or admirable equipment to get into war do not serve in the hard realities of fighting. Intellectual dishonesty is powerful in the field of emotion, but it does not count for such among tanks, airplanes and battles. The Administration is socially minded, but it is not economically minded. In war when that is translated to the home front, it means failure in administration because social measures in war are merely political fluff. The real thing is the hard economic fact. The Administration is unwilling to accept any of the economic experience won in blood and tears during the last total war on the ground that "this war is different." The whole thing, at times seems hopeless. Total war is won or lost on the home front. The last war was won by the collapse of the home front in Germany.

As to peace. The Republican Party as the opposition party will necessarily ride the reaction which is inevitable from the war. The problem is to establish certain accepted bases of party policy before the end. If W.W., instead of nebular phrase, would demand that our book should be accepted as the Republican policies, it would contribute to that end. I could get the other leaders to agree; they simply refuse to give W.W. the issue of opposing a proposal from them.

Incidentally, for your own information, a friend has put up the money to send 25,000 copies of the book free to high school and village libraries.

I hope Mrs. White will be coming with you to the white lights. (They are on until 7:00 p.m. only.)

Yours faithfully,
[Herbert Hoover]

CLAUDE R. WICKARD TO ROOSEVELT
November 7, 1942

Following the November elections, the rumor of Hoover's impending appointment as Food Administrator once again became the talk of Washington. In an effort to head off any discussion within the White House, the Secretary of Agriculture sent the following letter to the president. As Hoover predicted in conversations with Edgar Rickard, Arch Shaw, and others, nothing came of the rumors. [This document is from the Franklin D. Roosevelt Papers in the Franklin D. Roosevelt Library.]

November 7, 1942

The President
The White House

Dear Mr. President:

At a recent Cabinet meeting there was a discussion of the advisability of creating a separate Food Administrator and also mention was made of Mr. Hoover's name in connection with that post in the

last war. In that regard I thought you might be interested in knowing
Mr. Hoover's views on this subject. The following is a statement
Mr. Hoover made on December 15, 1941, when testifying at hear-
ings on the Emergency Price Control Act:

"I might say this as to the division in the last war between the
Food Administration and the Department of Agriculture: Prior to the
last war the Department of Agriculture had been practically an institution of scientific research; it had never engaged in economic
activities of any great consequence. It had some theoretical, economic services. The Department at that time did not want to undertake the multitude of economic activities connected with food
control; therefore, food was set up separately and at the express wish
of the Secretary of Agriculture. Since that time our Department of
Agriculture has developed enormous economic engines engaged in
the distribution of food, in the control of the price of food, in putting
price floors under agriculture, and so forth. It is in a considerable
degree a food administration in itself right now."

Sincerely yours,
/s/Claude R. Wickard
Secretary

ROOSEVELT TO HERBERT LEHMAN
January 2, 1943

It is not clear why Roosevelt asked James Rowe to prepare a background paper
on Hoover. Lehman was working in the State Department on international relief
matters and would later that year become director of the United Nations Relief
and Rehabilitation Administration. It is possible that the president was looking
for information to discredit Hoover and his private relief efforts. Lehman acknowledged receiving the report on January 25, returning the original copy to
the president. Not included below, there was nothing controversial in Rowe's
report; it was nothing more than a straight-forward chronicle of Hoover's public
service. [This document is from the Franklin D. Roosevelt Papers in the Franklin
D. Roosevelt Library.]

January 2, 1943

PERSONAL & PRIVATE
MEMORANDUM FOR HON. HERBERT H. LEHMAN

I asked Jim Rowe to prepare the enclosed. It gives the historical
and legal background of Herbert Hoover's activities during and after
the first World War.

I am sending you the original together with Jim Rowe's memorandum. Please send it back but you may keep the copy attached.

F. D. R.

Enclosures

ROBERT PATTERSON TO ROOSEVELT
February 20, 1943

Roosevelt also asked the War Department to look into Hoover's wartime service. In the following memorandum, Patterson transmits a document that purportedly shows that Hoover advocated food production over military transport. The document was misdated, however. Hoover had sent his memo to Edward M. House in February, 1917, several weeks before the U.S. declared war. The brouhaha that resulted from the use of the Hoover memo would last for four months.

February 20th, 1943.

Memorandum for the President:

There is attached a copy of a typewritten memorandum from Hoover to House under date of October 27, 1917. In it Hoover urged that shipping be devoted to shipment of food and munitions to Europe and that no soldiers (except air forces and engineers) be sent to France.

Hoover said that the safety of the world lay in our production of food and munitions, that this production would be injured by putting millions of men under arms, and that the men could do no good in France.

We know that if his advice had been followed, the Germans would have won the war in the summer of 1918. It was the arrival of large forces of Americans that gave the Allies the material and moral assistance necessary to victory.

The doctrines of Hoover today on the paramount importance of raising food and reducing the Army are parallel to those propounded by him in this 1917 memorandum.

/s/ Robert P. Patterson
Under Secretary of War

REPORT OF THEODORE GREEN
February 28, 1943

The War Department sent a copy of the Hoover memorandum to Senator Theodore Green, Democrat of Rhode Island. A vigorous Roosevelt partisan, Green used the memo to attack Hoover in the following report on his investigation of manpower. Green went so far as to state that if Wilson had followed Hoover's advice, the United States would have lost the First World War.

SOME AUTHORITIES WOULD DEFER
CONCLUSIVE VICTORY RATHER THAN
FULLY MOBILIZE

There are those who would so jeopardize the winning of the war by substituting their military judgment for that of the Combined Chiefs of Staff; who are willing to risk a protracted war or stalemate rather than take the steps necessary to mobilize ourselves for early and conclusive defeat of the enemy; who believe that we are not economically strong enough to wage total war on the same scale and at the same rate as our enemies. Foremost among these is the Honorable Herbert Hoover. Whatever Mr. Hoover's standing as a military expert may be, his record as an economist is known to all of us. He twice has attempted to predict the military future of the United States upon the basis of his analysis of the country's economic ability to produce all the things necessary for total war while raising, training and shipping an Army overseas to defeat the German army. Once was on October 27, 1917, in a memorandum of which I have a copy. He did it again on February 8, 1943, when he released to the press a summary of his testimony at an executive session of this subcommittee. A comparison of these two documents conclusively demonstrates that Mr. Hoover has learned very little about modern warfare in the intervening period of over 25 years. If the country had heeded his advice in 1917, it would have lost the first World War beyond peradventure of a doubt. . . .

IF WE HAD HEEDED MR. HOOVER'S 1917
ADVICE THE ALLIES WOULD HAVE LOST
WORLD WAR 1—HIS 1943 ADVICE IS THE
SAME

There is nothing new under the sun. He didn't think we could do it then. He doesn't think we can do it now. The leaders of the Imperial German Army—von Hindenburg and von Ludendorff stated that it was the presence of two million fresh American soldiers in France with others arriving at a rate of over a quarter of a million a month which was directly responsible for the defeat of the German armies in November, 1918. All military historians have agreed that it was only the interjection of an American Army between the spearhead of the German attack and Paris in June of 1918 which turned almost certain German victory at that time into an overwhelming defeat in five months. The Allies would have been defeated in 1918 if the United States had followed Mr. Hoover's advice: all the evidence indicates that they will suffer defeat or stalemate if they heed it now. . . .

The United Nations are engaged in combined military operations based upon strategic plans which require attacking the German Army in 1943 and 1944 with large enough ground forces to crush that Army and bring about the unconditional surrender of Germany.

The enemy now has overwhelming ground superiority. The United Nations, other than the United States, are already so fully mobilized for total war that they are unable to augment their own ground forces by sufficient numbers of units to allow them to undertake this task alone. Therefore, the United States must transport the maximum number of ground forces overseas in 1943 and 1944 which available shipping will allow. While this ground force is being built up, the plans require that the foundation of German military power be weakened by an overwhelming air force. Meanwhile, an active war of attrition must be maintained against Japan, the Western Hemisphere must be protected from attack, and a base of military operations must be built up in the United States to train, transport, supply and maintain armies all over the world.

This requires that an Army of 8,208,000 be built in 1943 and maintained in 1944. Any cut in this number means a reduction in the number of ground forces and a disruption of the plan. No one except Mr. Hoover has seriously questioned the validity of these military plans as the most effective way of bringing the war to an early and victorious conclusion. To do so is to impugn the judgment of the military leaders to whom we have entrusted the military safety of the country. His validity as a military prognosticator in 1943 is disposed of by his 1917 predictions. . . .

HOOVER PRESS STATEMENT
March 1, 1943

Hoover was furious when he learned of Senator Green's attack and a similar one by Vice President Henry Wallace. In the following wire service story Hoover rebuts these attacks and goes on the offensive himself.

Chicago, March 1, (UP)—Former President Herbert Hoover today accused Vice President Henry A. Wallace and Senator Theodore Green (D., R.I.) of misrepresenting his stand on sending armies to Europe in World War 1.

"Mr. Wallace made the statement and Senator Green echoes it in the morning papers," Hoover said in a formal statement, "that in October, 1917, I urged upon Colonel House (President Wilson's advisor) that we should not send armies to Europe. They say 'his advice, if followed, would have allowed Germany to win the war.'

"I have now had my files of that period examined, and I have the following report:

"1—That Mr. Wallace or Senator Green or somebody else has been guilty of a curious action in changing dates. That discussion of the outlook was not October, 1917 but nine months earlier, in the previous February—two months before we even declared war.

"2—That discussion does not bear the interpretation put upon it. It had to do with questions of priorities—use of the navy, finance and supplies. It was based upon the February, 1917, shipping outlook and the state of the submarine war.

"3—Both the British and French governments and President Wilson held until sometime after we actually declared war that we could not or should not send troops. Only in May, 1917 did our army and President Wilson conclude that we could transport more than a 'token' army. Later on the American system of convoys was so successful as to change the whole shipping outlook, and everyone's views changed as to sending larger contingents.

"I was a member of the American War Council and supported these policies. The press shows that in June and July of 1917, I am quoted as saying we can and must supply soldiers to the front to maintain the strength of Allied armies.

"But aside from the joy of pulling a red herring across the real issue of our food problem, what does all this have to do with our most dangerous food situation today?

"The food situation cannot be blacked out by speeches. Acknowledged facts are:

"1—We have been cut off by submarine and the Japanese from our normal large imports of food. Out of our larder thus depleted, we must supply Britain, Russia and the extra food required by our armed forces if we are to win the war.

"2—I believe we can ration down our consumption to support this drain if we could maintain the 1942 farm production.

"3—But we are faced with a serious decrease of farm products in 1943 due to taking manpower to the armed forces and munitions, to the lack of farm machinery and fertilizers and to decrease in protein feeds. In some farm products the ceiling prices do not cover the farmer's costs. He is apparently expected to work a 72 hour week for less than nothing. The prospects of short planting, short harvesting, short animal products in 1943 as shown by the reports of the country agricultural agents are most alarming. Already there are partial local famines in meat and dairy products in many parts of the country.

"Unless remedies are promptly applied, it is useless to talk of relief to the inevitable European famine after the war and even of a healthy supply to the American people."

ROOSEVELT TO WATSON
March 9, 1943

Roosevelt was also interested in the Hoover memorandum taken from the Edward House papers. He was informed by his aide "Pa" Watson that Theodore Green had used it in his report on manpower. [This document is from the President's Secretary's Files in the Franklin D. Roosevelt Library.]

March 9, 1943.

Memorandum for General Watson

Will you find out from Patterson if he is going to use the memorandum from Hoover to House of October 27, 1917?

F. D. R.

[Editorial Note: Two notes were scrawled across this memorandum: (1.) U[nder] Sec[retary] Pat[terson] said "He will Use it" (2.) Sen Green used it & Hoover said it was Feb. 1917–Before War declared. Green checked & reiterated Oct. 27, 1917]

PERRIN GALPIN MEMORANDUM
May 19, 1943

How did Senator Green obtain the copy of Hoover's memorandum to House? Through his associate Perrin Galpin, the former president demanded an answer and an apology from Charles Seymour, the president of Yale, and from the War Department. He received a letter of regret from Seymour on March 11, but the War Department was less candid. In the following memorandum, Harvey Bundy attempts to explain how the memorandum had fallen into Green's hands.

Memorandum Of Telephone Conversation
With Harvey H. Bundy, Assistant To The
Secretary Of War, 11:25 AM
Wednesday, May 19, 1943

Harvey Bundy telephoned me from Washington this morning. Charles Seymour was in his office at the time. He said that the War Department people, in the first place, did not understand the implications under which it was obtained from Yale. The document itself was not ticketed as confidential. Senator Green sent over to the War Department and told them that he wished to make a speech on the size of the Army and they provided a number of documents for him, including your memorandum. Bundy said the War Department did not write Green's speech for him. It was a clear misunderstanding and they are sorry.

As to the circulation by the Public Relations officer in the Sixth Service Command, the War Department says this was wrong and it has been stopped. They apologize and say it was a stupid thing to do. One officer, Bundy says, made a mistake and they can't find any evidence that it was circulated in any other place.

Bundy also said that he hopes that the Chief will not take his stand on the idea that a document written by him when he was a public official is private and confidential even during his lifetime. He feels that there are a number of Senators up on the Hill who would take issue with this point on the ground that the Senate has a right to use such documentation as it needs from former public officials in connection with its consideration of current business. It is his opinion, although he did not speak as a lawyer, that the Chief would not come out on top in a discussion with some of the blatherskite Senators.

Bundy reiterated that it was a clear misunderstanding in the War Department not to have indicated the confidential nature of the document. On the other hand, he says there is no doubt they could have obtained it by subpoena if it had been necessary. The man to whom Charles Seymour talked on the telephone about the document does not remember whether Seymour stressed the confidential nature of the House Collection.

I asked Bundy whether I would hear from him further and he said that he would prefer that this whole matter rest here on the basis of this telephone conversation. He said he hoped also that the Chief would not attempt to carry it further because he felt that if it became a public debate upon the Hill, the Chief's position would not necessarily be maintained and there might be continued unpleasantness.

He stated again that he was sorry that the War Department had anything to do with the circulation of the Green report and he stated that he did not know whether the officer who made the mistake had some political motive.

Harvey Bundy said he had been out of the city much of the time since my letter came and he was sorry he had not been able to answer it before.

Harvey also said that the War Department had its warning and would exercise more care in the future and for that reason among others he hoped that the matter would end here without further public action.

P. C. G.

HOOVER MEMORANDUM
May 20, 1943

Hoover's anger was manifest in the following brief that he drafted on May 20. "There are lots of things about this whole transaction that require further explanation," Hoover began. He then went on to ask nine penetrating questions. He would not let the matter drop.

5/20/43

There are a lot of things about this whole transaction that require further explanation. Bearing in mind that President Seymour admits sending the memorandum to Assistant Secretary Lovett of the War Department in February, 1943; bearing in mind that Seymour claims that Lovett asked for this specific document by telephone; bearing in mind that Seymour says he sent it confidentially.

Bearing in mind that the "memorandum" in question related to events of July, 1917 (25 years ago) and had no relation to this war.

Bearing in mind that only by distortion and misrepresentation could any faulty judgment be found; bearing in mind Lutz' report that Pershing, Bliss, Harbord and March were all of the same view, and that President Seymour supports Lutz' report.

Bearing in mind that there were only two copies of this memorandum in the world, in Hoover's files and the House papers at Yale; bearing in mind also that there are scores of memoranda between Hoover and House relating to methods and progress of the last war.

Bearing in mind that Hoover appeared before the Senate Committee on February 8, 1943, and made a decent, moderate recommendation that drafting of farm boys be postponed until after the harvest.

Bearing in mind that Wallace used this "memorandum" to smear Hoover on February 23rd; that the War Department admits sending it to Senator Green, who used it to smear Hoover on February 28th.

That Hoover denounced this action on the 29th of February with vigor.

That the War Department sent the smear out from Commanding officers on April 9th after this denial of Hoover's.

With these things in view, one can raise the following questions:

1. Who was it concocted the idea of distorting that memorandum for smear purposes?

2. How could the War Department know about and ask for this specific document of 25 years ago? Who informed the War Department of it?

3. If the War Department wanted information on the last war, the Secretary, the Under Secretary, the Assistant Secretary, all of them old colleagues of Hoover's, knew they could get it from him. They know every document that Hoover has is open to proper use to win this war. Why did the War Department not call Hoover? Why should they want this one particular document out of scores of others that are more important except for smear purposes?

4. It was obviously sent to the War Department and communicated after Hoover's appearance on the Senate on Feb. 8 and before to Wallace before he spoke on February 23rd. Hoover was in New York all this time. Why was he not consulted by the Yale authorities before they sent it?

5. President Seymour says Bob Lovett telephoned for the specific document. Lovett knows Hoover. Why was he not told to ask Hoover for it? In fact, is [it] not the truth that someone from Yale called the War Department and told them how useful it would be for smear purposes?

President Seymour says he stated to Galpin on February 28th, after Green used it, his dismay at violation of "confidence." Why had he not called Hoover before he sent it?

6. The War Department acknowledges that the document was sent to Green from them, when Green was making his "report." But Wallace had used this document for smear purposes five days before Green did. How did Wallace get it? Why was the War Department obviously industriously circulating and distorting the document?

7. The War Department says it was not "marked confidential" as Seymour purports. (That is no excuse for the distortion.) But what covering communication did Seymour send with it? Where is it? If not, did Seymour just put it in an unmarked envelope and send it? If so, why avoid confirming an enclosure to the Department?

8. If the War Department did not distort the document into a smear, why did they send it to Wallace, Green? Why did they send this smear distortion to the Commanding Officer of the Sixth Service Command for further publication? Do Commanding Officers circulate smears on a former President of the United States by Army orders or on their own volition? Is not the honor of the War Department involved here?

9. The probity of several people is involved also unless there is a lot of further explanation.

Is Hoover to rest under this on a telephone conversation from the War Department that says they are sorry and that he may be further smeared if he doesn't look out?

STIMSON TO HOOVER
June 14, 1943

The Secretary of War stepped into the controversy on June 3 with a letter disavowing any personal knowledge of the incident. Hoover responded on June 7 with a detailed account of what had happened and asking for the War Department to publicly repudiate what it had done. In the following letter, Stimson declined to make a public statement, but did agree to take a more direct role in reviewing how the Department handled such matters in the future. Hoover let the matter drop in his reply of June 18.

June 14, 1943.

Personal

My dear Mr. Hoover:

I have received your letter of June 7th and very much appreciate your words about the Army and about our personal relations.

I have carefully tried to look at this question of Senator Green's statement and the War Department's part in it from all possible angles and I have come to the conclusion that a further public statement by me would be unwise and unhelpful.

The officer of the War Department who asked for your memorandum of 1917 did not know that it had a confidential character. President Seymour unquestionably believes that he pointed this out but the officer who asked for it is equally sure that he did not. A public dispute on such an issue would be unfruitful, particularly as the officer who made the request had nothing further to do with the formulation of Senator Green's report.

The passage of Senator Green's report which you quote in your letter was never put out as a War Department statement although much of the material included in the report was made available to Senator Green by the War Department and his report was prepared with the assistance of an officer in the Department, the material and this assistance having been requested by Senator Green. In furnishing such assistance to the legislative work of a senator, the War Department followed a custom which has become routine.

The subsequent distribution of Senator Green's report in the area of the Sixth Service Command by a local Army officer of that Command was an error which was stopped as soon as my office in Washington learned of it.

I have now given definite directions that in the future any matters which might involve the War Department in a controversy or misunderstanding with you must be brought to my personal attention.

Very sincerely yours,
/s/Henry L. Stimson

Hon. Herbert Hoover,
420 Lexington Avenue,
New York, New York.

ROOSEVELT TO JAMES F. BYRNES
June 16, 1943

In spite of his and other efforts to discredit Hoover, Roosevelt continued to receive suggestions that the former president be made head of a new "food administration." In the memo below, he passes the buck to James F. Byrnes, the director of the Office of Economic Stabilization. A Roosevelt confidante for many years, "Jimmy" Byrnes was often referred to as "the assistant president for the home front." Byrnes had no answer for the president and the letter from Columbia University president Nicholas Murray Butler was never answered. [This document is from the Franklin D. Roosevelt Papers in the Franklin D. Roosevelt Library.]

June 16, 1943

Memorandum For Director Byrnes

How shall I answer this?

F. D. R.

Enclosure

Letter from Dr. Nicholas Murray Butler, President, Columbia University in the City of New York, [ ]/10/43, to the President, marked "Personal." States that it would be a step of greatest importance both administratively and for the satisfaction of public opinion if the whole matter of food administration could be centralized under Herbert Hoover himself, and all other agencies discontinued or abolished.

No draft of reply in file, 12/14/43

RICKARD DIARY
June 22, 1943

Further evidence that Roosevelt was being urged to establish a food administration came to Hoover over lunch with Bernard Baruch. Hoover repeated the gossip to Edgar Rickard who recorded it in his diary.

Tuesday, June 22

. . . H. H. shows me memo re lunch with Baruch, who has not been called in although he was largely announced by Administration. Baruch very discouraged and says Hopkins has large influence, and F. D. R. adamant against setting up Food Administration with necessary powers. Says H. H. has been proposed by Stevenson, Knox and Byrnes, but President only gets mad. . . .

ROOSEVELT TO HOOVER
January 7, 1944

The sudden death of Lou Henry Hoover elicited a heartfelt response from across the nation. Many Americans deeply appreciated this uncommon woman. Among the messages received at the Waldorf was the following telegram from the President and Mrs. Roosevelt.

January 7, 1944.

Honorable Herbert Hoover
Waldorf Towers
Waldorf Astoria,
New York, N.Y.

The radio has brought me word of the sorrow which has come to you with such overwhelming force. To you and all who mourn with you the passing of a devoted wife and Mother, I offer this assurance of heartfelt sympathy in which Mrs. Roosevelt joins me.

Franklin D. Roosevelt

ROY HOWARD TO STEVE EARLY
January 8, 1944

At the request of publisher Roy Howard, the White House arranged cross-country air transportation for Allan Hoover and Herbert Hoover, Jr., to allow them to attend their mother's funeral. Commercial air travel was severely limited during the war and without Steve Early's assistance, it is unlikely that the "Hoover boys," as Howard calls them, could have reserved flights from California to New York on such short notice. As Howard notes in the following letter, President Hoover was "deeply appreciative." There is no record of Hoover writing directly to Early. [This document is from the Stephen T. Early Papers in the Franklin D. Roosevelt Library.]

January 8, 1944.

Stephen Early, Esq.,
The White House,
Washington, D.C.

Dear Steve:

I want to thank you most sincerely for your very prompt cooperation last night in the matter of priorities for the Hoover boys.

Mr. Hoover was considerably moved and deeply appreciative when he learned of the quick action and the kindly and sympathetic spirit you so promptly manifest.

The fact that I was not in the slightest surprised at your reaction does not in the least minimize my appreciation of the typical co-operation which you have so often and so generously extended me.

My best to you.

Sincerely,

/s/Roy

[Editorial note: A handwritten note across the bottom of the page reads: "The girls in Mr. Early's office do not know how Mr. Early arranged this. Probably by phone."]

HOOVER TO ELEANOR ROOSEVELT
January 25, 1944

Hoover was deeply moved by the telegram, but responded in a somewhat surprising manner. He wrote first to Mrs. Roosevelt in his own hand, expressing great appreciation for "the fine sympathy and understanding which you send." There was no acknowledgment of the president, however. Mrs. Roosevelt considered it an "unusual" letter and penned across the bottom "file to keep." Three days later, Hoover sent a one-sentence, typed note to the president acknowledging the telegram.

Jan 25, 1944

/s/My dear Mrs. Roosevelt—

It was most courteous of you to write to me upon Mrs. Hoover's passing. I greatly appreciate the fine sympathy and understanding which you send and I am grateful for it.

Yours faithfully

Herbert Hoover

[Editorial Note: The following appears across the bottom of the page in cursive and block writing: "File to keep—UNUSUAL X Herbert Hoover."]

HOOVER PRESS STATEMENT
April 12, 1945

More than a year passed before Mr. Hoover wrote again on Franklin Roosevelt. This time it was to express sorrow at the death of his long-time rival. "While we will mourn Mr. Roosevelt's death,'' Hoover noted, ''we shall march forward.'' With these words, Hoover would begin to put Franklin Roosevelt behind him.

April 12, 1945

The Nation sorrows at the passing of its President. Whatever differences there may have been, they end in the regrets of death. It is fortunate that in this crisis of war our Armies and Navies are under such magnificent leadership that we shall not hesitate. The new President will have the backing of the country. While we mourn Mr. Roosevelt's death, we shall march forward.

HERBERT HOOVER

HOOVER TO ELEANOR ROOSEVELT
April 14, 1945

Hoover also handwrote a personal note of condolence to Eleanor Roosevelt on April 14. Most significant is the fact that Hoover refers to the passing of his beloved wife, Lou, in sharing Mrs. Roosevelt's loss. Mrs. Roosevelt responded with a thank-you note on April 18 expressing her gratitude.

April 14, 1945

/s/My dear Mrs. Roosevelt:

I need not tell you of the millions whose hearts are going out to you in sympathy. I want you to know that I join with them.

Your own courage needs little support but the whole country is extending it to you.

With Mrs. Hoover's passing I know the great vacancy that has come into your life and I cannot forget your fine courtesy in writing to me at that time.

Sincerely yours,
HERBERT HOOVER

Mrs. Franklin D. Roosevelt
The White House
Washington, D.C.

RICKARD DIARY
April 14, 1945

That Hoover was planning a return to public life was evident only two days after Roosevelt's death. In this passage from Rickard's diary, Hoover muses on taking up a position in a newly formed Truman cabinet. Although he would never hold cabinet rank in the Truman administration, Hoover would become a valued counselor to Truman on matters of famine relief and government reorganization. [See Timothy Walch and Dwight M. Miller, eds., *Herbert Hoover and Harry S. Truman: A Documentary History* (Worland, Wyoming, 1992).]

Saturday, April 14

. . . To dinner alone with H. H. Tell him I entirely approve of his statement to Press re F.D.R.; it was one of the very few that did not spill over. He thinks that Truman will prove a change for the better. He thinks that if he has intention to appoint new Cabinet he should do so without delay. If he does it person by person remaining members will gang up on him. H. H. would like to be Sec'y of War, and says in that job, with command of shipping, he could give relief to Europe in short order. Play Gin until late.

Conclusion

My Personal Relationship with Mr. Roosevelt

More than 13 years after FDR's death, Hoover wrote a brief, formal memoir of his friendship and rivalry with his successor. Most interesting is Hoover's deliberate use of the phrase "good friends" to describe their early relationship. Hoover also acknowledges that he and FDR disagreed on a great many issues from the health of the U.S. economy to Roosevelt's decision to enter World War II. Within the memoir, Hoover republishes a number of documents used elsewhere in this book. The memoir serves as a perfect coda on the long, tempestuous relationship between the two presidents.

September 26, 1958

MY PERSONAL RELATIONS WITH MR. ROOSEVELT

This memoir is concerned solely with President Roosevelt's foreign relations and foreign policies and their backgrounds. It is not concerned with his domestic policies. Nor is it an appraisal of his abilities or his character. But my personal relations with Mr. Roosevelt over the years are part of the backgrounds.

During the period of the American participation in the First World War, Mr. Roosevelt and I both served under President Wilson,—he as Assistant Secretary of the Navy and I as United States Food Administrator. At that time, he had no participation in foreign affairs. We had little official business together as my part in naval matters were with the Secretary of the Navy and naval officers directing food matters in the Navy. I was a member of the President's "War Council" of which the Secretary of the Navy was a member. We met socially during this period and were good friends.

After the Armistice I served on President Wilson's staff in Europe and we had little contacts during that period as Roosevelt's service was largely in the United States.

In September 1919 I returned from Europe and engaged myself largely in supporting President Wilson's effort to secure the ratification of the Treaty of Versailles, the emphasis being on membership in the League of Nations. I served as Vice Chairman of the President's second Industrial Conference from November 1919 until March 1920. I had a number of pleasant meetings with Mr. Roosevelt, who continued as Assistant Secretary of the Navy until 1921. To my surprise Hugh Gibson, our Minister to Poland, sent me the following letter which Mr. Roosevelt had written to him. [Ed.: See FDR to Gibson, January 20, 1920 above.]

In August 1921 Mr. Roosevelt suffered a severe paralysis from polio which left him with practically paralyzed lower limbs, and all his life thereafter he was compelled to use a wheel chair and steel braces when standing erect.

I greatly admired the courage with which he fought his way back to active life and with which he overcame the handicap which had come to him. I considered that it was a great mistake that his friends insisted upon trying to hide his infirmity, as manifestly it had not affected his physical or mental abilities.

I had become Secretary of Commerce in March 1921. With Mr. Roosevelt's recovery from his illness, he entered private business, and among his activities he was Chairman of the American Construction Council, a trade association engaged in forwarding the interests of those enterprises. I suggested to him that Department of Commerce would be glad to cooperate with the council in improving standards of construction, statistical services, etc. We continued this joint effort for several years. My files are replete with correspondence in these matters over the years 1924 to 1928. In that year I was the Republican candidate for President and Mr. Roosevelt was the Democratic candidate for Governor of New York. We were both elected—he by a majority of 25,000 and I by a majority of 100,000 in the State of New York. We exchanged telegrams of congratulations and good wishes. Mr. Roosevelt's telegram was as follows: [Ed: See FDR to HH, March 4, 1929 above.]

However subsequent to the election the original of the following letter came into my hands, which seemed to indicate less than fair play in political debate from a personal friend. [Ed: See FDR to Julius H. Barnes, September 25, 1928 above.]

During the period from 1939 to the attack on Pearl Harbor on December 6, 1941, I made many speeches in opposition to Mr. Roosevelt's foreign policies. From the ample lessons of the First World War and its aftermaths, I opposed every one of his steps toward involving the United States in war. I made many public addresses, the most important being at the time Hitler turned his forces upon Stalin. By this action the fate of Western civilization in Europe was no longer in jeopardy. In my speech on that occasion I stated—June 29, 1941:

In the last seven days that call to sacrifice American boys for an ideal has been made as a sounding brass and a tinkling cymbal. For now we find ourselves promising aid to Stalin and his militant Communist conspiracy against the whole democratic ideals of the world. Collaboration between Britain and Russia will bring them military values, but it makes the whole argument of our joining the war to bring the four freedoms to mankind a gargantuan jest. We should refresh our memories a little.

I urged that America stand on the side-lines while these demons—Hitler and Stalin—destroyed each other, and then with our gigantic strength intervene to give the world a lasting peace.

Once the United States had become involved in the war, like every other American I gave such assistance as I was permitted to win the war. There is no way out of war but victory. I offered my services to the President in any way or position where my experience would be useful. He made no reply. Despite the urgings of such mutual friends as Bernard Baruch and Mr. Roosevelt's Secretary of War Henry L. Stimson, he frigidly declined any association with me.

I did not blame him for this attitude as my speeches in opposition to his foreign activities were probably hard for him to bear.

Further Reading and Research

The story of the extraordinary rivalry between Herbert Hoover and Franklin D. Roosevelt has yet to be written. Glimpses of their friendship and conflicts over twenty-seven years can be found in a handful of memoirs and in a number of scholarly articles by historians and political scientists. Below is a selection of the publications that have appeared to date.

Berle, Adolf A. *Navigating the Rapids, 1918–1971*. New York: Harcourt Brace Jovanovich, 1973.

Best, Gary Dean. "Herbert Hoover, 1933–1941: A Reassessment," in *Herbert Hoover Reassessed*. Mark O. Hatfield, ed. Washington, D.C.: Government Printing Office, 1981, pp. 227–273.

———. *Herbert Hoover: The Post Presidential Years, 1933–1964*, 2 vols. Stanford, CA: Hoover Institution Press, 1983.

Burner, David. *Herbert Hoover: A Public Life*. New York: Alfred A. Knopf, 1979.

Cole, Wayne S. *Roosevelt and the Isolationists*. Lincoln: University of Nebraska Press, 1983.

Freidel, Frank. *Franklin D. Roosevelt: Launching the New Deal*. Boston: Little, Brown, 1973.

———. "Hoover and FDR: Reminiscent Reflections," in *Understanding Herbert Hoover: Ten Perspectives*. Lee Nash, ed. Stanford, CA: Hoover Institution Press, 1987, pp. 128–140.

———. "Hoover and Roosevelt and Historical Continuity," in *Herbert Hoover Reassessed*. Washington, D.C.: Government Printing Office, 1981, pp. 275–291.

Henry, Laurin L. *Presidential Transitions*. Washington, D.C.: Brookings Institution, 1960, pp. 23–29.

Hoover, Herbert. *Addresses Upon the American Road, 1933–1938*. New York: Charles Scribner's Sons, 1938.

———. *Addresses Upon the American Road, 1938–1940*. New York: Charles Scribner's Sons. 1940.

———. *Addresses Upon the American Road, 1940–1941*. New York: Charles Scribner's Sons, 1941.

———. *Addresses Upon the American Road, 1941–1945*. New York: D. Van Nostrand Company, 1946.

———. *Addresses Upon the American Road, 1945–1948*. New York: D. Van Nostrand Company, 1949.

———. *The Memoirs of Herbert Hoover: The Cabinet and the Presidency, 1920–1933*. New York: The Macmillan Company, 1952.

———. *The Memoirs of Herbert Hoover: The Great Depression; 1929–1941*. New York: The Macmillan Company, 1952.

———. *Public Papers of the Presidents: Herbert Hoover, 1932–33*. Washington D.C.: U.S. Government Printing Office, 1977.

Ickes, Harold L. *The Secret Diary of Harold L. Ickes, 1933–1936*, 3 vols. Jane D. Ickes, ed. New York: Simon and Schuster, 1953.

Joslin, Theodore G. *Hoover Off the Record*. Garden City, NY: Doubleday, Doran & Company, 1934.

Kennedy, Susan E. *The Banking Crisis of 1933*. Lexington, KY: University Press of Kentucky, 1973.

Lippmann, Walter, "The Permanent New Deal." *Yale Review* 24 (1935), pp. 649–667.

McCoy, Donald R., "Trends in Viewing Herbert Hoover, Franklin D. Roosevelt, Harry S. Truman and Dwight D. Eisenhower." *The Midwest Quarterly*, 21 (Winter 1979), pp. 117–136.

Moley, Raymond. *27 Masters of Politics in a Personal Perspective*. New York: Funk and Wagnalls, 1949.

Robinson, Edgar Eugene, and Vaughn Davis Bornet. *Herbert Hoover President of the United States*. Stanford, CA: Hoover Institution Press, 1975.

Romasco, Albert U. "Herbert Hoover's Policies for Dealing with the Great Depression: The End of the Old Order or the Beginning of the New?" in *Herbert Hoover Reassessed*. Washington, D.C.: U.S. Government Printing Office, 1981, pp. 292–309.

Roosevelt, Franklin D. *The Public Papers and Addresses of Franklin D. Roosevelt, 1928–1932. Vol. I*. Samuel I. Rosenman, ed. New York: Random House, 1938.

Rosen, Elliot A. *Hoover, Roosevelt, and the Brains Trust: From Depression to New Deal*. New York: Columbia University Press, 1977.

———. "Intranationalism vs. Internationlism: The Interregnum Struggle for the Sanctity of the New Deal." *Political Science Quarterly* 81 (June 1966), pp. 274–297.

Showan, Daniel P. "The Hoover-Roosevelt Relationship During the Interregnum." *Lock Haven Review* 1 (1961), pp. 24–50.

Smith, Richard Norton. *An Uncommon Man: The Triumph of Herbert Hoover*. New York: Simon and Schuster, 1984.

Tugwell, Rexford. *The Diary of Rexford G. Tugwell: The New Deal, 1932–1935*. Michael Vincent Namorato, ed. Westport, CT: Greenwood Press, 1992.

————. "Transition: Hoover to Roosevelt, 1932–1933." *Centennial Review* 9 (Spring 1965), pp. 160–191.

Wilson, Joan Hoff. *Herbert Hoover: Forgotten Progressive.* Boston: Little, Brown and Company, 1975.

Index

About the Editors

TIMOTHY WALCH is Director of the Herbert Hoover Presidential Library in West Branch, Iowa. Previously, Walch was editor of *Prologue: Quarterly of the National Archives* and co-director of the Modern Archives and Records Administration in Washington, D.C. Educated at the University of Notre Dame and Northwestern University, Walch is the author or editor of 16 books, including *At the President's Side* (1997), *Parish School* (1996), *Immigrant America* (1994), and *Herbert Hoover and Harry S. Truman* (1992). For his professional and scholarly work, Walch has received awards from the National Archives and Records Administration, the National Endowment for the Humanities, the U.S. Catholic Press Association, and the Teachers College of Columbia University.

DWIGHT M. MILLER came to the Herbert Hoover Presidential Library in 1964 after three years as an assistant archivist in the Presidential Papers Section of the Manuscript Division of the Library of Congress. As Senior Archivist, his experience at the Hoover Library includes co-editing *Historical Materials in the Herbert Hoover Presidential Library* and compiling and assisting in editing *The Public Papers of the Presidents: Herbert Hoover, 1929–1933*, 4 vols., and *Proclamations and Executive Orders: Herbert Hoover, 1929–1993*, 2 vols. Most recently he co-edited, with Timothy Walch, *Herbert Hoover and Harry S. Truman: A Documentary History* (1992).

Recent Titles in
Contributions in American History

ISBN 0-313-30608-7

90000>

EAN

9 780313 306082

HARDCOVER BAR CODE